Barossa Food Wakefield Press

This book makes you long for the days when the kitchen hummed throughout the day to the sound of laughter, accompanied by delicious smells and small treats snuck when no one was looking. It is a beautiful book about a quiet country lifestyle fast disappearing. Jeni Port, *Age*

Angela Heuzenroeder's knowledge of Barossa food comes from all the Barossa meals she has eaten in her lifetime. She was born in the Barossa Valley, came back to be married there and has lived there ever since. Angela has long been involved in keeping local history alive. As a teacher-librarian in local schools, she has collected materials and taught children about the history of their local area. She and food consultant Maggie Beer were founding members of an oral history group that took a tape recorder into people's homes and recorded their reminiscences, many of which were about food.

Eric Algra is an Adelaide-based freelance photographer. He particularly enjoys photographing landscapes and people. Eric was awarded the Ilford trophy (for the highest scoring print) and the Athol Shmith award (for black-and-white excellence) in the 1998 Australian Professional Photography Awards.

Mark Rosenzweig

Barossa food

Angela Heuzenroeder

Photographs by Eric Algra

Wakefield Press

Wakefield Press
16 Rose Street
Mile End
South Australia 5031
www.wakefieldpress.com.au

First published 1999
Revised edition published 2002
Reprinted 2007
This edition published 2020

Text copyright © Angela Heuzenroeder 1999, 2002
Original photographs copyright © Eric Algra 1999, 2002
Other copyright photographs are acknowledged in captions

All rights reserved. This book is copyright. Apart from any fair dealing for the
purposes of private study, research, criticism or review, as permitted under
the Copyright Act, no part may be reproduced without written permission.
Enquiries should be addressed to the publisher.

Designed by Liz Nicholson, design BITE, Adelaide
Typeset by Clinton Ellicott, Wakefield Press, Adelaide

ISBN 978 1 74305 803 9

 A catalogue record for this book is available from the National Library of Australia

To my aunt, Winifred Schulz, an excellent cook, and to the group called the Sunday School, who played cards in her back shed and told countless stories: Eric, Clem, Otto, Eugen, Frank, Wilf, Tiny

contents

Foreword by Maggie Beer	viii
Preface	x

wheels turn

Chapter 1	Beginnings	2
Chapter 2	Recipes for Change	13
Chapter 3	Menge and the Melons	22
Chapter 4	Küche, Kirche und Kinder	35

winter

Chapter 5	Winter Trimmings	56
Chapter 6	The Weekly Leavening	71
Chapter 7	Kuchen in a Warm Kitchen	86
Chapter 8	The Pig	100

spring

Chapter 9	Noodles and Cheese	126
Chapter 10	Food Outdoors	142
Chapter 11	Grand Entertainment	156

summer

Chapter 12	Hives of Activity	174
Chapter 13	Christmas Celebrations	191
Chapter 14	Summer Fruits	202
Chapter 15	Yabbies, Pickles and Sauces	217
Chapter 16	Mulberries, Drinks, Apples and Cucumbers	232

autumn

Chapter 17	Grapes and Wine	248
Chapter 18	Mushrooms, Quinces, Nuts, Figs, Olives	266
Chapter 19	Autumn Reflections	288

Author's Note	294
Sources	296
General Index	306
Index of Recipes and Described Dishes	314

Foreword by Maggie Beer

At last we have a book about the food of the Barossa Valley. Angela Heuzenroeder has recorded memories and delved into recipe notebooks and other documents to set down the recipes and changing history of Barossa food and its culture. Nothing could be more valuable than describing this culture before it is lost.

Nowhere else in Australia that I know of has such an identifiable regional food culture: the ties to the land hearkening back to European settlers of the Valley; the traditions of the seasons upheld; a 'peasant' culture in its closest possible sense. I give this last as the greatest of accolades, because it meant that the mixed farmers or vignerons were proud of their food and their culture and they worked hard yet, I suspect, effortlessly to marry their food traditions to our climate.

The other truly important factor in the Barossa food culture has to be the wine industry: that connecting with the wine, the winemakers, the enjoyment of the grape – and all that flows from there.

I have lived in the Barossa since 1973 and progress has its price. When I arrived *Barossa Deutsch* was still spoken in the streets by old and young alike; there was more time to gossip at the butchers and in front of the post office. But the sense of community I felt from the first day I arrived has never changed.

Traditions must be maintained and in the Valley we work for this with our annual shows and events such as the Vintage Festival and the Barossa Music Festival. There is no place like the Barossa for getting things done. The hospitality is legendary and there is a proud history of volunteering among the community.

I have always thought it was the luckiest accident of my life that I came to live in the Barossa. I had grown up with a love of food, thanks to a German heritage on my father's side and a tradition of great cooks in the family, but had not realised how that passive education of always eating simple but perfect food in season had shaped my life.

My husband, Colin, and I came to the Barossa for him to farm pheasants and grapes. A much more patient soul than me, Colin listened to his neighbours and learnt his vineyard skills. I was the city girl always in a hurry, but my nose for good produce slowed me down as Colin introduced me to neighbours like Ed Auricht, whose property we drove by daily. Ed would sit at night in his orchard of almonds, shelling the first of the season. He presented some to me and I understood for the first time the perfection of the new season. He planted turnips for me and walked with them across the bridge to our Pheasant Farm restaurant when it first opened. They were so young and crisp that we ate them raw. The yabbies had already gone from the North Para, which ran through our property, but locals used to bring them to us in wheatbags. We would lay them in the water on the side of the dam until we needed them. The contractor who sprayed our vines used to shoot the hares that nibbled the young shoots and bring them to our door. We raised our own pig and smoked the bacon in our own smokehouse attached to our very first home.

I enjoyed helping Angie research this book, testing the recipes and accompanying her on some of the visits to Barossa food producers. I especially recomend the *Mandeltorte* and the Hock pudding!

The Barossa has a special food heritage, and I think it has shown the way for other Australian regions to look around them to maximise their food potential. But tradition cannot be imposed – we have it in the Barossa Valley, and now we have it recorded!

Preface

It is a Sunday morning in March. At the annual Tanunda show, in the Barossa Valley in South Australia, judging for the dill gherkin and pickled onion championships is about to begin. The judges stand on the shellgrit floor of the show hall in the warm morning light, spittoons and plates of entry samples in front of them, with all the decorum that they would use for judging wine.

Further down the row, in another championship, slabs of German cake are being taken from their glass cases, cut and tested for texture and flavour. Does the knife drag through the doughy yeast base? Does the crumbly *Streusel* topping fall off too easily? Is the colour even, both on top and underneath?

Now a judge moves to tables where the *Rote Grütze* entries are glistening in cut glass bowls. The *Rote Grütze* dessert is made in the traditional Barossa manner with red grape juice and sago. Like a rich, red wine, it is examined against the light. The judge can tell which variety of grape was used and whether it is the best one for colour and flavour.

Meanwhile, smoky, spicy, garlicky smells from the sausages in the smallgoods section are drawing people to the judging of the traditional wursts: the black pudding or *Blutwurst*, the white pudding or *Leberwurst*, and the *Mettwursts*, garlic-flavoured or plain.

When the judges have examined all the entries and awarded prizes, the stewards unmask the names of the entrants and announce the winners. The Dill Champion is a newcomer this year. And to think that the winner of the German cake section stayed up all night baking for this moment!

These traditional competitions in the annual Barossa Valley shows continue part of the local food culture. Not only the cucumbers are preserved; so also is a sense of tradition about local food. Along with legendary wines, a love of music and religious traditions, the characteristic foods of the Barossa Valley give a unique character to the place and the people whose families have lived there for generations.

The Barossa food culture is based on the ingredients that have grown well there since European settlement as well as on the traditions brought from the other side of the world in the middle of the nineteenth century. It came mainly from central eastern Europe, brought by German-speaking Prussians, long before Germany was a single country. English settlers brought their traditions too. Over the years, as people in the Barossa used old ingredients in a new way, food traditions mingled and the Barossa earned a reputation for outstanding and inventive cuisine. Indeed, people in the Barossa have developed some original local dishes not made in quite the same way in any other part of the world. And even in the 1930s, the *Barossa Cookery Book* was claiming that the district was 'celebrated throughout Australia for the excellence of its cookery'.

My own interest in the traditional foods of the Barossa Valley stems from a lifetime of eating. I was born in the Barossa and went back to live there after I married. I am familiar enough with the food prepared by local people to recognise a Barossa meal when I am served one. Even as a young child I was aware that the food we ate in the Barossa was not quite the same as food I tried in other places. After the Second World War, my parents may have leaned towards an Australian way of life that borrowed much from the English, but that did not obliterate certain customs, like having blood pudding for Sunday morning breakfast, and the ritual consumption of fresh *Streuselkuchen* on Saturdays.

The post-war era brought many German-speaking immigrants to

the Barossa, and they brought new ways and new foods. The 1970s saw the promotion of tourism across Australia. Reports promised prosperity if we could attract tourists, and the Germanic character of the Barossa suddenly became an important means of luring visitors to the area. Anything German would do, as long as it was colourful and jolly. At festive times, local people began to sport imitation Tyrolean hats made out of cardboard and imitation *Lederhosen*, which might more accurately be called vinyl-hosen. Restaurants and shops began to sell German foods that the locals had never seen before. Visitors and locals alike began to believe that Black Forest cake and *Mandelbrot* were all part of the traditional Barossa food culture. The distinctions were blurred.

It must have been during those same years that I started to realise how many of the food customs common in the Barossa of my childhood were no longer around. Where were the cups of *Kochkäse* or boiled cheese that we used to buy as a savoury treat? Had the bakers forgotten that fresh sultana grapes went under the *Streusel* on the *Kuchen* in autumn? How long was it since we'd had noodle soup, claws and all, made from a hen from our own fowl yard? Nostalgically, I thought of the expanse of honey biscuits and machine biscuits spread across the kitchen table before Christmas when I was a child.

I decided to start compiling lists of the foods I knew local people had been making for generations. There were certain techniques and flavour preferences that made them typical Barossa cooking. The world needed to know about them before they disappeared! Visitors and local people alike needed to be reminded about the traditional food of the region. After all, having such a strong sense of regional identity coming from its distinctive European culture, its shared festivals and its unifying wine industry, the Barossa could lay a very strong claim to having a continuing regional cuisine starting from earliest white settlement. It was probably the only place in Australia that could do so.

The year 1992 marked the celebration of 150 years of European settlement in the Barossa. Working in consultation with noted chef, restaurateur, food consultant and food producer, Maggie Beer, I began a search for people who knew and prepared traditional Barossa food. I interviewed them and spent time in their kitchens until I could identify dishes, brought by the settlers, that are still made or remembered. The memories of people I interviewed bridge back into the nineteenth century. They give an insight into the culture surrounding the preparation of food on the so-called mixed farms that kept farming families in the nineteenth and early twentieth centuries self-sufficient even in hard times.

Letters, diaries and written reminiscences of early settlers give a picture of the kinds of foods they grew and prepared, including foods – like kangaroo – that were new to them but that became familiar in a new land. Some local families still possess the hand-written recipe notebooks that women compiled around the end of the nineteenth century and the beginning of the twentieth. I have made a collection of about ten of these, copied and used with the kind permission of the owners. (I would love to collect copies of more.) They are fascinating documents because they are written in a mixture of German and English by people whose language was in a state of transition. They reveal as much about the development of the Barossa food culture by the recipes that are not included as by the recipes that are common to all of them.

The *Barossa Cookery Book* and other recipe books printed over the years have proved to be useful points of comparison, especially viewed in the context of the time when they were produced. The *Bremisches Kochbuch* is a recipe book published in Bremen, Prussia, in 1834 and brought to Australia in the luggage of a family who settled in the Stockwell-Light Pass area of the Barossa. The recipes on its use-stained pages provide an insight into the different methods of cooking dishes that are similar to some which survive today. The *Universal-Lexikon der Kochkunst* and its English equivalent, *Mrs Beeton's Book of Household Management*, in their several editions, are good for comparing food from different eras and cultures.

Many food writers in Germany have gathered information from areas once the home of the Barossa settlers. In the case of Silesia, several people in the west, who were refugees in 1946 when the area was handed back to Poland, have compiled recipe books to document traditional Silesian cooking. Some of the recipes in such books strike a chord of recognition for people who know Barossa dishes. Clearly, these are the traditional foods that have survived the transplant from one country to another.

Barossa Food

Using these sources, I discovered a core list of foods brought by the early Prussian settlers that are still made, or at least commonly remembered by elderly people.

But I also learned that to look at the history of the food of a region is to sample a movable feast. At different times in the history of the Barossa, some foods gained prominence while others retreated into the background, at least temporarily. Sometimes particular foods were connected to stories about particular people. Many of these foods, I decided, were worth recording, along with the circumstances in which they flourished. Some are included to symbolise influences from cultures other than the central and eastern European. They may not have appeared in the Barossa until well into the twentieth century. Yet, they are all part of the history of Barossa food.

For everything there is a season and in a food culture the seasons more than anything else shape people's lives. After describing early settlement, original dishes and early ways of cooking, the book follows the seasons to look at the foods made in the Barossa at different times of the year in different eras. The history of food eaten over the years is one of love and marriage, politics, war, finance and community life – for ultimately it is the story of changes that have happened to people themselves, to those who prepare the food and eat it.

Some recipes (in italics) are here purely for interest's sake. But where a recipe is really worth making in a modern kitchen, an updated version, for a manageable quantity, is given in detail, with comments or serving suggestions. Many of the recipes were tested with the help of Maggie Beer, from whom some of the comments come. We had great fun and learned a lot in discovering some of the dishes that may not have been cooked in the Valley for a century, as well as trying more recent favourites. Following suggestions from readers of the book's first edition, I have modified some of the old recipes. I hope that other people will make them, in home kitchens or in restaurants. Enterprising producers might consider developing some of them for export. I hope that my book will help bring the Barossa to the rest of the world.

Angela Heuzenroeder, Tanunda, 2002

wheels
turn

Chapter 1

Beginnings

The Barossa Valley is a rumpled quilt of vineyards that slope down from the flanks of a very old range of hills. Just recently, up there on the range, I stood by the wall of the Mengler Hill lookout, viewing the houses and towns scattered across the land below. Close at hand, at the foot of the hill, it was easy to make out the early settlement called Bethany and farmhouses that seem to have been sitting comfortably forever amongst their vines.

To me, the road below leading towards Tanunda and beyond is a timeline between past and present. Starting from Bethany, the first village of German-speaking settlers, I can trace the Barossa towns that grew later, each one showing evidence of its European origins. Today, these towns attract people who find it remarkable that places with such a distinct German influence can be found on the other side of the globe, translated into an Australian setting.

What would visitors observe about the Barossa that makes it different from other parts of Australia? First of all, a number of names on buildings and street signs are those of people who came from central and eastern Europe: names like Rothe, Hage, Keil, Schrapel and Fiedler. These appeared on the very early shipping lists to South Australia and have ever since been well-known in the local community.

Then visitors would be struck by the number of Lutheran churches in the settlements: four in the small town of Tanunda alone, and no fewer than two substantial Lutheran churches in the hamlet of Light Pass, which is too small even to have a shop.

In the streets near the churches, and out in the countryside, visitors would see examples of the early settlers' cottages. Some of them were built by English settlers but many were built by people from central and eastern Europe. They are long and narrow with high-pitched, European-looking gabled roofs. Once most of these had thatched roofs and some barns still have roofs of silvery straw. People who built them, from the middle of the nineteenth century onwards, came from European farms that were made in a similar way.

Talking to any long-time residents, visitors would learn that a definite Barossa Valley accent still exists. They would hear English spoken with the rhythm and some of the word patterns of German. It is nothing like the accent of the German immigrants who have arrived since 1945, though. Rather, it harks back to the language spoken by much earlier generations. Its sing-song, slightly nasal twang is disappearing among younger generations, but even in their speech the occasional sentence lets slip an affinity with the grammatical structures of German. You can still hear some people ask, 'Are you coming with?' This is a direct translation of the grammatically correct German question: *'Kommst du mit?'*

A visit to the bakery and butcher's shop in any of the local towns would complete the impression that the Barossa's cultural identity is distinctive. The yeast cakes are literally 'German cake'. The wursts, too, are much the same as the ones made on farms back in Silesia, Brandenberg and Posen in the nineteenth century.

There are many other aspects of community life in the Barossa directly connected to the origins of the early settlers, such as a love of choirs and band music, and an apparent passion for neatness and order. However, it is the European-based food culture of the Barossa Valley, which first began with the arrival of the Prussian settlers, and developed with British and other influences, that is the subject of this book.

The place to begin the Barossa story is with the arrival of the first German-speaking community who settled as a group in the hamlet of Bethany.

On 11 July 1841 the sailing ship *Skjold* edged its way uncertainly out of the port of Cuxhaven downstream from Hamburg. It was carrying about 270 people from the provinces of Posen, Brandenburg and Silesia in Prussia. They had sold their possessions and left their homes to begin a risky venture on the other side of the earth.

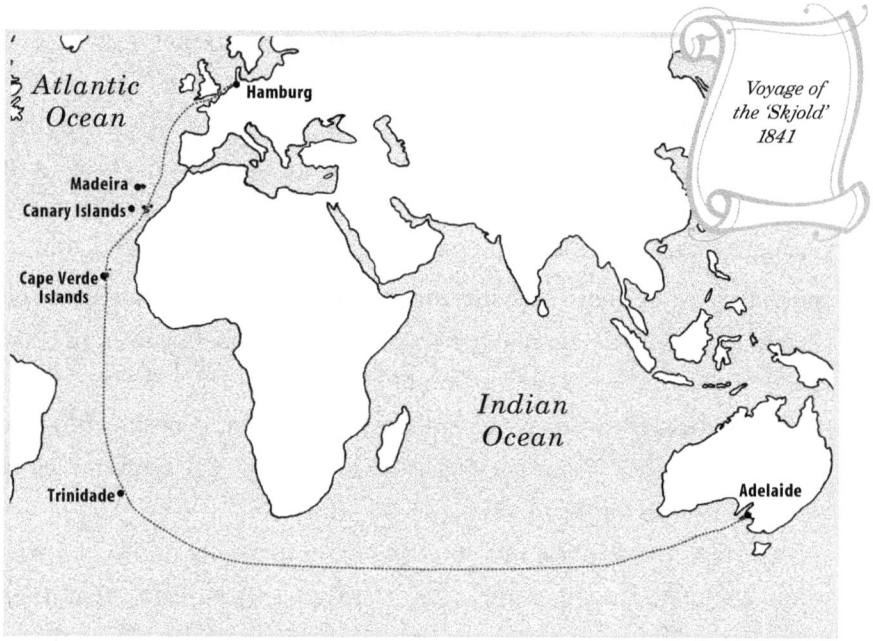

The passengers had come from different villages in central Prussia, and probably did not know each other well before being thrown together in the narrow confines of the wooden ship, but they had common bonds. They were all Lutherans who did not take kindly to the changes being forced on their church by King Friedrich Wilhelm III, and they had a common leader, Pastor Gotthard Daniel Fritzsche, who had ministered to their several parishes in Prussia. Now, no longer willing to put up with secret church meetings and the risk of arrest, these people had decided to leave Prussia with their pastor and set up a parish in a new land.

During the voyage they shared the ghastly experience of an epidemic of dysentery. Over 50 of them died. Every day adults and children gathered together on the deck to pray and, often, to witness sea burials. The birth of some babies during the voyage would have contributed to a growing sense of community. By the time the ship berthed at Adelaide in South Australia, they must have felt as though they had been together forever.

After a few months recovering from the journey in settlements near Adelaide, about half the passengers were prompted by their leader to band together once more, this time to set off for the foot of the Barossa Ranges and take up land 80 kilometres north-east of Adelaide. They stacked their belongings, tools and building materials into ox-drawn waggons, covered them with canvas and, with dogs and children capering beside them, trudged off on foot to find the place for their new village. In the Barossa, they made their way past a handful of farms newly started by a few English and German-speaking families until they reached the site intended as theirs. Some were already calling it *Bethanien* (Bethany) after the village outside Jerusalem mentioned in the Bible. Other people, feeling a sense of anticipated proprietorship, referred to the area as *Neu Schlesien*, or New Silesia.

Subsequent groups from the same part of Prussia and from neighbouring regions continued the settlement of the Barossa. Prussian shipping agents circulated booklets with glowing descriptions of life in South Australia. Family members read letters from the adventurers who had gone on ahead. They learned that the climate was warm and that there was plenty of food. There did not seem to be as much illness over there. They felt reassured to read that the farms had by and large the same animals as their own: cattle, horses, geese, ducks, pigeons and hens – even the same sorts of cats and dogs! They looked at the situation around them in Europe, which had been in the grip of drought and famine and where there were rumblings of yet another war. They were encouraged by the thought that they could worship as they pleased and own their own land without bureaucratic interferences. They had bought their land at a high price from the British but, all in all, it was not so very difficult to decide to settle in another part of the world.

More districts in central and eastern Europe were drained of people as lines of emigrants lengthened. They left on ships via Hamburg, Cuxhaven and Bremerhaven. Most were heading for the United States but a good many were bound for South Australia.

Some emigrants left parts of Prussia from which other people had already departed. Many came from places that today form part of Poland, like Grünberg (now Zielona Góra), Klemzig (Klępsk), Züllichau (Sulechów). They also left places further south in Silesia: towns near Liegnitz (Legnica), towns along the Oder River closer to the capital city of Breslau (Wrocław); towns further east in the province of Posen, like Nekla. A sizeable number of Wends, of slavic origin, came from between Dresden and Cottbus in Saxony and from near the Spreewald south of Berlin in Brandenburg. They settled in the north and west of the Barossa district. A large number of people arrived from the grand-duchy of Mecklenburg–Schwerin, which was not part of Prussia at all, and imposed memories of the old land upon the new by naming the area they settled *Neu Mecklenburg*. Later settlers came from the Harz mountains in Hannover, attracted by the copper mining in South Australia.

Each of these areas had regional dishes of its own that must have been familiar to the people who were leaving, and some European ways of preparing food and drink that were common to them all. Some local families still recall the German names for these dishes with pride, even the ones they no longer make.

What did the emigrants eat on board ship? Captain Hahn, who commanded one of the first ships of German-speaking immigrants, later wrote in his diary about the voyage of 1838:

Their provisions for the period indicated consisted of 26,674 gallons of water, 24,400 pounds of bread, 27 barrels of pork, 27 barrels of beef, 10 casks of herrings, 38 barrels of flour, 60 casks of dried peas, 7 bags of coffee beans, 5 large barrels of sugar, 50 cheeses, 17 quarters of butter, 29 bags of rice, 5 barrels beans, 2 barrels plums, 2 barrels pearl barley, 7 hogsheads of vinegar, 10 bags of salt, 8 hogsheads of sauerkraut, 1 hogshead wine, 50 bottles cognac, 105 bottles port wine, 25 bottles bitter brandy, 50 pounds tea, 50 pounds arrowroot, 1 small barrel lamp-oil.

Johann Daniel Thiermann wrote on 5 May 1848 about his voyage to South Australia in 1844:

The normal ship menu included coffee from 7.00 am – without milk – with sugar to taste, butter, cheese as well, then at midday peas, beans, groats and prunes, wine sago, different kinds of soup; as vegetables: sour cabbage, green salted beans, dried peas, potatoes etc. The potatoes ran out long before we reached Rio and so the Captain bought for the cabin passengers 4 sacks of potatoes and doled out 2 or 3 potatoes every midday.

The lower deck passengers were far worse off in every respect: no sugar for their tea, and between 3 to 8 pounds of butter a week, which came rapidly to an end, and a little syrup. Some had brought so many supplies with them that they only rarely relied on the ship's supplies. On Sundays and Thursdays after chicken soup we had 4 roasted fowls or ducks (for 28 people in the steerage) and a pudding on every table.

This book concentrates on the Barossa food culture although it does refer to other areas as well. The Barossa Valley was not the only place in Australia, nor indeed the first, where Prussian immigrants went in the nineteenth century. Further south in the Adelaide hills, German-speaking newcomers, led by Pastor August Kavel, had already settled at Hahndorf, and towns like Lobethal and Blumberg (Birdwood) sprang up soon afterwards. Large numbers migrated from Europe to Victoria from 1849 onwards, and to Queensland from the 1860s. From the Barossa itself, families needing more land packed their goods and journeyed to other parts of South Australia and to Victoria,

New South Wales and Queensland. But the original German culture remained strongest in the Barossa Valley, and historians have described the district as a 'unique centre of continental traditions and culture in an otherwise English-speaking community'.

All the elements were there in the Barossa to keep the original culture intact for a good long while. The early settlements were individual congregations. They each had a pastor and a schoolteacher to keep people aware of the Lutheran faith that bound them together. Young people were urged to marry within the local congregation. Even individual arrivals joined the fold rather than face social isolation in a country community.

The congregations were also sufficiently remote to remain separate from Anglo-Saxon and secular influences for at least one generation after settlement. As late as the 1930s, the non-Lutheran partner of an interdenominational marriage could be treated by a Lutheran family as a social outcast. A friend told me only recently that in the 1930s her English father had to stay out in the car when her mother, descended from an original Barossa family, went back home to visit the parents.

A quick count of the electoral rolls of 1884 shows that many polling centres in the Barossa had extraordinarily high ratios of German names to English or non-German. Of the Barossa townships, the ratio in Tanunda was about 10:1, in Nuriootpa it was 6:1, in the tiny hamlet of Stockwell it was 25:1. By comparison, closer to the capital, in the other areas where the original settlers had also been German-speaking Lutheran congregations, the township of Hahndorf had a ratio of about 3:1 of German names, Lobethal a ratio of 4:1 and Birdwood, originally called Blumberg, had two German names for every English name on the roll.

Another small sign of how effective this inward-turning approach was at keeping German culture alive in the Barossa can be seen in the book-lending patterns that were part of the Institute Library's country lending service in South Australia in the nineteenth century. From the 1860s, boxes of books written in German were sent to communities across South Australia populated by German-speaking settlers. In the 1890s, this practice came under review and the Institute board members recommended that it was no longer necessary to send books in German because most people in those areas now spoke and read English. The only exception was the Barossa, where it was suggested that the service of lending books written in German might be continued.

You can see from these instances why the food prepared in the Barossa had a chance to stabilise in a strong cultural base of European origin before beginning to develop characteristics of its own. So now is a good moment to look at a list of foods from the early communities that numbers of people make or at least remember today.

Streuselkuchen – German Cake
From Silesia
Yeast cake with crumbly topping of flour, sugar, butter and spices (still found in Berlin, Northeim, Osterode, and surrounding areas, brought there by refugees after the Second World War). Very important in Barossa daily life. Versions had fresh fruit under topping. The Barossa version is sometimes made with fresh sultana grapes under Streusel.

Schlesisches Himmelreich – Silesian Heaven
From Silesia
A dish of stewed, smoked pork (eg bacon), dried fruits (eg apples, plums and pears) and dumplings. The Barossa adaptation used pie-melons called *Pompenbrei*, or stewed quinces instead of dried fruit. Still known to some elderly people.

Quittengelee – Quince Jelly, Potroasted Quinces
From Silesia, Brandenburg, Mecklenburg
Whole quinces simmered very slowly in sugar and water produced both the jelly and the dessert of quinces. Fashionable once again.

Sauerkraut – Pickled Cabbage
From many areas of Germany
An important part of settlers' diet, but made less often after the First World War.

Dämpfkraut – Steamed Cabbage
From Silesia
Cabbage lightly steamed and seasoned with bacon, vinegar, pepper, salt, sugar and caraway seeds.

Gurkensalat – Cucumber Salad with Vinegar and Cream
From Silesia
An essential part of Barossa Christmas dinner.

Weihnachtskuchen – Ammonia Biscuits
From Silesia and eastern Europe
Honigkuchen – Honey Biscuits
Schaumkuchen – Meringues
From many parts of Prussia
Spritzgebäck – Wurst-machine Biscuits
From Brandenburg
These are all Christmas biscuits.

Berliner Pfannkuchen – Kitchener Buns, Berlin Buns, Sugar Buns
From Brandenburg and other areas
Deep-fried balls of yeast dough with jam in the middle.

Blutwurst, Leberwurst, Mettwurst, Lachsschinken, Knackwurst, Zungenwurst – Smallgoods from the Pig-killing
From a wide area of central-eastern Europe
Most of these were made on Barossa farms a generation ago. The preparation of *Lachsschinken* was more refined, prepared for particular people or occasions.

Saure Gurken, Salzgurken – Dill Cucumbers
From Silesia, the Spreewald and other areas
The Barossa ones are laid in vine leaves with brine and dill, like the Silesian ones. Liegnitz (now Legniza in Poland) was once famous for its dill pickles.

Quark, Kochkäse, Stinkerkäse – Peasant-style Cheeses
From many parts of Europe, including Brandenburg, Silesia and Posen
Cottage cheese; 'boiled cheese' ie fermented cottage cheese gently heated to become a creamy spread; 'smelly cheese' or balls of *Quark* allowed to ferment and gather a coating of jelly.

Kartoffelsalat – Warm Potato Salad
Possibly from Brandenburg
Warm peeled, cooked potatoes dressed with vinegar, bacon, onions and cream.

Quarkkuchen, Käsekuchen – Cheesecake
Attributed to the Wends south of Berlin
A saffron-flavoured cheesecake on a yeast base.

Rote Grütze – Red Berry Dessert
From Mecklenburg, Brandenburg and north Germany
Red berries or gooseberries thickened with some sort of grain, mainly sago since the nineteenth century. The Barossa adaptation used red wine grapes instead of wild berries.

Nudeln – Noodles
From many parts of central-eastern Europe
Flour, salt and eggs made into dough, cut with a knife or machine and dried for soup and puddings. An essential part of fowl and noodle soup, the classic starter for Sunday dinner.

Meerrettichsoße – Horseradish Sauce
From south of Berlin
Grated horseradish in a condiment sauce.

Backobst – Dried Fruits
From most parts of Europe
A favourite dessert. Vegetables, like peas, were dried in the sun in the same way.

And, of course, the practices of making wine and beer . . .

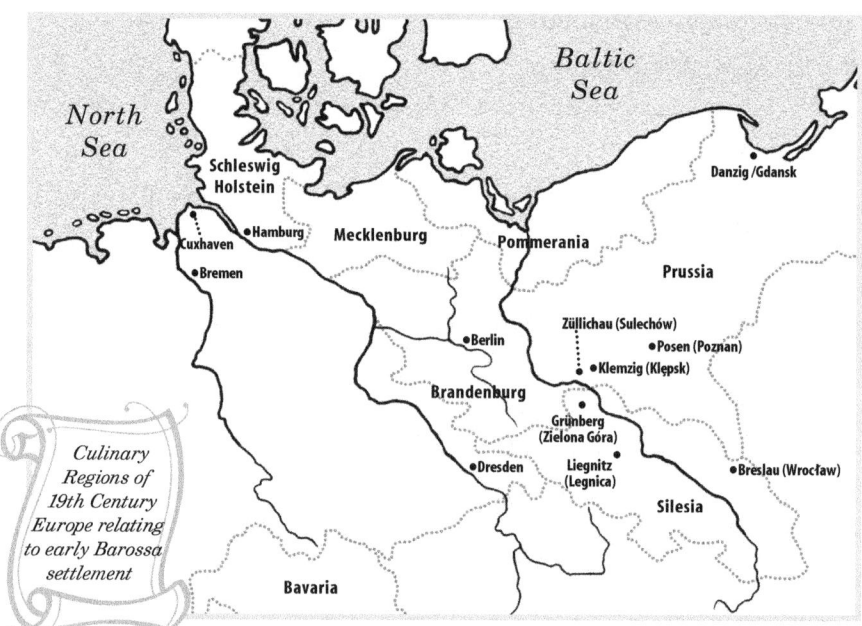

Culinary Regions of 19th Century Europe relating to early Barossa settlement

Chapter 2
Recipes for Change

Towards the end of the nineteenth century, Prussian dishes in the Barossa started to have competition from English recipes. Farming families, who by now were coming to terms with the English language, frequently subscribed to newspapers like *The Chronicle* and improved their English skills as they read practical advice about cropping and land management. But *The Chronicle* had a popular recipe page, too, and the recipes were mainly Anglo-Saxon. Many a farmer's wife cut out the ones that appealed to her and put them in her recipe notebook. A century later, out they flutter when the book is opened, flagging the fact that old recipes were once being challenged by new – as they always are, with an inventive cook.

The English invasion into Barossa kitchens continued as, little by little, children in the third generations of Lutheran families began to marry partners outside the Lutheran church. Even within groups from the first settlements who had kept themselves to themselves for so long, sons and daughters in the third generation were marrying people with English and Irish names: for example, in the family of Linke, the first of whom who came out on the *Zebra* in 1838 and died in Moculta in the Barossa in 1879, surnames like Jack, Peters and Branson crept into the family tree as the nineteenth century rolled into the twentieth.

The melding of German and English cooking shows best in the ways people preserved their food. In the days before refrigeration, of course, people ate a good deal of food that had been preserved in some way in a season when it was plentiful. Prussians had always been keen on fermented foods. Their baking of cake relied on fermented yeast cultures; the cheeses were fermented milk; the wine fermented; the beer, cucumbers, *Sauerkraut* and *Mettwurst* fermented. English people, on the other hand, had a taste for sweet jams and pickles. They were making good use of the sugar that came from the British colonies. The flavour of curry that pepped up some of their pickles was no doubt a legacy from the British Raj in India. Of course, the Prussians *did* use sugar in their food preparation and the English *did* make cheese, beer and wine. It is, rather, a question of emphasis. In the early twentieth century, many recipes cut or copied from English newspapers into notebooks (which were otherwise written in German) gave directions for making sauces, pickles and jams that were sweeter than much of the Prussian food had been.

The English brides certainly got their way on the foods prepared for Christmas. The fish dishes and poppyseed dishes of eastern European origin gave way to roast poultry and plum pudding. Some people can recall the traditional Silesian *Mohnklöße* being prepared from poppyseed and bread soaked in milk, and dishes made from the salt herring that had been imported from Europe in little wooden casks. By the time the first *Barossa Cookery Book* was published in 1917, however, Christmas pudding and rich Christmas fruit cake were firmly on the menu, submitted for the publication by cooks with names like von Bertouch and Koch. Families who once knew only German recipes were by now tucking in to English fare, as well.

If any dishes were declining in popularity, the 1914–1918 World War and its aftermath sent them underground. Suddenly it was not a good idea for people to show their German background. If you criticised the Australian government, especially if you spoke German, you might find yourself arrested and interned for years. Soldiers made raids and house searches and nobody could say for certain who in the community had acted as informers. A foment of hatred spread

in the wider South Australian community towards people with German-sounding names or German backgrounds, even though these people had never thought of themselves as anything but Australian. Everyone became extremely wary.

All too sensitive to the general climate of opinion, Barossa people did try hard to change, although they found it difficult to drop the German language overnight. It was just too easy to slip into *Deutsch* at unthinking moments. When a local farmers' society met, the president gave a directive to the members that from now on they had better conduct the meetings in English instead of German. Then, calling for the financial report, he said, 'Now, Hugo, how much money do we have left in the *Kasse*?'

Some people anglicised their names, especially if they moved away from the district. If Prussian foods were going to be sold, it was probably safer to follow government policy and anglicise the food names, too. So *Berliner Pfannkuchen*, those round balls of yeast dough with jam in the centre that are deep-fried and rolled in sugar, achieved respectability under the name of Kitchener buns, in honour of the English general whose name was in everybody's newspapers.

More frequently, as Vera Bockmann wrote in her memoir *Full Circle*, foods of German origin were generally despised. 'Better not to talk about these things in public.' So with German names concealed and German customs repressed, families tried hard to meld unnoticed into the broader community.

A generation later, many people were surprised to learn that their family originally had a German name and had come from the Barossa. One woman I interviewed described how she grew up in Gladstone, a town in South Australia's mid-north. She married and came to live in Tanunda in the Barossa. It surprised her to see how her mother wolfed down the pickled cucumbers that she would bring as a present when she went back to visit. One day the mother said, 'Is old Hulde Schmidt still living in Tanunda?' The daughter asked how her mother could possibly know Hulde. To the daughter's amazement she discovered that her mother had been born in Tanunda and had completely hidden all traces of her past. The dill cucumbers gave her away!

The *Barossa Cookery Book* was born on 'Tanunda Australia Day', 8 September 1917. How it came about makes an interesting story. The front cover of the first edition announced that the proceeds of the book were to go to the South Australian Soldiers' Fund. The second edition, which is undated but must have appeared soon after the war was over, proclaimed that the proceeds of this new printing would now be devoted to: 'The Tanunda Soldiers' Memorial, in the form of a Hall costing many thousands of pounds.'

The hall in question had already been built – but paying for it had become extremely difficult, for a reason that had to do with the climate of the times. Next door to the hall is the Tanunda Club, which in 1907 was a thriving centre where the men of Tanunda could meet, play billiards, sample the local wines and converse and sing in German. Having built their own substantial club-house, the members had decided to erect a town hall and theatre where touring companies could perform plays and where local schools, bands and other groups could put on concerts. In May 1913 the hall, with its theatre dressing-rooms and movable scenery, was officially opened. The 500 or so Tanunda Club members were confident that they would soon be able to pay off the building.

Then came August 1914 and England and Australia declared war on Germany. In spite of a public meeting held in the Tanunda Club to declare the citizens' loyalty to King and country, the military became concerned at rumours of disloyalty in the town. People reported that members of the Tanunda Club had expressed anti-English sentiments. The German language spoken there suddenly seemed to have threatening overtones. Rumours, accusations and resignations of committee members followed and by 1915 the military authorities were ordering that the club be closed. By 1916 the closure was permanent. The Tanunda Club members were not even allowed to use their hall from that date onwards. With no more Tanunda Club existing and no more access to the hall, the committee that had built the hall in the first place had no way of paying for it. They had no choice but to sell it to the Institute Committee. Their decision and the subsequent sale took place from 1919 to 1920.

As one of the many patriotic projects being carried out in the town, the *Barossa Cookery Book: 400 Tried Recipes* had first been produced by a committee headed by the local doctor. Along with knitting socks for the Red Cross and so on, people contributed their recipes for this little book. The ladies of the local Cheer-up Society folded and collated the pages.

It is not surprising to find that the first edition of this book does its bit to show the flag by offering recipes of a decidedly British flavour: dishes with names such as Exeter Stew, Dolly Vardon Cakes and Thornton Pudding. There is even a recipe for 'Trench Porridge', in which Anzac biscuits are soaked then boiled to a mush, to be eaten as they were by soldiers in the trenches. The contributor is Private Offe, a brave soldier risking his life for his country in spite of his despised German name. But the contributor who gave the recipe for 'German Sausage', the only recipe in the book that dares to show any Teutonic connections, was Miss Crawford of Angaston, whose Anglo-Saxon name clearly made her immune to any charges of disloyalty.

By the time the second, undated, edition of the *Barossa Cookery Book* appeared, the war was over and the Tanunda Institute Committee had bought the grandiose hall that needed to be paid for. This time the sales of the book could reduce the debt. However, the project would still be a patriotic one, for the hall was to be named The Tanunda Soldiers' Memorial. It would still be supporting the memory of the war, so that was all right.

I wonder if anyone saw the irony of the situation. The building of the hall was deemed to be a most patriotic cause, in spite of the fact that the project had been begun by a group of men who as club members had been accused of disloyalty to their country. And I wonder, too, if anybody in 1917 saw how the first edition of the *Barossa Cookery Book* could be read as a political document reflecting the sensitivity of the times.

Except for a slight rearrangement of the recipes for fish, a new introduction and a new cover, the second edition of the *Barossa Cookery Book* is very much like the first. It was the third edition — basically the one still sold today — that was the enlarged deluxe edition containing 1,000 recipes. It first appeared in the mid-thirties and by this time fears of anti-German feeling must have abated. Here at last, alongside the Chow-chow and the Genoa cake are recipes for cucumbers pickled in dill and vine leaves, and several versions of German cake. For a while, at least until the next world war, Barossa Valley cooks were no longer shy to share the foods of their Prussian ancestry.

Here, too, are countless recipes for cakes. The Barossa, like the rest of Australia, launched into the Age of Cake, that time between the wars when middle-class people enjoyed the leisure activity of taking afternoon tea. Even women working on mixed farms periodically found time in their busy day to mix up a sultana cake, lamingtons or a batch of scones for church meetings and for visitors. How they managed that along with the fowls, cows, pigs, garden and work inside the house defies the imagination.

Cooks in the 1940s deserved to be called accomplished if they could make Napoleon cake. Layers of thistledown sponge interleaved with layers of feathery pastry, sandwiched around layers of cream and raspberry jam could make a person's reputation, as it did for winemaker Peter Lehmann's mother. During the Second World War, American clergy servicemen based in the army camp at Sandy Creek on the edge of the Barossa enjoyed visiting Pastor Lehmann and his wife, especially if the Frau Pastor served Napoleon cake, her crowning achievement. I'm not sure how she did this when there was rationing of butter with coupons and when most of the sugar supplied was raw. But people on farms had their own cows and although much of the farm produce, as well as flour from the local flour mill, had to be sent off to feed soldiers in other places, there still seemed to be enough to keep cooks going.

In Tanunda, especially, food was available to help feed the soldiers who were billeted with every family as a way of keeping the locals under tabs or so some thought. It was a lively and busy time when the house was full of soldiers from all over Australia, from all walks of life, and there were more trainees in a tent city down at the park. Local families welcomed their guests with a fine dinner, in many instances with wine served at the table (especially for the officers, billeted on the eastern side of the main street). The hosts entertained them at concerts and tennis parties and could count on their help in the house. It was a time of thrift – nothing useful or edible was wasted – but the concert-goers still enjoyed plates of cake and sandwiches for supper afterwards. Brown sugar no doubt caused the creation of new recipes.

After the Second World War immigrants from Europe brought with them all sorts of exciting ways to prepare food that Australians did not know. Many from Germany chose to settle in the Barossa, and for the first time local people of the post-war era tasted such delicacies as *Pumpernickel* bread and *Sauerbraten*. The locals poked and prodded the packaged *Stollen* that enterprising German delicatessen owners had imported from Europe. They tried the bags of *Pfeffernüsse* dipped in thin white icing, so like their own honey biscuits and yet so different from them. They developed an instant enthusiasm for *Bienenstich*, a yeast cake with an almond and toffee topping. Along with the rest of Australia the Barossa Valley people began to learn a great deal about the food culture of a wider Europe.

As the pace of life speeded up from the 1970s onwards, it was less common to find people in home kitchens with the time to devote to traditional Barossa cooking. When it takes several hours for yeast cake to rise and prove before being baked, women who also go out of the home to paid work are not going to make it very often.

This means that butchers and bakers and other commercial food producers have become increasingly important for promoting the Barossa food culture. Most people only taste the sausages and cake served to them over the counter of a shop (they might be quite surprised to discover that versions made a generation ago in private kitchens were quite different: that the *Kuchen* was much flatter, for example, and the *Streusel* often thicker and softer). We rely to a large degree on local bakers and butchers to keep the traditional foods alive.

And who would have guessed that the new commercial thrust on the Barossa Valley food scene would produce other dishes to be firmly associated with the region? For example, from the 1990s, Barossa Valley Pheasant Farm pâté became so widely known through export nationally and overseas that many people living in those places would associate that food with the region without knowing of any other.

The other large commercial influence on food in the Barossa since the 1970s has been the growth of the restaurant trade. It began with the Weinstube, built between Tanunda and Nuriootpa, and Gramp's Weinkeller Restaurant at Jacob's Creek. From these to the caterers and eating-houses of the present day, the public food ventures established in the Barossa have brought to local cuisine sophistication and a sense of adventure. A creative interest in food and catering among people in the wine industry has also shown that good food and good wine go together, a concept that is very important for the Barossa food culture.

Every one of these commercial ventures into food presentation has influenced Barossa food, yet none would have made any impact without an appreciation of the quality of food that existed in the region from the time of European settlement.

Chapter 3

Menge and the Melons

There are pumpkins growing in the tree outside this window. Seeds that were in the compost sent out long runners, which wired themselves into the branches and now heavy blue pumpkins are sitting up there along with an old bird's nest.

I am fairly sure that pumpkins were among the first vegetables cultivated in Barossa Valley gardens. Melons certainly were. When the first Europeans came to settle, these plants began to flourish in an experimental garden set up beside the creek later known as Jacob's Creek, a name we associate today with the best-selling red wine. And really the Barossa food culture begins right there, with vegetables growing by the creek.

The first known garden was planted by Johannes Menge, an eccentric geologist from Hessen. If anyone knew what was hidden in the earth and ways to take advantage of the South Australian soils and climate, Menge would have been the man. He had come to the Barossa in 1839 with instructions to examine its mineral wealth and farming potential – and he was passionately interested in gardening.

This little man with a big hooked nose and pointed chin had set up a shelter for himself under an overhanging cliff close to the spot where Jacob's Creek joins the Little Para River. People today call the place Menge's Cave, although it is not a cave at all, just a depression underneath the cliff. An alluvial river flat lay nearby in an elbow of the creek. Energetic Menge set to and, with the help of some labourers, dug a channel, diverting the creek water, so that the river flat became what he called Menge's Island.

This was where Menge established his garden. In between his forays into the ranges, he planted, weeded and watered and watched with delight as vegetables began to grow. A year later, he wrote a letter to one of his employers, George Fife Angas, living in England, about all the food he had produced:

You will easily comprehend that my garden is stocked with the finest vegetables, whilst the gardens around Adelaide are dried up.

One plant of melons producing two or three fruits round Adelaide has yielded twenty to thirty on Menge's Island, tangibly confirming my opinion that your land is, even respecting the fertility of the soil, worth more than land round Adelaide. As to the size, my largest melon this day weighed about 16 lbs, and I should have had some weighing 20 lbs if the rats had not interfered and nibbled off the vines on which they grow.

People today still visit the places where Menge had his cave and his island, the spot where he set up his lean-to against the cliff, surrounded by gardening tools and the heaps of minerals he had taken from the nearby hills.

He must have sat there often smoking his pipe, writing his reports and recording the results of his soil and mineral tests. Perhaps he sometimes sat with his feet in the water of the creek, munching a piece of *Wassermelone* and spitting out the pips. More than likely, though, he kept the seeds of the melons and pumpkins to give to newly arriving settlers, as he had done with seeds from his earlier garden on Kangaroo Island.

And indeed settlers were now beginning to move into the area. An English family – two brothers, William and John Jacob, and their sister, Ann – also took up land at Jacob's Creek in 1839. Other families were pitching tents and building cottages. For many of these settlers, like the Kleemann family who lived upstream on the other bank, a visit from Menge must have been quite common.

He would appear at their doorways, mostly at meal times, the eccentric little man who looked like Mr Punch. Sitting down at their tables he probably harangued the families with his theories about how colds and fevers came from demons, but many would have listened to his expert advice on growing different plants for food.

From the start, the early German farmers produced food for themselves and to sell to other colonists. In the first years of settlement around Adelaide, nobody else seemed very interested in agriculture. They were too concerned with land speculation. People were importing staples like flour and potatoes from Van Dieman's Land at great expense. For meat they killed wild birds: ducks, emus and painted and stubble quail. Surviving by hunting or importing supplies, not many settlers actually grew food.

What an opportunity for the German farmers! Old reports say that it took them only a few months to establish a village of whitewashed, thatched cottages at Klemzig on the outskirts of Adelaide. From their vegetable gardens and dairies, they were soon supplying food for the rest of the people; and when they set up villages at Hahndorf, to the east, and later in the Barossa Valley to the north, one of their first concerns was to plant vegetables, fruit and wheat on their narrow strips of land leading down to the nearest river.

Times were hard until the farms were established and not all the crops succeeded. Yet, a writer of the time calling himself 'Old Colonist' (thought to be a Henry Jones, Esquire) who visited Bethany in the Barossa Valley in 1851 said that most of the farmers around this little German village had gardens and were doing very well.

Old Colonist visited an elderly Mr Fiedler, who grew abundant crops of peaches, nectarines, plums, pears and apricots. Fiedler also had a vineyard and made his own wine. Old Colonist tried the wine, as well as some spirit that Fiedler had distilled from the grape skins. It sounds from the report as though this spirit had a kick to it and that Old Colonist left Fiedler's farm far merrier than when he arrived. The Turkey Flat Winery on the way to Bethany is where this meeting

Peter Lehmann in his orchard

between Old Colonist and Fiedler took place. It is easy to imagine Fiedler sitting in front of the little cottage next to the present winery, offering a drink to a passing visitor with a twinkle in his eye.

Old Colonist's visit to the Barossa already shows a pattern in the way people lived: a pattern which, for many families, was to continue until half-way through the next century. They worked hard to be self-sufficient, but many also knew how to enjoy the good things of life: good food, good wine and warm hospitality.

They had mixed farms and could produce almost everything they needed. The farm would carry livestock: pigs, cows, poultry, perhaps a few sheep. Fruit trees grew: quinces, apples, pears, apricots, plums, as well as vines. Old walnut, mulberry and almond trees are still dotted around the district. Where wheat could be grown successfully, it was. And everybody had a vegetable garden.

What delightful places those vegetable gardens were, with their orderly rows of peas and beans on trellises and the radishes, turnips and beetroot laid out in precise rows. Lay the rake handle across the newly tilled dirt, put seeds in the fingerholes poked along the line at intervals, and you get that order, that precision. You also experience some of that feeling of closeness to the origins of food that forms the basis of a true food culture. People in the Barossa had that feeling.

I can remember an old lady talking years ago, with tears in her eyes, about the smell of cucumber seeds. Even in the seed, she said, you could smell the scent of the cucumber which it would one day produce. For her, the promise in that smell affirmed her religious beliefs and, in a similar way, working the land was related to the religion of the early Barossa settlers. They believed that they were God's stewards of the land, and that they should make it fruitful, enjoy its bounty and pass stewardship on to the next generation.

Growing vegetables for them was a duty and a pleasure; and for many local people it remains so to this day. Many collect the seeds from the produce they have grown and give them to other people to try in their garden plots.

Some of the seeds have been passed on through the generations.

Anna Geier, aged 97 when I interviewed her, described how seeds were handed down in her family:

The green cucumber seed, you can't buy that. It's more like an apple cucumber in flavour, but short and green. We keep that seed every year. Spread it out on paper to dry. I have seen it done for fifty years. A lot of people come to me for the seed. They say: 'Auntie Anna, have you got some of your nice cucumber seed?' They all want that seed because that cucumber was a lovely one to eat and you can't buy that seed. We've been keeping it for years. We take the seed nearest the stem and we use that cucumber for making salads.

Back on the farm, the vegetable garden was part of a microcosmic food web, in which one item of food contributed also to the production of another. The vegetables would go to the kitchen, where they would be prepared for the table. The peelings and scraps would be fed to the pigs and poultry, which also grew fat on skim milk from the dairy and the fruit dropped from the trees in the orchard. Surplus vegetables were chopped up for cow fodder. Then, manure from the pigs, fowls and cows would go back to the gardens and vines.

In due time, the pigs and poultry would be slaughtered. The pigs were made into sausages, hams and bacon, which would be preserved in the smoke-house, absorbing the curls of smoke rising from the smouldering almond shells. The lard would be rendered for use in cooking and for making soap.

Out in the sheds, grapes were turning into wine, and any failed wine into vinegar. Some farms had grindstones for making flour. In the dairy, the farmer's wife turned milk into cheese and cream into butter.

So, in good times, into the farm kitchen would flow a supply of different kinds of meat, milk, butter, cream and cheese, eggs, fruit, vegetables, cooking fats, nuts and flour. You could preserve, pickle, bake and roast using almost entirely supplies from your own farm.

Talk to anyone who lived on one of these productive farms before the Second World War, and you discover that their shopping lists were short indeed. These folk visited the towns only to buy goods like sugar and clothes and to go to football and church. Even if their own farm lacked one or two of the food supplies, their neighbour would be bound to produce them.

It would be easy to romanticise all this, but keeping the show going was very hard work. People I have interviewed say what a relief it was when the pigs were gone for good. Suddenly, they had less work and one less bad smell. When central dairies were set up and trucks came to pick up the milk in cans, people felt nearly as glad as they did when they finally sold the cows altogether.

And yet, those same families still enjoy producing food for themselves and most of them still have a vegetable garden. So the vegetable garden is the last element of that bountiful farm life to go, which is curious, since it was the first thing to be established.

Which brings us back to the melons. Having grown in the district's vegetable gardens ever since Menge introduced them so many years ago, they and pumpkins and cucumbers are a basic part of the region's food culture. Here is an old Barossa saying about when to plant them:

Pompen und Melone
Gurken und Bohne
Wassermelone, Zuckermelone
und Kurbis.

The secret of the rhyme is not so much in the meaning of the words but in the way you say them. The words are simply a list of vegetables: different kinds of melons, cucumbers and beans, watermelon, rockmelon and pumpkin. You have to chant the first three lines in a resonant voice and roll the 'r' sound on the last word. Then you have a good imitation of frogs serenading each other in the local

Mona Doering in her vegetable garden

waterhole. The message is clear: when you hear the frogs in early spring, it is time to plant these seeds in the garden.

And when the fruits ripened, what did people do with them? Watermelons and rockmelons they just ate and enjoyed, or sent to market in the city – unless it happened to be young Johannes Kleemann, who with his brothers in the early 1850s discovered that they could roll them down the cliff into the Aboriginal encampment by the creek, causing everyone there to scatter. Then they themselves ducked and ran, terrified lest they should be discovered and punished.

Pie-melons were different. They arrived in South Australia long after the first German-speaking settlers, who invented the name *Pompen* for them. It is not a name or a plant known to people in Germany today. Their market price was first listed in the *South Australian Register* in 1855. They originate in countries to the east of the Mediterranean and must have arrived in South Australia by a haphazard route. The seeds grew easily and the melons multiplied promiscuously, right through South Australia to south-western Queensland and western New South Wales.

At a time when any source of food was valuable to pioneer families, cooks discovered that pie-melons were adaptable. You could do all sorts of things with them. Because they were so easy to grow, pie-melons could feed large numbers, and they became a staple of family meals. They lasted in storage for months on end, provided that their stalks were quite dried out at harvesting time. The bland-tasting flesh absorbed the flavours of whatever the cook added to pep it up. Mixed with lemon, currants and spices, pie-melon pulp was very often baked into sweet pastry cases for dessert.

People with long memories say that they never want to see another pie-melon pie ever again! Yet pie-melons have a pleasant texture for cooking and hand-written recipe-books show that by the early 1900s cooks were using them in all sorts of puddings, jams and pickles. Mostly, these recipes were written in English, alongside others in German. Some came from newsclippings taken from English-language newspapers. Right across the state, inventive cooks seem to have been determined to make the best use of pie-melons.

In about 1910 Frau Pastor Stolz of Light Pass wrote a recipe for melon and pineapple jam into her notebook. She attributed the recipe to a Mrs Wallent and wrote the comment *Sehr gut!* under the heading. The recipe below is adapted from her original.

Melon and Pineapple Jam
Delicious, if you can get a good pie-melon! A food processor takes away the tedium of cutting up the fruit.
800 g melon | 3 lemons | 6 cups water | 6 cups sugar | 1 small fresh pineapple

Puree melon in the food processor. Zest lemon rind and set aside. Juice the lemons and add juice to the melon. Pour the water over the melon and lemon. Let all stand a few hours and then boil for half an hour. Remove from heat. Add sugar and stir until dissolved. Boil briskly for about $3/4$ hour, stirring all the time, until a little gels on a saucer. Meanwhile, peel and puree the pineapple and add for the last 15 minutes of cooking. Add grated lemon rind last of all. Pour into heated jars and seal.

Four years later, as war was breaking out, Annie Heinrich wrote out a recipe for pie-melon jam with oranges and ginger that must have made enough to feed the army going off to the Dardanelles!

Pie-melon Jam with Oranges and Ginger
45 lbs pie-melons and 35 lbs sugar | 12 lemons and 12 oranges |
2 oz whole ginger | 1 heaped tsp acid

Slice, peel and cut the melons the night before and mix well with the sugar. Cut up the lemons whole. Peel and cut up the oranges and put with the melons. Cut the orange peels fine and put in a dish of water. Pour off the water in the morning and add the peels to the other ingredients with the ginger and acid. Boil well for two hours.

In 1920, the pie-melon avalanche was continuing. A cutting from the *Chronicle* newspaper of that year shows the Polst family of Light Pass near Angaston with huge waggon-loads of melons setting off for the Adelaide markets. The caption suggests that the melon harvest, which followed the vintage, might bring a price as uncertain as that which farmers managed for their grapes. Vignerons today might wonder if anything has changed.

Pie-melon Chutney
A good accompaniment to bread and cheese or to spread in ham sandwiches. Makes 2–3 jars.

470 g minced pie-melon ┃ 85 g brown sugar ┃ ½ tsp salt ┃
¾ cup vinegar ┃ ¼ tsp pepper ┃ 115 g onion ┃ 60 g sultanas ┃
½ tsp ground cloves ┃ 1 tsp minced garlic

Gently simmer all ingredients except garlic about 45 minutes until a rich brown colour. Do not let it burn. Add finely minced garlic and simmer until garlic is tender.

Well, then, what ever happened to pie-melons? In the following decades, they were still being used. Thrifty cooks discovered that you could add a bottle of raspberry essence to the jam mixture and call it Mock Raspberry jam! Today, however, they are no longer as common as they once were, although they are still around. Greengrocers say that a few people still grow them and, in April and May, some still ask for them in the shops. But it appears that the tide that began in 1855 has been stemmed, and that people no longer have to find inventive ways of cooking them.

Pumpkins! Now they were a common sight years ago. If you went out in the family car for a Sunday drive, you often saw pumpkins on the tops of underground tanks, their squat, heavy shapes holding down the corrugated iron. Or, if you called at a farmhouse, you would see them on the verandah on old wire bed-frames. They were cut up and baked with the Sunday roast or boiled then mashed to a pulp and masked in parsley sauce. Some families had a delicious way of cooking pumpkin, baked in layers with poultry stuffing. This next recipe is a very old one from the Roennfeldt family.

Layered Pumpkin Bake
The lemon zest is a good balance to the pumpkin.
2 or 3 cups steamed, mashed pumpkin, seasoned with salt, pepper and a nut of butter ▮ 2 or 3 cups of seasoning made with $1/2$ loaf white bread, 1 small onion, finely chopped, 1 dsp of fresh, chopped thyme, 1 tsp fresh, finely chopped sage or marjoram, $1/3$ cup fresh, chopped parsley, grated zest of $1/2$ lemon and 1 tbsp melted butter ▮ grated, sharp-flavoured cheese ▮ extra butter for the top

Grease a casserole dish. Place pumpkin and seasoning in layers, finishing with pumpkin. Top with grated cheese. Dot with butter. Bake at 160°C for 20 minutes or until cheese browns.

People who lived on farms remember the long trough hewn from a tree-trunk into which they would tip the pumpkins of the giant variety grown especially to feed the cows. They remember standing with one foot braced on each side of the trough, chopping up the pumpkins with a spade and watching the cows eat them with gusto.

Finally, many early recipe notebooks give directions for making a spiced pumpkin pickle that can be served as an accompaniment to hot or cold meat. Similar recipes still form part of the repertoire of traditional cooks in many parts of Germany today. The next recipe is adapted from the 1907 recipe-book of Mrs Stolz of Light Pass.

Sweet-and-sour Pumpkin Pickle

This pickle would go well with ham, pickled pork, a coarse meat loaf or a terrine. A spoonful of the pickle juice can add flavour to gravy for veal and other meats. Makes about 2 jars.

350 g pumpkin, not too ripe, halved, seeded, peeled and diced ❙ 350 ml wine vinegar ❙ 350 ml water ❙ 300 g sugar ❙ grated zest of 1 lemon ❙ 4 cloves ❙ 1 stick cinnamon ❙ 10 g fresh ginger root, peeled and finely chopped ❙ 8 peppercorns ❙ 2 tsp salt

Boil vinegar, water, sugar, lemon rind and spices together for 15 minutes. Add the pumpkin and simmer for 30 minutes or until the pieces are tender and glazed. Cover and let stand overnight. Next day remove the pumpkin and pack it into jars. Boil the juice until it forms a thick syrup. Sieve and cool. Pour it over the pumpkin and seal the jars. Best if kept for a few weeks.

Chapter 4
Küche, Kirche und Kinder

Whenever I travel over the hill at Lyndoch and see the Barossa Range ahead, I think of how the early settlers, both German and English, came in their waggons along this same route. I wonder if the first glimpse of those hills gave them the same sense of arrival as I always have when I see them stretched out ahead of me.

I think especially of the women, and how they had to adjust to living in a strange new land. Imagine the first settlers reaching Bethany in early March, the harshest, driest time of the year! Looking at the grey bush from their European perspective they probably wondered if they would ever again know a home like the ones they had left.

Of course, it was up to them to make any sort of home at all. That meant making everything as much as possible like the life they knew back in Europe. Within ten years, they succeeded so well that, by the winter of 1851, the German traveller Friedrich Gerstäcker was able to write of his visit to a Barossa house:

At the stove sat an old grandmother with a white-haired child on her knees. The old woman was a faithful, excellent example of an elderly German peasant woman of the kind found only in the centre of Germany ... Not only that, but everything in the room was German: oven, chairs, tables, cupboards, footstool, spittoon, earthenware pots, plates decorated with texts, dishes and verses from the hymnbook.

The women who lived in these buildings must have felt pangs of homesickness in their European farmhouses amidst alien bushland, but this was no time to sit and brood: there was too much to do! Just keeping track of the children, getting the house in order and the meals prepared would have made each week hard enough, without all the extra farm work as well. Women helped clear the land, hitched themselves to the plough alongside the ox in harness, and traipsed off to market in distant towns to sell butter, eggs and vegetables.

They must have been tired, those settlers, coming back to the farmhouse at nightfall – in time no doubt to prepare the evening meal. Trudging home along the track, they probably had plenty of time to wonder, as most cooks do, 'What shall we have for tea tonight?' As a matter of fact, in my own great-grandmother's written account, 'tea tonight' by the end of the week sometimes meant fried bacon and onions – all other foodstuffs had run out.

Two good starting-points for seeing how newly arrived settlers did their cooking are George French Angas's picture of the first village of Bethany, settled by the passengers of the *Skjold* in 1842, and the historic little cottage built by the Luhrs family at Light Pass in 1846.

Young Angas, in about 1845, took his sketch pad and paints to places in the antipodes and left us a personal record of life in those times. The lithograph of his painting of Bethany really does tell a story about cooking arrangements. Out in the open, with fowls and goats scratching around nearby, and with other women walking past lugging various containers, a villager is tending an open fire and a large, bubbling pot. Perhaps it contains water for the washing but it could just as easily be food, because not all the cottages in the picture have chimneys. That may mean that they did not all have a place to cook indoors. Family records show that often people did the cooking outside first of all and that this arrangement might continue for at least a year until a proper indoor fireplace could be built.

The original Luhrs kitchen is just one step up from this most primitive arrangement. Unless some cooking was still being done in

Luhrs Cottage, built in 1846

Luhrs Cottage

the open air at Luhrs Cottage, meals for a large family were all cooked on one small fireplace in the narrow kitchen. Instead of an oven, there was just an iron frame, a *Vier-Fuß*, over the coals on which to rest the saucepans – great, heavy, cast-iron affairs that would wrench your wrists. These pots, including black-bellied 'witch's cauldrons', were the main sorts of containers the pioneer German women had for all their cooking, even for baking bread.

Anna Rosina Luhrs was the mother in charge of the tiny kitchen at Luhrs Cottage. There was just enough room for a few small cupboards, a little table and the fireplace at one end. Bending down towards the fire to lift off the pot of soup, with young children clinging to her skirts, she must have had a strong heart as well as strong wrists. What if one of the children fell into the fire? No wonder Anna Rosina used a sharp tongue to keep the family in order! She was a strong-minded person: as 24-year-old Anna Scholz, she had made her own decision to migrate to Australia in 1845 to work as a serving girl for another family from her district.

Later, in the cottage built for her and Heinrich Luhrs, the schoolteacher she married in Australia, she must have stood for hours in front of the fire. Even though no known photograph of her exists, her presence will always be there – on the slate hearthstone is a hollow groove, worn by Anna Rosina's feet.

Eventually, the tiny kitchen and open hearth at Luhrs Cottage could no longer cope with the needs of a large family. A separate building, almost as large as the cottage itself, was built a few metres behind the cottage and this was the new kitchen. At last the cook (Anna Rosina or her successor) had room to swing a rolling pin! It must have been like heaven for her. She also had a long kitchen table on which to spread the trays of *Streuselkuchen* – and even an oven in which to bake it.

But there was still no hot-plate. The oven door was at the back of the fireplace, about 30 centimetres above the floor of the hearth. In front of it, the fire was lit and the saucepans were still placed on a rack over hot coals. It was the kind of cooking arrangement that was

Küche, Kirche und Kinder

The bread oven

common throughout the Barossa Valley and other places where German-speaking pioneers had settled. Whether the kitchen was in the central body of the house, or whether it was built outside, the opening to the bake-oven was at the back of the fireplace and people cooked the daily food on the fire in front.

Kitchens with bake-ovens like this are dotted all over the Barossa Valley. Some you can see from the road, often just parts of the ruined shells of farms, looking for all the world like fossilised steam engine boilers. Having the oven projecting from the wall of the house like this was a good way to keep the heat of cooking out of the kitchen, and people no doubt built ovens like this not only to reduce the risk of burning down the house but more especially to cope with the Australian climate. Externally protruding ovens may have existed in Prussia at the time the settlers left, but there do not seem to be obvious remains of them today. Certainly, on my travels in 1996 to historic villages in parts of Europe where early settlers originated, I did not see bake-ovens extending outside like the Australian ones.

The new Luhrs kitchen was not nearly as elaborate as some of the others in the neighbourhood because it did not have a place indoors for smoking sausages, a 'black kitchen', as many farmhouses had. But it probably had an outside smokehouse and it did have a cellar, where the cook kept her jars of *Sauerkraut* and pickled cucumbers, ripening cheeses, calico bags of dried apricots, pears and apples, and jars of wine in their wicker coverings. Hooks and wires hanging from the ceiling held rows of sausages. Bunches of aromatic herbs from the garden would be hanging up to dry: dill for the cucumbers, caraway seeds for the quark, thyme and marjoram for seasoning the poultry and wursts. The combination of these cellar smells was complex and unforgettable. It leaves an imprint on the mind as permanent as the groove on Anna Rosina's hearthstone.

Naturally, if your oven is designed for baking bread and cake once a week, and your daily cooking is confined to saucepans and pots placed over hot coals, this arrangement is going to influence the sorts of meals you prepare. Yet it is not easy to find out exactly what meals people made in early kitchens. The trouble is that people did not often write down recipes for the dishes they cooked in those pots. They just knew how to make them and put in a pinch of this and a cup of that.

Many early cooks did not even know how to write. Caroline Herbig, who raised her children in the famous Herbig Family Tree at Springton, could sign her name only after her children had taught her. Anna Rosina Luhrs herself may not have known how to write, even though her husband had studied languages at Oxford, for the birth details of the children entered in the Luhrs family birthday book are written in English, and in English handwriting, as early as 1848. Heinrich probably wrote them himself.

But many of the pioneer German women *were* educated. To read some of the old commercially printed German recipe-books would have required a high level of literacy. Girls would have learned to read not only in school but also in their catechism classes. In many families this was a significant time in a girl's life. My own great-grandmother spent six months in 1872 boarding in Tanunda, preparing for her confirmation, after her family had moved 50 kilometres further north. The experience would have given her a great deal of practice at reading and writing. Anna Geier of Greenock showed me the exercise books she filled with writing at her catechism classes in about 1910. By the time her confirmation day arrived, Anna had become a fluent reader and writer of German.

I must tell the poignant story, too, of Miss Dorchen Nehrlich, who was an educated woman and a clever pianist engaged to be married to Pastor Fritzsche. Some rather supercilious English visitors to the township of Klemzig on the outskirts of Adelaide in 1841 saw her grand piano in the parlour of the house they were visiting, and requested to hear her play. She was called in from the creek where she had been washing the family clothes. Wiping her soggy hands on her petticoat, she sat down and tossed off a fantasia before leaving the room hastily to get on with her work. She was no rustic simpleton!

An early kitchen

Sometimes old diaries talk in a very general way about the wild game that ended up in settlers' cooking pots. They mention parrot pie, wild duck and rabbit. Family history books say that settlers clearing scrubland ate a good many kangaroos and wallabies while these were plentiful. Combining these foods with ones from their traditional food culture, they made dishes like kangaroo served with bacon and garlic.

I have found no specific recipes for preparing native game foods, however. Cooks probably had no time to record their successful meals. Besides, they probably considered wild game to be a stop-gap until they were able to produce the ingredients for traditional foods – and they were clearing land, bringing in livestock and planting as fast as they could to make this possible. It would take several generations eating a good deal of kangaroo and parrot to make these part of a region's food culture. Much of the game did not survive for a long enough period to become an essential ingredient in a widely made dish.

Roast Kangaroo with Bacon and Garlic

This is what G.R. Juers said his parents ate at the early settlement called Hoffnungsthal. I assume that the dish was similar to 'Bush Kangaroo' or 'Kangaroo Steamer', made by many colonists in Australia and so I give an adaptation of that dish. Wild garlic grows along many Barossa roadsides: not all the early settlers' crop went into the pot.

Line a pot with fatty strips of bacon and in it put alternating layers of finely sliced kangaroo, onion, garlic, salt and pepper. Cover with a tight-fitting lid. Cook over a moderate heat 10 minutes to sear the bacon. Reduce the heat to extremely low and cook for 2 hours. After 2 hours, add a cup boiling water. Do not stir: just shake the pan. Simmer 20 minutes. In a small pan, blend 1 dsp flour with $1/2$ cup water. Strain off liquid from the cooked meat into the flour mixture. Stir rapidly to make gravy. Cook gravy gently for a few minutes and serve with the slices of kangaroo. A traditional Barossa way to liven up the gravy would be to add a little juice from a jar of pickled figs or pumpkins, or perhaps a few drops of vinegar and a pinch of sugar.

Very soon the settlers were putting some of the foods from the old country in their heavy, black cooking-pots. A few elderly people can still recall one or two of their early traditional European dishes. Some have even put them down on paper, to capture a fading memory of foods their families once loved.

The first is *Schlesisches Himmelreich* (Silesian Heaven). This dish is still made in Germany. Not surprisingly, people who remember it can trace the origins of their families back to the land near the River Oder. Made with smoked pork, dumplings and dried fruits, it was an extremely rich dish. A little goes a long way. It filled adults who ate it with nostalgia, but some of their grandchildren reacted very differently. Vera Bockmann, who was 90 when she spoke about it early in 1993, said that she ate it only to please her grandmother.

Schlesisches Himmelreich – Silesian Heaven

The combination of the smoked pork and the sweet-sour dried fruits is good. The pears, especially, marry well with bacon. So do the prunes. But it is rich. The peasant version used a purée of dried peas instead of cornflour to thicken the stew.

MEAT AND FRUIT

250 g *Backobst* (dried apples, pears, prunes) ❙ 500 g smoked *Speck* trimmed into cutlets (or bacon, or *Kassler* from a good butcher, or a roll of pickled pork) ❙ freshly ground black pepper ❙ juice and rind ½ lemon ❙ ¾ cup stock or water ❙ 1 tsp cornflour ❙ dash of brandy

DUMPLINGS

¾ cup mashed potato ❙ ¾ cup flour ❙ 1 egg ❙ 1 tsp salt

If the *Backobst* is hard, soak it overnight in a little water. Next day simmer fruit, meat and seasoning gently together in the stock or water for about 15 minutes until soft. Thicken with cornflour, add brandy and check the seasoning.

Mix together the dumpling ingredients, form dough into little balls and drop them into boiling salted water. Simmer until dumplings float on top, drain and serve with the pork dish.

Küche, Kirche und Kinder

Now, the dish that is mentioned most often when old people remember the meals prepared by their grandparents is one that must have been adapted from *Schlesisches Himmelreich*. It is called *Pompenbrei mit Klöße* (pie-melon puree with dumplings). 'Ah, the *Pompenbrei*,' they say nostalgically. 'We loved the *Pompenbrei*!'

Why, though, did people make *Pompenbrei* for their pork and dumplings in preference to the dried fruit version that they brought with them from Silesia? Dried fruit must have been available to use. Did they just prefer the taste and texture of the pie-melon flavoured with lemon? Or was there so much flesh on pie-melons that the farmers could not bear to see good food go to waste?

Pompenbrei mit Klöße – Pie-melon puree with dumplings

DUMPLINGS
2 cups plain flour | 1 tsp cream of tartar | ½ tsp bicarbonate of soda |
1 tsp salt | 1 tbsp butter | about ½ cup buttermilk or water

MEAT
500 g smoked pork spare ribs or pickled pork | 1½ L good meat stock

POMPENBREI
500 g pie-melon | rind and juice 1 lemon | ½ cup currants or sultanas |
½ tsp cinnamon or a small piece cinnamon bark | ⅓ cup water |
1 tbsp sugar or golden syrup

Make the dumplings or *Klöße* by working the dumpling ingredients into a stiff scone dough, and gradually adding a little buttermilk or water. Simmer meat in 1 cup meat stock over a very low heat for about 20 minutes. Meanwhile, in a separate pot, boil the rest of the stock. Shape the dough into walnut-sized dumplings and drop them into the boiling meat stock to cook for about 20 minutes.

Peel and cut up pie-melon. Place in a saucepan with other *Pompen* ingredients. Cook until soft.

To serve this dish, you arrange the cooked, drained meat and dumplings on the plate, and over them you spoon the puree of *Pompen*. Just before serving, some families poured a little red wine over the food. But I wouldn't.

From the time of earliest settlement, much of the culture of food preparation was based on the keeping of pigs. The German settlers needed the lard from fattened pigs to make soap, as well as for their basic cooking fat. The meat they ate most often was pork, prepared in various ways and preserved by smoking or pickling in brine. The Prussians do not appear to have eaten as much lamb or mutton last century as the early English settlers did, but as well as pork they did favour poultry, beef and veal.

Bertha Hahn, who lived at Marananga and at Vine Vale as a girl, has written out for us the recipe of *Sauer G'schlinge*, made when a young calf had been slaughtered. The recipe is a good example of the way everything remotely edible was used to advantage in a farming food culture. After the stomach lining had been used to produce rennet for cheese-making and the veal for roasting, this recipe dealt with the lungs.

Sauer G'schlinge

1 set of lungs from a young calf fed on pure cow's milk (the calf should be 6–8 weeks old and should not have any infection or congestion on the lungs)
2 onions, chopped ǀ salt and pepper ǀ allspice ǀ vinegar to taste ǀ
3 or 4 medium-sized potatoes, peeled and diced

Cover the lungs with water and bring to the boil. Lift the lungs from the water and tip the water out to remove any scum that may have formed. Cover the lungs with fresh water and cook gently until tender. Remove from water and chop into bite-sized pieces. Return to water, adding other ingredients. Simmer gently until the soup or stew is nicely thickened by the potatoes. The meal is served in deep bowls and eaten with a spoon.

The cook always had a pot of soup on the go and most often it was noodle soup, made with broth from a boiled fowl. People swore by noodle soup's ability to settle upset digestive systems and to ease anything from constipation to bilious attacks. Besides, it made a delicious start to one of the grander Sunday meals. In its simplest form, it was made without vegetables, although often it contained carrots and an onion as well as nutmeg, a commonly-used spice in Barossa food.

Fowl and Noodle Soup

The fresh celery gives good flavour to this soup. Having an excellent chicken is also important. An old-fashioned soup would have been made from an old bird, and would also contain the giblets, claws, comb and brains.

1 corn-fed chicken with a good covering of yellow fat | water to cover | 2 tsp salt | 6 black peppercorns | 3 celery stalks with leaves | 2 or 3 sprigs thyme | handful of home-made noodles | 1 onion, chopped | 2 carrots | 2 tbsp butter | ½ tsp nutmeg | 1 tbsp plain flour | parsley

Wipe the chicken. Prick fat all over with a skewer, but do not pierce the meat. Melt 1 tablespoon chicken fat in a pan with a heavy base and to release the fat slowly brown the chicken on all sides over a gentle heat with the lid half on the pan. Cover with water, add salt, peppercorns, 3 celery stalks and thyme. Simmer until the chicken is tender. The length of time depends on the age of the bird – you might have it going for half an hour for a young chicken or for a few hours if the fowl is old. Do not overcook.

Remove the pot from the fire and let it stand until next day. Take out the celery. Remove the chicken from the stock (use the chicken in another dish) and skim some of the fat off the surface. Melt some of the chicken fat in a stock pot and gently fry the chopped onion, the carrots peeled and chopped and add stock and extra salt and pepper to taste. Bring to the boil, simmer until the vegetables are soft, add noodles. Simmer 5 to 7 minutes until the noodles are tender. Remove from the heat.

In a little pan, melt butter with nutmeg and brown it without burning. Stir in the flour. Add a little of the broth and blend. Pour the mixture into the soup. Return to the heat. Stir until it is slightly thickened. Stir in a good handful of chopped, fresh parsley and correct the seasoning.

We can work out people's eating habits in the early years of settlement because some of the customs continued into the next century.

For instance, people always had their main meal in the middle of the day. This remains the case in many Barossa families today. Peter Lehmann, the well-known winemaker, remembers how he had to race home from school at lunchtime, bolt down a large roast dinner and pudding and rush back to school to fit in a game of football before the bell went for afternoon lessons.

From the leftovers of the midday dinner, an evening meal of cold meat and salads was put on the table at night. The cook might make soup to go with it, possibly turnip soup with dumplings. This soup was made simply by boiling turnips, onions, potatoes, parsley and celery in good stock until quite soft, putting the lot through a sieve, and adding milk, salt, pepper and perhaps a little nutmeg. The dumplings, for which recipes have already been given, would be cooked in the soup or in boiling salted water and added later.

Here are two other soups commonly made by descendants of the Prussians:

Rote Rüben Suppe – Beetroot Soup
The quality of the stock is crucial.

375 g beef or marrow bones ⁞ 5 cups water ⁞ salt, pepper and sugar to taste ⁞ 1 corn of allspice ⁞ 1 bay leaf ⁞ 1 dsp chopped, fresh marjoram ⁞ 500 g beetroot ⁞ 1 tbsp red wine vinegar ⁞ 1 tbsp flour ⁞
1 cup sour cream

Make a good brown stock by browning the bones in a little fat, then simmering with water, salt and pepper and other seasonings until the meat is cooked. Drain and reserve the meat for another meal. Strain the stock into a pot. Allow to cool. Skim off the layer of fat. (Or use chicken stock made from the previous recipe before vegetables and noodles are added.)

Wash beetroot. Place unpeeled in a pan with water to cover. Simmer until tender – about 3/4 hour. Drain. Peel beetroot while still hot. Mince. Place in a dish and sprinkle with vinegar.

Return stock to the heat. Mix flour with sour cream. Add to heated soup. When it has thickened, add beetroot with more vinegar, sugar and seasonings to taste. Reheat but *do not boil*.

Sauerkohlsuppe – Sour Cabbage Soup
This is a good peasant soup, if the meat and cabbage are not overcooked.

375g fresh pork ribs | 125 g smoked belly bacon | salt and pepper | 5 corns of allspice | 1 bay leaf | 1 L water | 375 g white cabbage, shredded | 1 tbsp flour | 1 cup fresh sour cream | sugar and vinegar to taste

Make a broth by simmering meat, salt and pepper, allspice, and bay leaf in water until the meat is cooked. Skim the scum. Add shredded cabbage, then simmer until cabbage is just tender. Remove the piece of bacon. Mix flour and cream and add to soup. Season to taste with sugar and vinegar. Serve with fresh, crusty bread.

Farmers needed a hefty breakfast. Elderly people recall platters of fried eggs and bacon, pancakes with syrup, bowls of porridge, *Blutwurst* and *Presswurst* fried in the pan. Nothing, someone said, is as delicious as fried *Presswurst* (not even bread dipped in egg and milk, fried in lard and called *Arme Ritter*).

A Sunday breakfast treat would be *Mettwurst* or *Knackwurst*, pricked with a fork, boiled gently in water, then served in steaming slices. If the skin of the *Mettwurst* split because the water was too hot, you certainly did not waste the rich ingredients, you simply ate the lot as *Wurstsuppe*, or *Mettwurst* soup, instead!

Peter Lehmann has – almost – the final word on breakfasts:

Years ago, my mother would fry potato left over from the day before, with onions, bacon and tomato. She would top the lot with a fried egg. I used to have that breakfast every day of my life. And what's more, I still do!

'Not if I can help it!' says Margaret, his wife. 'He's meant to be on a diet!'

The days of the week imposed their own rhythm on food preparation. Each day was set down for different activities in the house and on the farm. The week began quietly on Mondays and Tuesdays, when the women were busy washing and ironing. That rule was almost sacrosanct and still is for many. Often, people I interviewed for this book would say, 'Well you can't come on Monday because that's my washing day.' So the meals were simple on Mondays, probably made from leftovers of the mammoth Sunday roast. By Thursday, however, mighty preparations were being made for Friday, the day for baking bread and *Kuchen* and Friday's flurry of activity might continue the next day as well, leading up to the culinary climax on Sunday, with its huge midday dinner, often followed by an afternoon of entertaining visitors and an equally large late afternoon tea.

The pot-roast must have been an important part of the main meals of the week even for the early settlers. Old records of the Kleemann family describe women from neighbouring farms coming after 1839 to the Kleemann home to buy a joint of meat and taking it back to their own farm, neatly pinned up in a calico bag. At home, they would hang the bag on a hook in the shade of the verandah until cooking time. This practice continued for generations. A tiny girl on one farm, seeing the bag hanging in the breeze, ran and told her mother that there was a baby in a nappy pinned up to the clothes-line!

The way that roast was cooked shows just how long old habits continued to hold sway. On the early campfire and in the first kitchen fireplace, Anna Rosina Luhrs would have used a camp oven with little feet on it. The wallaby, beef, hen, or leg of goat – goats feature strongly in the Angas pictures – would go into the camp oven with a little water, salt and pepper and some added fat. For hours, Anna Rosina would brown and turn it, brown and turn it gently over a low heat. From time to time she would add a little more water or fat. By dinner time, the meat was tender and juicy, almost falling off the bone. She might add some carrots, pumpkin, parsnip or potatoes to the pot for the final half hour. She might make gravy using scorched,

Küche, Kirche und Kinder

brown 'baked flour', the brownings in the bottom of the pot and some of the stock made from boiling other vegetables.

Some time in the latter part of the last century, or even later, a huge, black, iron, wood-stove would have been installed in the fireplace, possibly even covering the bake-oven door or sitting alongside. Its arrival was an occasion for rejoicing. Now there was a broad, flat surface on top of the firebox, and a large oven underneath. You could fit a goose or a turkey into that oven. But is that what people did? No. They cut the legs off the camp oven and continued to turn and brown, turn and brown on top of the stove. They continued to use the camp oven to roast the geese, ducks, fowls, beef, turkeys and mutton. It is not easy to turn a huge turkey over the fire, but of course every wife had Herculean wrists from years of wrestling with those great black saucepans!

Harry Schmidt by the bread oven

And now came Sunday, which towered above the successive weeks like a giant exclamation mark. From the moment the church bell started ringing across the paddocks on Saturday evening, Anna Rosina and the rest of the congregation knew that the next day was intended to be a day of rest. You weren't supposed to do any heavy work, and yet you were expected to dish up the crowning meal of the week.

What skilled timing must have been required to get the family ready for church and the meat in the oven without appearing to break the observance of rest! Did mothers sometimes stay home from church so that they could baste the roast leg? Certainly some of the irreverent card-players who met on Sunday mornings for a hand of euchre, hearing the bell being rung in church at the moment that the Sanctus was being said, referred to it as 'the potato bell' – time for Mum to put the potatoes in with the meat.

Finally the service was over. The children, who had sucked conversation lollies while the pastor delivered his long, impassioned sermon, came filing out of the church. They stood around while the adults exchanged news; then hopped into the waggon or the buggy or, later, the new car to go home to the delicious smells in the kitchen.

If the pastor was coming as the honoured guest, the meal would be even more bountiful than usual. It opened with grace:

Komm Herr Jesu Christ,
sei unser Gast
und segne was du uns
aus Gnaden bescheret hast.

After the bowls of noodle soup, the dinner plates would appear, covered from edge to edge with roast potatoes and marrow, *Sauerkraut*, beans, cauliflower with white sauce and a spoonful of stewed quinces, and, if the meat was to be roast pork, dumplings boiled in hot lard – to say nothing of the slices of meat and cascade of gravy. And there was pudding to follow.

Küche, Kirche und Kinder

It is hard to imagine how people could manage to eat so much, but these were farm people who had worked exceedingly hard during the week and required a great deal of energy from their meals. The poor Pastor would have been very rude if he had refused any. When some pastors, like Peter Lehmann's father, died young of heart attacks, it was said that they had dug their grave with their teeth.

Now the eating was over, for the moment. The left-over meat and vegetables were whisked off into the safe for future meals and everyone stood up from the table. Probably the girl who helped in the house did the washing up, using water from the big black fountain on the stove. She turned the tap and steaming water streamed into the tin basin over soap encased in a wire strainer.

The pastor was bid a cordial farewell as he climbed into his buggy and stowed the family's gift of firewood on the buggy floor. After all that food, no doubt he undid a few buttons in relief as he drove out of sight.

winter

Chapter 5
Winter Trimmings

The Barossa Valley is supposed to have a Mediterranean climate, with warm, dry summers and cool, wet winters. At least, that is what the children are taught at local schools and that is generally how it is.

Sometimes, though, winter begins by being dry, so dry that the cold air hangs like a dead weight and gardens seem starved for water. Then the local people anxiously peer at the sky wondering when the rain will come, and old-timers bring out their wisdom about the *Siebenschläfer*.

The *Siebenschläfer*? The name refers to a superstition that came to this district with the early settlers from Europe. People say that if it rains on 27 June, the rains will continue for another seven weeks. Does the theory hold any water (so to speak)? Farmers used to claim that it did. Strange to say, a wettish period often does seem to follow if there are rains around that date but then who has ever counted the days accurately or given it more than a passing thought? Perhaps we should! Even if people remember the weather predictions associated with the name and talk about them at the beginning of winter, I don't think that many actually know who or what the *Siebenschläfer* were.

The story of the *Siebenschläfer* or Seven Sleepers is a very old one, and it spreads across many countries and many cultures. It is found in tales from Arabia, North Africa, Europe, Scandinavia and Scotland.

In one version, the sleepers are persecuted Christians from the third century who slept for 200 years after being walled up in a cave near Ephesus. In the Arabian story, the Sleepers – who in this version had a dog – foretold the coming of Mohammet. In many of the legends, people said that when the sleepers moved in their sleep a disaster would surely follow, or at least a change in the season. It is this last bit of the story that came to the Barossa Valley with the early settlers.

The funny part is that, like all seasonal stories brought from the other side of the world, this is a legend relating to a different hemisphere. Yet here in the Barossa it fits perfectly well into the scheme of things and everybody hopes that the Seven Sleepers will roll around a bit in their slumbers, to bring an end to an unwelcome dry patch of winter.

It would have pleased the early settlers that, with good winter rain, they could grow their beloved cabbages with ease. They were probably surprised to learn that you could have cabbages ready to pick in the winter. Such a luxury they did not have in the old country, which is why the Prussians had pickled their cabbage as *Sauerkraut*. (Not that they had invented the skill; it had come to Europe from Asia, brought by the Romans and then later by Mongols invading from the south-east in the thirteenth century. In fact, in the southern hills of Silesia you can visit the ruins of old fortresses that were built in an attempt to keep out the Mongols in the time of the son of Genghis Khan. It is fascinating to think that here, indeed, may have been the entry points in space and time for *Sauerkraut* coming into the German part of Europe.)

No matter who made the world's first *Sauerkraut*, the settlers coming from Europe to Australia by sailing ship would have been much worse off without it. The letters of advice sent by Pastor August Kavel to other congregations in Prussia thinking of booking their passages show that it was an important part of the food on board ship:

I would strongly advise you to take also preserved green beans – they are obtainable in Hamburg – [and] sauerkraut, dried green cabbages in jars . . .

Pastor Kavel made it quite clear that eating *Sauerkraut* would prevent months of sickness from scurvy. He knew very well how seafarers had become ill in the past from the lack of fresh fruit and vegetables. The people thinking of migrating probably did not need his advice, though, because they were already used to making *Sauerkraut* and they brought their cabbage slicers with them to Australia. Several of these lethal-looking contraptions are on display in the Historical Museum in Tanunda. Once again, here is food being preserved by people of Prussian origin using a process of fermentation.

Sauerkraut

Rinse the *Sauerkraut* before eating to remove the salt, if necessary.
For every 5 kg cabbage you need 250 g salt and a dsp of caraway seeds.

Slice the cabbage very finely, put it in a dish and sprinkle salt over it, working it with your hands until the juices start to run. Lay a whole outer cabbage-leaf at the bottom of an earthenware crock and pack in layers of the sliced cabbage, sprinkling each layer with a few caraway seeds as you go and ramming the layer hard. (Some people had a stick called a *Stampfer* to do this.) Leave enough room at the top of the crock so that the juice does not overflow. Cover the top layer with some more great big cabbage leaves and a plate that fits the width of the crock. Weigh down the plate with some heavy weights inside a clean glass jar so that the cabbage is immersed in its own brine. Cover with a cloth. Store it in a place with an even temperature. In warm weather, leave it ten days. In colder weather, it takes three to five weeks to ferment.

Different families had their own variations on the basic method of preparing *Sauerkraut*. The large cabbage leaves needed to have the bloom of yeast on them to start the fermentation, but it was possible

Bertha Hahn makes Sauerkraut

to speed things up by putting a lump of unbaked bread dough in the bottom of the pot. Some people made a calico bag that fitted into the crock and rammed the cabbage into that. The bag helped to keep out the air. Others placed a white cloth over the fermenting cabbage before putting on the plate and weights. This helped to lift off the crust of fermented matter. Some people who still make it today, so I'm told, freeze the *Sauerkraut* in plastic bags when it is done. But this is unnecessary, for the whole reason for fermenting the cabbage is to make it keep. As long as it stays immersed in the brine and has been properly made, it can last for months.

When the *Sauerkraut* was ready, cooks had their own pet ways of preparing it for the table. They might drain it, rinse it in clear water and eat it cold. They also made it into a hot vegetable dish by heating it in a saucepan with a few more caraway seeds, a little white wine, some ground pepper and a pinch of sugar. Some cooks simmered it gently with a little honey and smoked bacon. But whatever they did, they all agreed that it made a beautiful accompaniment to roasted meats, especially pork. It also goes well with grilled steak.

Although many people in the Barossa made *Sauerkraut* in the nineteenth and early twentieth centuries, by the end of the Second World War the custom was much less common. There are a couple of reasons for this. First of all, two wars against Germany caused people to stop eating foods that were obviously German – for a while, at least. But I think that a more important reason was the fact that people could pick cabbages fresh in the winter in this country and so they no longer needed to pickle and preserve them.

That did not stop local people from liking their cabbage cooked to have a sweet-sour, almost fermented, taste, and most families ate a variation of a recipe for fresh cabbage cooked with bacon, onion, vinegar, pepper and sugar as an approximation of the flavour of *Sauerkraut*.

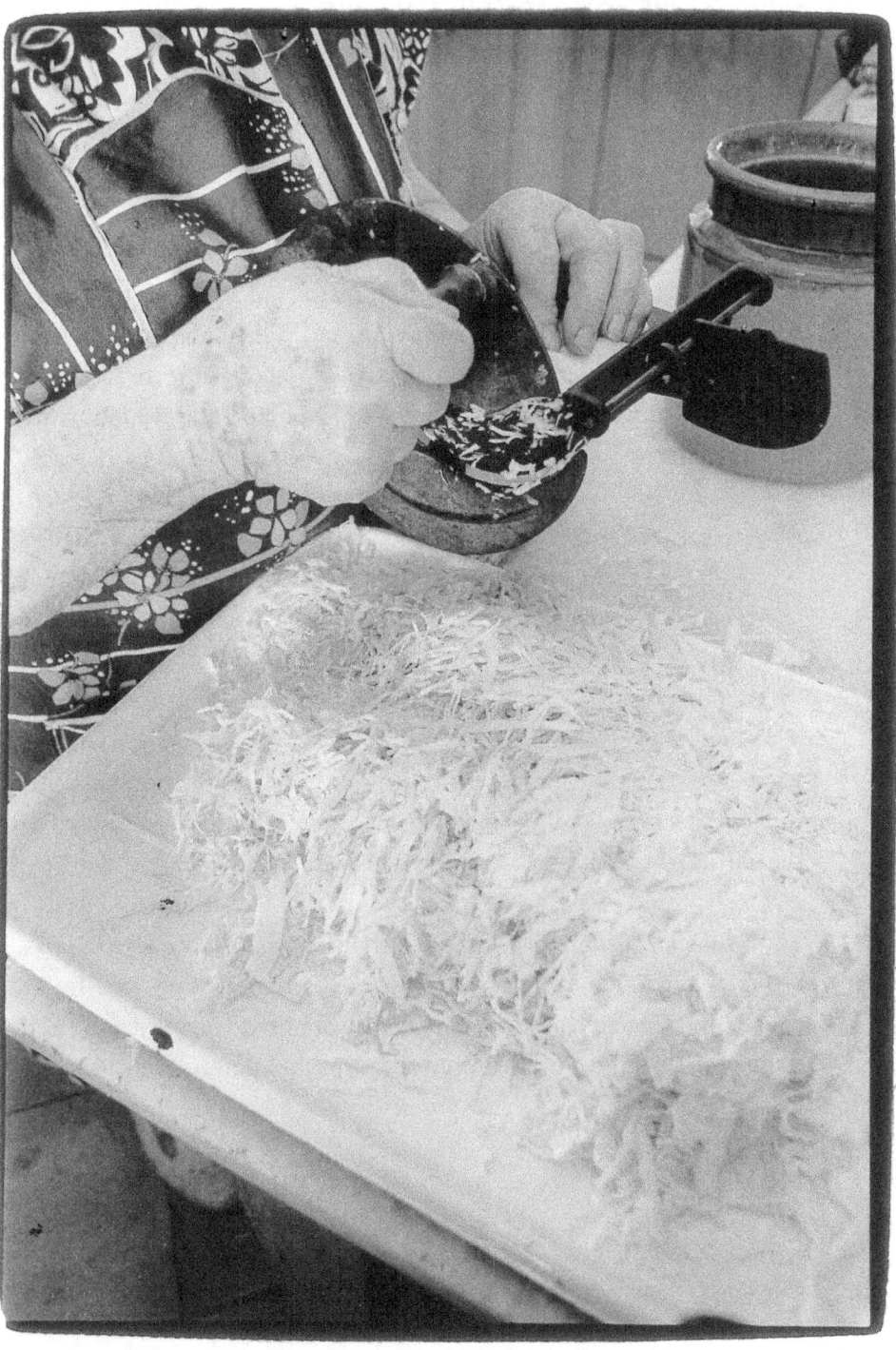

Dämpfkraut – Sweet–sour Cabbage
One of my favourite childhood dishes. The recipe serves six.

4 cups finely shredded cabbage | 2 tbsp lard or butter or water | 2 or 3 tbsp vinegar | $\frac{1}{2}$ tsp freshly ground pepper | 1 tsp sugar | $\frac{1}{2}$ tsp salt | 2 rashers bacon with rind removed, diced | 1 small onion, chopped | extra butter | $\frac{1}{2}$ tsp caraway seeds

In a frying pan heat lard, butter or water. Add cabbage and cook gently until it is just tender. Drain. Add vinegar to taste, ground pepper, sugar and salt. In a separate pan, fry bacon and onion. Add these to the cabbage. Lastly add a generous lump of butter and the caraway seeds. Return to a very slow heat and simmer until the cabbage is transparent, stirring frequently. Be careful not to burn it.

As with any recipe, a great deal depends on the length of time the food is cooked. The crisp, separate shreds of flavoured cabbage produced by one cook are quite different from the softer, fragrant pulp dished up by another. It's a matter of trial and individual taste.

People preserved beans and turnips by the same fermentation process as they used for *Sauerkraut*. They rammed them into earthenware jars, packing them down with salt. They ate the beans and turnips raw or cooked, but had to soak them in water first to take out the salt. The beans were served with cream and a sprinkle of pepper.

The Prussian settlers brought with them to Australia a love of broad beans, a vegetable still grown today in the regions they left. In late winter and through spring, people often ate broad beans served with the sweet-sour flavour so dear to the Prussian palate.

Broad Beans
The flavour of the beans is enhanced by the tart-flavoured glaze.
The recipe serves six.
3 cups broad beans (if they are tiny and tender, keep them in their pods; if they are older, peel them and prepare 3 cups of the bean seeds) | water to cover | 1 tbsp butter | $1/2$ tsp sugar | $1/2$ tsp salt | $1/2$ tsp pepper | 1 tsp vinegar | 1 rounded tsp plain flour

Boil the beans in water until just tender. Remove from the heat. Drain the water, leaving just a little in the bottom of the pan. Add a nob of butter the size of a walnut, a good pinch of sugar, a good pinch of salt, a sprinkling of fresh ground black pepper and a teaspoon of vinegar. Shake the pan and taste to see if the flavours balance. Finally, add a good teaspoon of plain flour or cornflour, stirring and shaking until it is combined with the stock and melted butter. Return the pan to the heat until the sauce thickens.

Tucked into one corner of most local vegetable gardens was a little patch of horseradish and this root vegetable was ready to be dug up and used in winter, although it was there for other seasons as well. Back in Europe, horseradish sauce was a traditional accompaniment to fish. Horseradish also went with roast beef. Some people can recall members of their family eating grated horseradish as a salad, too.

Horseradish was native to Eastern Europe and loved by Russians, Poles and Prussians. *Mrs Beeton* says it was native to England, too. A common Prussian method was to mix it with white sauce. It could also be added to mayonnaise. Later cooks discovered that you could make horseradish sauce simply by mincing the root, adding vinegar and a tin of condensed milk. But many continued to make it using fresh horseradish and fresh cream, the fresher the better. After all, in winter and in spring when people might be sneezing their heads off, what better cure than a jolt from the juice of freshly grated horseradish?

Meerrettichsoße – Horseradish Sauce

From the *Barossa Cookery Book*. Pleasant with crumbed fish or chicken. The only early example I have found of olive oil used in a recipe.

1 or 2 horseradish roots | 1 egg yolk | 3 tbsp Lucca (olive) oil |
2 tbsp vinegar | 2 tsp prepared mustard | 1 tbsp cream |
pinch cayenne pepper | pinch salt

Beat egg yolk in a basin, gradually beat in oil, first drop by drop, then in a slow stream. Add vinegar, cream, mustard, salt and pepper. Peel and grate horseradish roots and stir them into the sauce.

Horseradish Sauce made with Cream

Serve with poached or grilled salmon or salmon mousse. Makes a small bowl full.

1 tbsp grated horseradish | 1 tsp prepared mustard | 1 dsp vinegar |
1 tsp sugar | 150 ml whipped cream | salt to taste

Combine all ingredients and add the whipped cream and salt last of all. Make just before serving.

In the cold days of winter, food had to be filling to keep people warm. The most filling food devised in the cold countries of Europe, where fresh vegetables were scarce in winter, was the dumpling. Immigrants from Silesia, Brandenburg and Mecklenburg must have known many different kinds. Books of traditional recipes from these regions invariably devote a whole chapter to dumplings. They include dumplings made from flour, egg and mashed potato, dumplings like tiny *choux* puffs, called *Schwamm-Klöße*, in meat broth, and yeast dumplings simmered or steamed, served with stewed dried fruit. English and Irish cooks, too, must have brought with them to the new land a repertoire of dumplings.

Although Australia was of course a much warmer country where fresh vegetables were still available in winter, the dumpling habit did not completely die out – as we have seen with the *Pompenbrei mit Klöße*. Occasionally someone thought to write out the ingredients in her recipe notebook, possibly at the direction of grandmother. By the time the recipe for potato dumplings was set down in the Scholz recipe-book, the writer was no longer using German handwriting, and the German spelling had become a little unusual:

Kartoffelklöße – Potato Dumplings
Mehl geriebene Kartoffeln Eier Milch Sals and Muskatnuß ungefähr halb Kartoffel und halb Mehl, der Teig muß ziemlich steif sein daß man ihn kann in Bälle rollen.
Flour, grated potato, egg, milk, salt and nutmeg, about half potato and half flour, the dough must be stiff enough to roll into balls.

These dumplings seem to have been simmered in water, or perhaps in the broth in which smoked meat was cooked for *Schlesisches Himmelreich*.

Sometimes the cook made more highly seasoned dumplings and dropped them into a good meat-and-vegetable stew cooking in the oven or on top of the stove: an utterly delicious country meal to warm you after a day 'tying on' in the vineyards.

Dumplings to go in the Stew
This quantity of dumplings would be the right amount for a stew made with 1.5 kg meat, 2 onions, 2 carrots, 2 parsnips, a turnip, and 1 stick celery.

$1^1/_2$ cups self raising flour ❙ 45 g butter or suet ❙ 1 tsp dried mixed herbs or 1 tsp each of chopped, fresh thyme and parsley ❙ pepper and salt to taste ❙ $^1/_2$–$^3/_4$ cup milk

Blend all ingredients except milk in a food processor. Tip mixture into a bowl. Make a well in the mixture. Stirring with a fork, add enough milk to make a stiff paste like scone dough. Pat out onto floured board. Cut off pieces, roll into walnut-sized balls and add to stew for the last 30 minutes of cooking, with the lid on.

Related to dumplings, especially to the potato kind, were potato pancakes. Made from grated potato, eggs and onion back in Europe and eaten with stewed apple, in the *Barossa Cookery Book* they were coyly called Mock Fish and recommended as a savoury substitute for meat by Mrs Edwin Kleemann. In the original, she slips from one language to the other, saying that the grated raw potatoes must be as fine as *Nudeln*.

Potato Pancakes
The fat would have been lard but these are just as delicious cooked in olive oil. Serve with home-made tomato sauce for a truly Australian meal.

4 medium potatoes | 1 large onion, grated | 4 eggs | salt to taste | 2 tbspn lard

Peel and grate potatoes. Add onion. Place in a sieve and press with the back of a spoon to remove some of the liquid. Beat in eggs. Add salt. Drop tablespoons of the mixture into boiling fat and fry, turning once, until brown on both sides. Drain on brown paper and serve.

As if all these foods were not filling enough, main meals, especially in winter, were not complete without a solid pudding. People's recipe-books devote pages and pages to puddings: date pudding, canary pudding, cabinet pudding. *Mrs Beeton* and the food columns in the *Chronicle* newspaper seem to have had an enormous influence on this end of the meal, and most of these recipes have been copied out in English, sprinkled with the odd German word or misspelling, like 'Cabinetspudding', showing the cook heroically coming to terms with the language of the new country.

Pudding recipes also came with the German-speaking settlers. They are even mentioned as part of the shipboard meals by some of the passengers. The first one of these was rice pudding with prunes and syrup. Directions for making rice pudding appear in both English and German in some of the early twentieth century recipe notebooks that I have seen.

Another very old recipe that appears time and again in people's notebooks is bread pudding. It is hard to say which country the recipe came from, as both *Mrs Beeton* of 1860 and the 1834 *Bremisches*

Kochbuch contain their own versions. All that you can tell is that the German families must have been bigger than the English ones – while the English recipe calls for four eggs and half a pound of grated bread, the German counterpart deals with lots of twenty eggs, all separated and whipped, added to three pounds of soft white breadcrumbs.

Bread Pudding
This recipe is typical of many in the notebooks. It makes a lovely, light dessert. It is worth making and quite different from bread and butter pudding. The recipe serves six.
3 cups milk | 1½ cups crumbed, stale bread | 2 tbsp butter | 2 eggs | small handful candied peel | ¾ cup sugar | a little salt | 1 tsp vanilla essence | handful currants

Scald the milk. Add crumbs and butter. Let stand 10 minutes. Separate eggs. Whip the whites. Sprinkle a greased pie-dish with peel. Stir egg-yolks, sugar, salt, vanilla and currants into the bread mixture. Fold in the beaten whites. Pour into pie-dish. Stand in a pan of very hot water. Bake at 160°C about 40 minutes. Do not let boil.

As the years went by, bread pudding seems to have lost its popularity to baked bread and butter pudding.

Bread and Butter Pudding
The crisp, buttery, baked bread-crusts make this recipe different from the previous one. It serves four to six.
3 thin slices white bread, cut in halves or quarters and lightly buttered | ½ cup mixed dried fruits of different kinds | 2 whole eggs | 3 tbsp sugar | 1 tsp vanilla essence | 1 cup milk | ½ cup cream | fresh nutmeg

Line a greased pie-dish with the buttered bread. Sprinkle dried fruits over the top. Beat lightly together eggs, sugar, vanilla, milk and cream. Pour mixture over the bread and fruit. Grate fresh nutmeg over the top. Bake at 170°C for 25 minutes or until golden-brown and just firm. Do not burn the fruit (cover it with foil towards the end of cooking if necessary).

Later, when the English influence was making itself felt, German families often enjoyed the delights of steamed pudding or baked roly-poly. All these foods can be found in the hand-written recipe-books used in the region, whether in German or English.

Pie-melon Roly Poly

Lemon-flavoured pie-melon puree freezes well and seems to increase in flavour for the freezing. Although considered old-fashioned, it makes a palatable dessert. The recipe serves four to six.

FILLING

700 g pie-melon flesh, seeds removed ǀ ½ cup water ǀ grated rind and juice 2 lemons ǀ ½ cup sugar ǀ ¾ cup sultanas ǀ ½ tsp grated nutmeg

CRUST

60 g butter ǀ 1¼ cups self-raising flour ǀ ⅔ cup milk

JUICE

60 g butter ǀ ¼ cup sugar ǀ ¾ cup water

Dice melon and chop up in the food processor. Add water and lemon juice. Cook slowly, stirring often, until melon is tender and thickens (about 20 minutes). Add sugar and sultanas. Stir until sugar is dissolved. Remove from heat and add grated lemon rind. Allow to cool. Freeze half for another occasion.

Rub butter into flour. Add milk gradually to form a soft dough. Roll out and place in buttered baking dish. Let mixture hang over the sides. Place strained fruit in centre, sprinkle with grated nutmeg and fold sides in over fruit.

Combine ingredients for juice in small saucepan over the heat. Pour it over the fruit pastry. Bake in a moderate oven (180°C) for 35 minutes. Serve warm with cream.

Good winter rains help to plump out the citrus fruit on trees down in the back yards of the Barossa. To have orange and lemon trees growing out in the open must have been a delicious luxury for the settlers; back home such trees were grown in tubs and brought indoors during the cold weather. When one immigrant arrived in South Australia in 1860, he saw from a distance many green and golden bushes. Ah! he thought. These must be the oranges and lemons people have been talking about. He disembarked from the ship only to discover that the bushes merely bore some fluffy yellow flowers, which he later learned were called wattle.

The Barossa immigrants must have looked forward to using citrus fruit in their cooking. The Anglo-Saxon settlers made marmalade, for which there are many excellent recipes in the *Barossa Cookery Book*. The one I love best is for mixed citrus marmalade given by Mrs Gladys Plush. The Plush family members were well-known orchardists right from the very earliest days of English settlement in the Barossa Valley. The recipe below is modified to be made in a food processor.

Mixed Citrus Marmalade

Pick the fruit and make the marmalade early in the season. Do not refrigerate the fruit. The recipe makes about eight jars. The original recipe is for double this quantity. To make it you would need a larger preserving pan and the boiling time at each stage would be one hour.

2 grapefruit | 2 oranges | 2 lemons | 2 mandarines | 2¼ L water | 2 kg sugar

Grease the bottom of a 5-litre pan. With a sharp peeler, thinly peel off the fruit rinds. Chop them up in the food processor and place in the jam pan. Peel off the rest of the pith. Halve all the fruit and pick out the pith core and pips with a knife. Blend the fruit in the food processor. Pour the juice and pulp into the pan. Pour over the water, stand overnight then boil ¾ hour or until the rinds are tender. Turn down the heat to very low to stop the jam from boiling. Add sugar – which you may care to warm first in a bowl in the oven. Stir over low heat until all the sugar is completely dissolved. Try not to let the wooden spoon scrape the bottom. Then increase heat and boil about 35 minutes. Keep watching to see that it does not burn and scoop off any scum that forms on the surface. Test to see if the marmalade has set by holding the dripping jam spoon over the pan. When the last drop clings to the spoon and does not fall, the jam is done. While still warm pour into clean hot jars using a little jug. The jam shrinks as it cools so keep topping up the jars. Seal.

Finally, here are recipes for candied peel and lemon syrup. They are typical of the ones women copied into their notebooks in about 1950 but cooks also made these treats in the 1830s when people were loading their chattels onto sailing ships and embarking for the new land.

Candied Orange Peel
This recipe shows that people wasted nothing. From the *Bremisches Kochbuch*
Soak 2 cups orange peel in salt and water for 4 or 5 days then bring to the boil 3 or 4 times changing the water each time. Make a syrup of 450 g sugar to 550 ml water. Gently simmer the peel in the syrup 1 hour for 2 days in succession or until transparent. Remove peel and put in the sun to dry. Store peel in airtight jar with a few drops of cooking oil to keep moist.

Lemon Syrup
Cooks have been experimenting with recipes for lemon cordial for 150 years. Twentieth-century recipe notebooks contain concoctions of lemons, sugar and such chemicals as sodium benzoate, citric acid, epsom salts and sodium metabisulphite. This delicious lemon syrup recipe from 1834 contains none of these. Use no metal utensils unless they are stainless steel.
Equal parts lemon juice and sugar ǀ grated or zested rinds of half the lemons ǀ a little water

Mix lemon juice and rinds in a pottery jug. Allow to stand overnight in a warm place. Next day, in a glazed (or stainless steel) pot dissolve sugar by adding a small amount of boiling water and stirring over a low heat. Strain the juice and add it to the sugar syrup. Bring just to the boil. Seal in sterilised bottles. The syrup will keep for several months.

Chapter 6
The Weekly Leavening

Sunday afternoon in the 1920s was visiting time in the Barossa and had been since earliest settlement. For both German and English families, it was often lonely working long and hard on the farm during the week and Sunday afternoon was a time to relax, catch up on family news and share advice about the land and the household.

When I think back to my own childhood, growing up in the 1940s and 1950s, I often remember the visits we made on Sunday afternoons to our grandparents, aunts and uncles. We would spruce ourselves up and pile into the back seat of the car to make the journey of an hour or so to our grandparents' place in a town north of the Barossa. I can't pretend that I always embarked on this visit with enthusiasm. After all, I could have spent that day knocking about in the back paddock or chasing my mother's turkeys or cruising around on my bike with friends.

Once we arrived, and after the initial formalities, the afternoon did improve. At first we perched awkwardly on the edge of the autumn-brown moquette suite in the sitting-room as our parents discussed Grandpa's health and the farming season. But Grandma was fond of a practical joke and soon she would offer round chocolates that squirted water in your eye as you reached for them. Then we would seek out the realistic artificial spiders that she had stuck on the lace curtains and on the framed German texts. Finally we would be sent out to play in the garden and I knew that Grandma would first of all find for us the two dolls she had made for her own children. Their bodies were of old stockings that Grandma had handpainted, and she had dressed them in frilly mob caps and gowns made of scraps of stuff from my aunts' childhood clothes.

Out in the garden we would wander around the neat plots, admiring Grandpa's beans trellised on bamboo wigwams, measuring ourselves against the towering hollyhocks, picking poppies and folding the petals down to turn them into one-legged dancers.

When the poppies – yellow, pink, red and white – had gone to seed, Grandma would shake the dried seed pods in our ears. Then she would pick off a pod and give to us this elegant little pepper-pot with a dry rattle. I wish I had kept one. I did not realise then how much poppy seeds were a part of the traditional food culture, important for making certain dishes in earlier generations. (I have only recently discovered, too, that some of the other varieties grown in South Australia were related to the opium poppy, *papaver somniferum*.)

Whether our visits were to this house where my grandparents had retired in the town, or to the old farm; whether uncles, aunts and cousins were there, too, or whether they in turn all came to visit us at our house, the crowning point of the Sunday afternoon was an elaborate high tea. We would gather around the table that was decked with an array of food so vast that you could hardly see the white tablecloth beneath.

Once Grandpa had said grace, we made short work of the feast before us. I remember the platters of cold ham and cold fowl – the real kind of poultry that bore no resemblance to the insipid meat of today's commercially raised chickens. I liked the sandwiches made with *Mettwurst*, pickled cucumbers or Grandma's special boiled cheese. There was bread spread with black blood-sausage and plum sauce. My brother headed straight for the cream puffs and jelly cakes and if Auntie Jean was the hostess we enjoyed slabs of the most delicious fresh *Streuselkuchen*, its topping scented with spices and sprinkled with almonds. Nobody could make *Kuchen* like Auntie Jean.

Not every family indulged in the luxury of Sunday-afternoon

visiting because some were too busy to stop work. Yet there were other farms where the children had to stay in their good Sunday clothes until two in the afternoon, just in case visitors should arrive. If nobody had appeared down the track by that time, they were allowed to put on their old clothes and go off to the waterhole to play. I wonder if their mother felt disappointed to spend the afternoon alone, or if she saw it as a rare chance to put her feet up and doze.

On Sunday afternoons in the 1920s when buggy-loads of people did arrive, a buzz of activity thrummed through the whole place. The men sat on the front verandah in their navy pin-striped suits with hats on, smoking and discussing the rainfall figures. In the house, the women were talking, showing the new cushions, comparing the excesses and achievements of their children. The youngsters could be anywhere, although on a farm they always visited the cowshed, especially at milking time, to let the new calves suck their fingers with sandpapery, slobbery tongues. The aroma of freshly roasted, freshly gound, freshly brewed coffee drifted through the rooms. If there was no coffee to be had, people roasted and ground kernels of wheat or barley instead. In wine-making households, if it was cold, you could be sure that *Glühwein*, made from mulled red wine and spices, was served.

After high tea, there might be some music in the sitting-room. Everyone had to be quiet when a talented musician in the family played Schumann and Beethoven, while at Christmas time they would all sing carols around the piano or the harmonium.

In some houses the men, especially, played bagatelle or card games like euchre and *Skat* but this depended what Lutheran congregation the family belonged to. Some were much stricter than others and did not permit the evils of card-playing or dancing. (Even in my own adolescence, I remember some socials where, when it came to the body-pressing bit in a Canadian barn-dance, we grabbed our partners' hands and whizzed round and round at arm's length instead.)

At last, when night had well and truly fallen, the visitors from town said their farewells and burrowed under travelling rugs in the chilly buggy or car to make the trip home – not too late because the new working week was about to begin but not too early, either, because it had been fun to spend time with family and friends.

Sunday, indeed, was the religious and social pinnacle of the week and its culinary success depended on preparations made days in advance. Cooks had to make ample bread and cake, not only for Sunday but for the following week as well and that is why most households had one or two huge baking bouts just a few days before.

In Harry Schmidt's family in the 1920s, Friday was bread-baking day, and look out if the firewood for the oven had not been chopped the night before! Thursday night was *Backholzhacken* night for young Harry. With shouted instructions from Mum and Dad ringing in his ears, he swung the axe in the shed, trimming the lengths of wood to go in the *Backofen*. Seventeen long branches he needed to trim so that they were about one and a half metres long – 17 branches for 14 loaves of bread. Sheoak branches were the best, or mallee, if it was obtainable. Then he had to stack them on the wheelbarrow and cart them to the kitchen, ready for Mum to stoke up the fire early next morning.

Meanwhile, Mum and her helpers had already been preparing the yeast mixture for the morning's baking. They needed to prepare a 'sponge', a mixture of flour and yeast leavening in a basin, which they would wrap in blankets and set to rise overnight in a warm place. Winter weather really presented no problem in most houses because there was always a warm nook at the side of the wood-stove, away from draughts, where the sponge could begin to work.

The cooks could make the yeast leavening to go in this sponge in several different ways, depending on whether the household belonged to the 'starter-in-a-bottle' school, the 'sour-dough' school or the 'dried-froth-from-fermented-grape-juice' school.

If the bread-makers favoured the bottle, they needed potatoes, hops, sugar, water and flour. Among the myriad recipes for this brew, quantities varied and so did methods. Some cooks just poured the boiling water over the finely chopped potato and other ingredients, adding the flour at the end, before pouring the lot into a bottle that they corked very securely and left to ferment for 13 hours.

Most commonly, though, people cooked the ingredients to make a liquid starter. They tied down the corks securely on the bottled brew. This was a wise instruction, for the liquid in the bottles could ferment for several weeks if necessary. Down in the cellar, this living monster, straining to be let loose, pushed against the corks with such power that one night, unless the string was firmly tied, explosions were bound to resound like pistol shots, causing the sleeping occupants of the bed in the room above to waken with a gasp.

'*Mutter, hast du etwas gehört?* Someone has been shot!' the father would say. When they discovered that it was just the yeast bottles, they would go back to bed before facing the task of cleaning up in the morning.

Bottled Hop-Yeast Starter
Keep the bottles airtight.

210 g peeled potatoes (ie 3 potatoes about the size of a lemon)
3 cups water | 2 tbsp hops | 2 tbsp sugar | 1 tsp salt
1½ handfuls strong unbleached bread flour

Boil the peeled potatoes in water. Drain, reserving water, and mash. To the hops – obtained from the brewery – which could be in a muslin bag, add the boiling potato water. Allow to infuse for ten to twenty minutes. Pour this infusion over the mashed potatoes to macerate. When lukewarm, strain the liquid and throw out the hop/potato mixture. To 1¼ cups of hop liquid add sugar, salt and flour. Break it up in the liquid with your hands. Pour the mixture into bottles. (Some people put a raisin in each bottle, one with the bloom still on it, for this is a source of yeast.) Tie down the corks very securely. Store in a dark place for about a week until it bubbles when opened.

Storing the yeast brew in a bottle for a while made it portable, and this was a great advantage for the pioneers who moved from place to place when they needed more farming land for their families. A great deal of bread last century was made on the move. At first light, before camp was struck, the women would mix the dough and wrap the wooden dough-bin carefully in blankets for the journey. At the midday halt, they would knock the dough down and knead it, put the cover back on the dough-bin and finally prove and bake the bread in camp ovens on the evening fire. Whether at home or on the move, when they poured in the yeast, they always left a little in the bottom of the bottle as a starter for the next brew.

It was not necessary to put the fermenting mixture in bottles if they were going to use it all in next morning's baking. Then, they could just leave the brew in a saucepan behind the wood-stove or to one side of the hearth all night in a place that was warm. In the morning it had frothed up and went in with the bread ingredients in a deep dish ready for mixing.

However, if you followed this method, you would need a lump of raw sour dough left from the previous baking: a lump about the size of a crumpet to begin the fermentation. That dough would have been allowed to dry quite hard, then crumbled into flakes and stored in an air-tight tin.

Wine-making families had a much easier way of starting yeast culture for bread (but more often for cake) and that was simply to use the froth from the fermenting vats of frontignan wine during vintage. This was said to make good yeast dough, with a dark colour and a delicate flavour.

Many cooks relied entirely on the foam from their wine vats to make their bread and *Kuchen*. What is more, they spread it out on trays lined with clean muslin cloth to dry in the air, crushed it into chips and stored it in sealed tins to be used instead of sour dough as the yeast starter for baking throughout the year.

At times neither hops nor fermented grapes were available. Then people had another way of cultivating yeast from lemons and many people did this during the Second World War when supplies of hops were irregular. The author of this recipe for lemon yeast claims that it makes excellent white bread.

Lemon Yeast

Mix 5 heaped dessertspoons of bread flour with 2 heaped dessertspoons of sugar and the juice of two average lemons. Add 1½ cups warm water and pour into a bottle kept for the purpose. After each lot of yeast, leave a little in the bottle as a 'starter'.

With all these methods, the hardest part, it seems, was getting the first culture to work, although with the bottle method it is possible to help the first starter by priming the bottle with a small quantity of boiled hop liquor a few days before actually making the hop-potato brew. Even so, for the first lot you made, you had to have patience. When you mixed the yeast with the flour, you just kept punching and kneading until it was suitably elastic. But how long did your patience have to last? Many cooks tell the story of how the dough just would not react, in fact showed no interest in rising, and so they buried it in the garden. Three days later, what did they see? The earth rising in an unholy mound, like a thing possessed: the yeast had at last begun to work.

Once a culture like this has been successful, though, nothing is quite so like perpetual motion as the action of continuing to make the yeast starter. I am thinking right now of a very old lady, well into her nineties, who still makes bread. At every baking, she transfers that little bit of life from the old batch to the new, and fermentation goes on in the same old bottle year after year. I am quite sure that it is this process of transferring life that gives her her own longevity.

The last thing on the previous night or the first thing on the morning of baking day, the cook added to the yeast culture enough unbleached strong bread flour 'to make a nice sponge so that it does not run off a spoon'. Allowing the yeast to work on a small amount of flour like this was a good way of telling whether it was still an active rising agent. After a while, she poured the sponge in with the bread ingredients, then mixed and kneaded the dough and set it to rise. The amount of flour used to the amount of liquid would vary according to the weather conditions.

Bread Sponge and Dough

SPONGE

250 ml active bottled yeast | 1 tbsp sugar | $3/4$ cup strong unbleached bread flour | $1/2$ cup lukewarm milk or water

Mix into a batter. Beat this about 100 times, lifting the spoon as you would for making batter. Cover it with a plastic bag and put it in a warm place to rise for several hours.

DOUGH

In the bottom of a large basin or wooden dough bin, smear 1 tablespoon softened butter or lard, mix in 5 cups of unbleached bread flour and 1 teaspoon salt. Make a well in the middle, add the bubbly-looking sponge and add $1^{1}/_{2}$ cups of lukewarm water. Mix into a flexible dough, pulling the mixture from underneath up and into the centre of the dough as the bowl turns. When the dough is combined, place it on the table and knead, taking the dough from the back pulling it up and over towards the front like a pasty, giving it a quarter turn then pushing it forward with the heels of the hands. Put flour on your hands as the dough gets sticky, not on the dough or the table. Continue to knead with this rhythm for 20 minutes. Grease the mixing bowl. Place the dough in the bowl with the seam side down. Cover and set in a warm place to rise for about 2 or 3 hours. When it has doubled in size, punch down the dough about 20 times, cover and leave in a warm place to rise again for another 20 minutes. Turn the dough out onto a board. Shape it into two oblong loaves. Place them side by side in a greased baking dish. Allow to rise again 10 minutes. Bake at 220°C for 10 minutes, then 180°C for 30 minutes.

While the dough was rising, the cook put wood to burn in the oven so that it reduced to coals and the oven could maintain a regular heat. As the dough was proving for the last time, the cook raked the coals out of the oven onto the hearth in front of the oven opening. She tested the oven temperature with a handful of flour on a tin plate. If it browned too quickly she sprinkled water in the oven to cool it. If it browned too slowly, she put some hot coals back in for a while. When the temperature was satisfactory, she raked out the extra coals, slid the loaves in their tins on long-handled paddles into the oven and baked them. The amount of time depended on the oven, the daily temperature and other variables.

Today we can only admire the expertise of those early cooks who, using the most primitive equipment, coped with a complicated cooking procedure and produced a food that was not just the family's staple diet but a marvel to eat as well.

In the Barossa Valley not too many people are left who bake their own bread by first making their own yeast culture. When commercially prepared compressed yeast became available, its slow-rising qualities seemed to produce bread that was as good as the old hop-yeast variety. Compressed yeast started to become popular by the 1930s and many quite elderly people do not remember anything else being used in their families.

In these days of dried-yeast baking, when doughs are forced to rise quickly to suit the baker's convenience, one of the few places left where you can enjoy the flavour of slowly proven bread made with compressed yeast is the Apex Bakery at Tanunda.

In all sorts of ways the Apex Bakery is a unique place to visit. It is a family business run by the three Fechner brothers, whose father, Keith, nicknamed 'Chiney', took his first job there as a twelve-year-old when the bakery began in 1924. Keith learned his trade by watching and working with the older bakers, who had no time to stop and explain things to him. He bought the business when his boss, Baker Hoffmann, retired some years later.

Chiney's conservative nature meant that he was reluctant to change any of the bakery methods. When suppliers tried to sell him the new oil-fired ovens he did not think he could afford them. It was his view that people should not buy anything unless they had cash in hand to pay for it. When other bakers were changing to the new dried yeasts, Keith stalled again. He knew the art of bread-making so well with the old yeast. Just by the feel of the dough, he knew how it was coming along. With dried yeast, it simply wouldn't be the same.

People may shake their heads at this reluctance to move with the times but here is one situation where extreme caution has paid off, for customers now come from near and far to buy Apex Bakery loaves. When you sink your teeth into the delicious crust of the kibble or feel the elasticity of the dough of a freshly broken white dinner roll, you soon know why. This is the real thing. Visitors to the Barossa return to Sydney and write back to the Fechners saying, 'We miss your bread!'

Early one morning, I go to watch the bread and cakes being baked in the wood-fired oven. The bakehouse is a bustle and flurry of activity as wood is fed into the firebox at the side of the oven. Trays of dough as palpable as white flesh sit waiting to be lifted in through the oven door on a long paddle.

Sawn mallee is the fuel for the 70-year-old oven, taken from allotments on the Murray Flats by the Fechners themselves, for their old wood suppliers have all gone. Nobody goes down and chops wood any more for a living so the Fechners have a licence to get their own. That way they are able to make sure that the mallee trees are trimmed without being destroyed. Within six or seven years each tree is back into strong growth, like a pruned vine.

Back in 1924 Baker Hoffmann built the oven himself with a firebox made in Adelaide. The design is called a Scotch oven. Unlike most of the old farmhouse bake-ovens it controls the flow of heat with a system of dampers directing the draught so that the heat flows from the firebox in a compartment at the side of the oven right down and around the oven interior.

Between them Nipper, Johnny and David Fechner carry on the traditional way of making bread through the night. At least, it is Johnny who comes in during the night and prepares the dough. He does not sleep there, though: not like his father, Chiney, who as a young man was so anxious that he might miss the time when the dough needed to be knocked down that he would put his bedding on the hinged lid of the dough-trough built against the wall. There he

Stoking the fire, Apex Bakery, Tanunda

slept the first part of the night. As the dough rose, it lifted the lid, tilting it and rolling Chiney towards the wall. He would wake up and punch the dough down, then go back to sleep. It always amazed him that the dough had the strength to lift his weight on the lid, yet sank back so easily when it was knocked down with his fist.

It's not an easy life being a baker because the work is constant and so many people depend on their supply of bread. Chiney would never go away because he would worry about what was going to happen home at the bakery. One year, when Nipper had just joined him as a new recruit, Chiney was persuaded to go to a wedding in Canberra with his wife. 'I don't know what happened', sighs Nipper as he tells this story:

That's the thing with a wood fire: you just don't know how the bread is going to go, so you've got to watch it all the time. Bread can take half an hour to cook, or it can take two hours. Anyway, Dad rings up in the morning to see how things are going back here and I tell you that bread hadn't been in five minutes and it was absolutely black! I don't know how it happened. Harry Stelzer from down the road walked in and he stopped to ask how things were going and then he saw the bread and said 'Ooop!' So when Dad rang, we had to say we'd burnt the bread and it looked absolutely shocking but there was nothing he could do about it. We shouldn't have told him, because I don't think he's been away since. And he's only 81!

By now the baking is over, the oven door has been swung open and Nipper is pulling out slides of freshly baked bread and rolls, filling the bakehouse with a heavenly smell. The bakers are greeting the shop assistants who are arriving for the day and calling out comments to each other. The atmosphere is warm and *gemütlich*.

Throughout its 70 years, the Apex Bakery has been an important part of Barossa Valley life. To end this chapter, try one of their horseshoe-shaped *Salzteig* pretzels, first produced by Baker Hoffmann himself. Generations ago, he supplied them free to drinkers in local

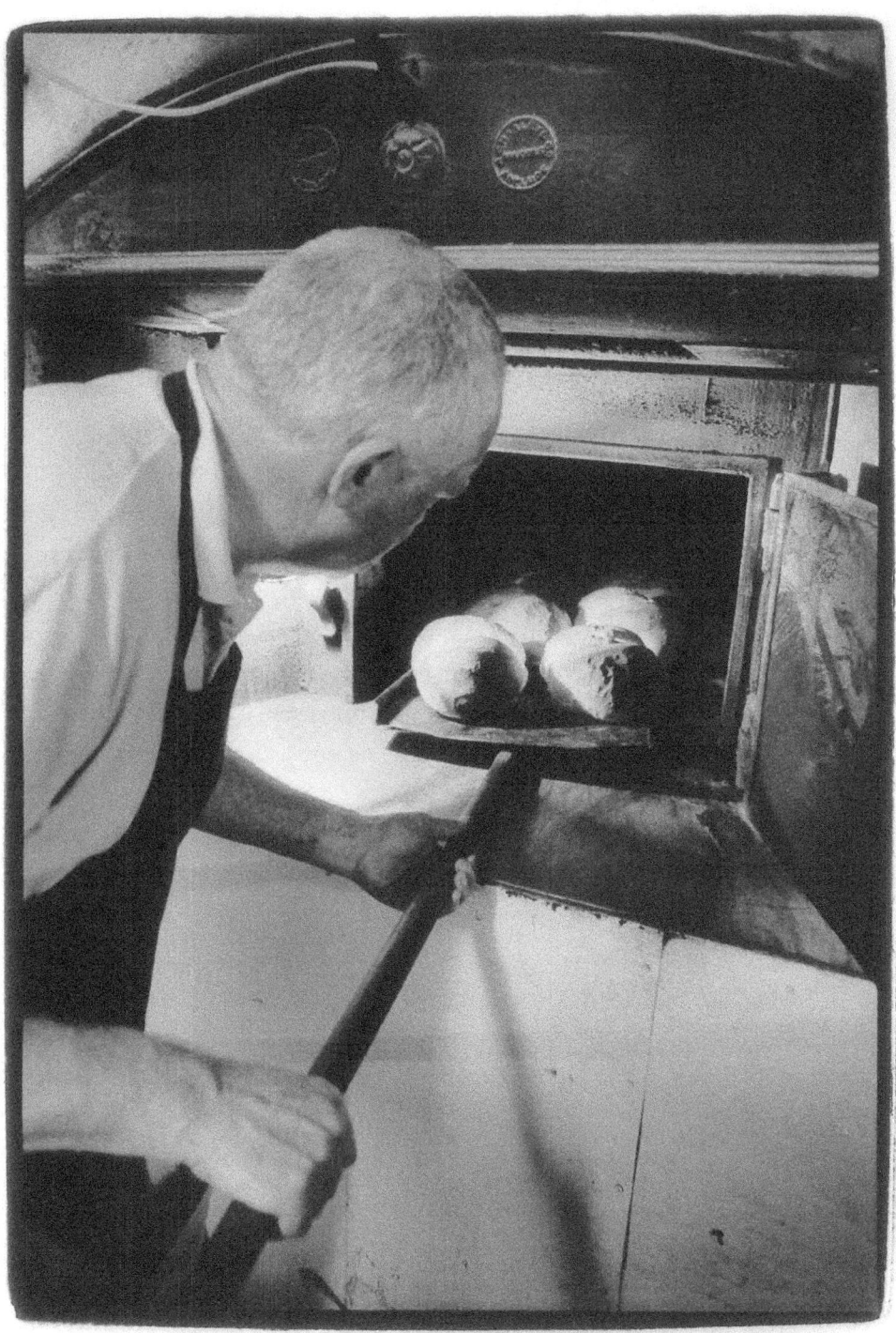

Brian Fechner, Apex Bakery, Tanunda

pubs and to children Chiney encountered when he was out on the delivery round with Baker Hoffmann's horse-drawn cart.

Although pretzels were not generally baked by Barossa Valley families, certainly not the curly Bavarian ones, local bakers did make and sell horseshoe-shaped pretzels. They sprinkled the pretzels with caraway seeds, a typical Barossa Valley flavouring.

Horseshoe Pretzels
A good accompaniment to dill cucumbers.
15 g compressed yeast ❙ ³/₄ cup warm water ❙ 225 g plain flour ❙
¹/₂ tsp salt ❙ 1 egg for glaze ❙ sea-salt flakes ❙ caraway seeds

Have all the ingredients at room temperature and the flour slightly warmer. In a warm saucepan, mix together half a cup of warm water and the yeast. Sift the flour and salt into a greased bowl, add the yeast mixture and enough warm water (try ¹/₄ cup) to form a fairly firm dough. Knead for 10 minutes. Place dough in a greased plastic container with a lid. Set to rise for 1 hour. Roll it out to about 7 mm thickness and cut it into strips. Twist the strips together to form a rope. Cut the rope into 20 cm lengths to form horseshoes, tapering and pinching at the ends. Or you can leave them straight and use them as 'salt-sticks'. Place on a greased tray, cover with a cloth and let rise 30 minutes. Brush with beaten egg and sprinkle with salt flakes and caraway seeds. Bake at 230°C for about 10 minutes.

Chapter 7

Kuchen in a Warm Kitchen

Sträselkucha
Schläscher Kucha, Sträselkucha,
Doas ihs Kucha sapperlot!
   ('*Streuselkuchen*/Silesian cake, *Streuselkuchen*/this cake
   is superlative!' – well-known Silesian verse)

My mother never baked the traditional *Streuselkuchen*. Even though her grandmother spoke German and had been brought on a ship from Silesia at five months of age in 1859, my mother's father had married a fierce English woman and so that cultural line was broken.

It was at a time when Anglo–Irish influences were seeping into the Australian German communities and giving them a totally different flavour. Talk about the cultural melting pot! As many other German-speaking women must have done, my great-grandmother actually taught herself English so that she could converse with her new daughter-in-law.

A few years later came the First World War, which gave the adoption of English ways another boost. One day soldiers came bursting into my grandparents' house and ransacked it, looking for guns. (This was in Eudunda, about 40 kilometres north of the Barossa.) My mother, aged about eight, and the other children huddled in a corner but their tiny English mother, livid with fury and indignation, made the soldiers put everything neatly back in the drawers. She laughed when one soldier stuck his bayonet up the chimney and was rewarded with a headful of soot. It served him right! And she made another soldier hold the crying baby.

Still, it was clearly in people's best interests to appear more English than German. So there was no incentive for my mother's mother to learn to make the old traditional foods of her husband's family.

Yet for all her Church of England upbringing, my own mother adored her Silesian grandmother. It was bliss to go and stay in that ordered, busy household when her mother was producing yet another baby. To be cosseted by all the grown-ups, to wander round the store, the cheese factory and the bustling delivery carts in the yard, to be in the kitchen when all the girls were preparing delicious food made a huge impression on my mother.

So, even though she did not make some of the more elaborate German fare, as a cook and housewife herself she copied many habits she had observed in her Silesian grandmother's kitchen – maybe without even realising it – and even though she did not bake *Streuselkuchen*, a fresh slab of it was ritually bought and eaten in our Tanunda household once a week.

Every Saturday morning one of us would ride our bike to collect the *Streuselkuchen*, commonly called German cake, from the kitchen of Elsie Schwarzkopf, who lived in a cottage on the other side of the town. Elsie's talent for making *Kuchen* brought many local customers to her back door. As Elsie shook icing sugar over the *Streusel* and wrapped up the large, flat slab of cake, its wonderful scent would fill her house.

That smell is one of the distinctive features of old German–Australian kitchens. You walk in and become aware of the enormous table, the tall wooden clock with its harsh metallic chime on the mantelpiece and, above all, the pervading smell of yeast, vanilla and spice from the *Kuchen*, which lasts long after baking day is over.

The scent really does permeate everything. When Elsie went to live in the local Rest Home, her cottage remained uninhabited for

Streuselkuchen

several years. Then she died and the house was put up for sale. Many people came to inspect the former shop. No furniture was in the house, not even in the front room where once Elsie had sold Rawleigh's products and pink sugar mice with string tails from the glass cabinet under the counter. Well, in fact, one piece of furniture did remain; the enormous, stone kitchen table had been too heavy to remove. That table, which must have held thousands of slabs of German cake during Elsie's life, still gave off its distinctive smell of yeast and spice even though the house had been unoccupied for so long.

It was a miracle if our slab of *Kuchen* reached home without holes where lumps of *Streusel* had been picked out of it. Who could resist having a taste to see if this week's batch was as good as the last?

As we sat around the kitchen table at home and polished off the rest with cups of coffee, we would talk about how the cake must have been made. Elsie surely could not have put so many trays of it inside her warm bed that morning. We knew that was the traditional way to get this yeast cake to rise but at the same time we somehow couldn't bear the thought of it.

I must say that none of the people I have interviewed in the past few years has ever actually carried out the practice of proving the dough in a still-warm bed, although one or two have said they tried and found more effective places to do the job.

One person who talked about this was Janet Nitschke of Greenock. Janet, like Elsie, has earned a reputation for making the most beautiful *Streuselkuchen*, much in demand for parties and weddings. When Janet's cake is around, people can't stop cutting off more and more bits and soon the slab has disappeared. As one Barossa friend said – while he was doing just that – the thing about Janet's cake is that it has the right *Glumpsch*! You don't have to speak any German to work out from the sound of that word what the texture of Janet's cake is like.

One Saturday afternoon Janet talked about baking while she was putting through a batch of her *Kuchen* for a party that evening. (The best time to eat it is soon after it has come out of the oven.) The room was warm and spicy from the first trays, which now sat basking along the ledge in the porch.

Janet was talking about how she kept the room – as well as the ingredients – warm, an important requirement for yeast cookery. You must not have it too cold but it is just as disastrous to have it too hot. The very first batch that Janet made just after she was married was a dismal flop because the heat of the room killed the yeast. This could have damaged Janet's confidence both as a cook and as a bride – local folklore says that a girl is not ready to marry until she can bake good *Kuchen*. Fortunately, Janet mastered the technique soon afterwards.

Years ago, Janet claims, maintaining the right room temperature was not an issue because in her mother's house the wood-stove kept the kitchen temperature constantly at 98 degrees Fahrenheit, summer or winter, so there was no problem about letting the cake rise. These days, Janet sets up a fan heater in the laundry where there are no draughts, and the whole process, with many batches at different levels of rising in different pans and bowls, flows smoothly from one stage to the next.

I asked Janet to talk about some of her baking techniques:

First of all, it's very important to use proper, milled flour because the ordinary flours that you buy from the supermarket are made from a different type of wheat and the gluten level is different. You must have a flour with a high gluten level. Usually I buy bread flour from the local flour mill.

The next thing is that I use only compressed yeast. It's a bit of a problem getting the yeast but one bakery in the Valley has it and you can buy it in food halls of some large city stores. If I'm buying yeast from the city I divide it up and freeze it – although, well-wrapped, it will keep for a good month in the refrigerator. For each lot of German cake, if I'm doing the normal batch, I use two ounces of compressed yeast. *It must be reasonably fresh otherwise it doesn't rise properly or it takes too long and, in my limited time before I go off to work in the morning, I haven't the patience to wait.*

Next you must consider what kind of fat to use. Most people use butter these days, which gives a lighter dough, but years ago people included at least some lard, which made the dough more moist so that it kept fresh longer.

The other important thing is the way you knead the dough. First you mix it with a spoon until you can't stir it any more. Then you add a couple of handfuls of flour and pull the dough from the back of the dish towards you, folding it over and gradually rotating the dish. Keep adding flour as you rotate until the sides of the bowl are quite clean and your hands, too, are clean of all the dough. The action is one of lifting the dough and using the palms of your hands to push it down into the dish.

When the dough is ready, it looks and feels like satiny skin. Janet laughs as she says, 'I usually knead by the clock and while I knead I read the local paper. By the time I've read it from cover to cover the ten minutes are up.' She did not say whether she was a fast reader.

Streuselkuchen

Janet Nitschke's recipe for four slides of cake. The quantities may be halved. *Kuchen* **essence can be obtained from Barossa pharmacies. It tastes like butter, rum and vanilla.**

KUCHEN
(A) 55 g compressed yeast | $1/2$ cup warmed milk | $3/4$ tbsp sugar
(B) $1 1/2$ cups of milk | $1 1/2$ cups plain flour | $1/3$ cup sugar
(C) 230 g butter or butter/lard combined | 9 cups plain bread flour | $1 1/2$ cups sugar | 1 tsp salt | 1 tsp cinnamon | $3/4$ tsp mace | 1 cup sultanas | 4 eggs | 2 cups milk | 40 drops *Kuchen* essence or vanilla

In a warm saucepan, mix together the ingredients in (A). Put the lid on the saucepan and put it about half a metre away from a fan heater for five to ten minutes. Keep the ambient temperature around 37°C. Now in a bigger saucepan mix the ingredients in (B) and the contents of the other saucepan. Again, put a lid on the saucepan and put it in front of the heater for another ten to fifteen minutes.

Meanwhile, gently melt the butter/lard. Into a large warm dish, sift plain bread flour, sugar, salt, cinnamon and mace, and stir in sultanas. In a smaller dish, beat together eggs, milk and *Kuchen* essence. Now combine the egg mixture, the melted shortening, the flour mixture and the yeast mixture in a big bowl and knead it for ten minutes.

Unless you have a dish big enough to let the whole mass expand, it is a good idea to divide it into four at this point. Weigh the dough into four equal portions, put each portion into a large plastic container with a lid and put the containers back near the fan heater for an hour. By that time, the dough has risen just about to the top of each container.

Prepare the baking trays by greasing them or lining them with baking paper. Pat the portions of dough onto each tray, gently using a rolling pin to make the dough level. Cover with large plastic bags or calico flour bags and stand them in front of the heater again for another half an hour.

Some juggling goes on at this point to make sure that the trays of dough do not all rise to the same degree at the same time because you can over-prove the dough. If you leave the risen dough for too long the cake does not rise well as it cooks and the texture is altered. So keep two of the trays a little way from the heater and bring them in closer while the others are finally having the *Streusel* put on top, ready for the oven.

STREUSEL

3 cups sugar ❙ 680 g of butter ❙ 6 cups plain flour ❙ 2 tsp each of cinnamon and nutmeg ❙ 2 tsp vanilla essence

Using your fingertips, rub the sugar into the butter, add the flour and then the remaining ingredients. It must not be too dry or it won't form the *Streusel* lumps, and you must knead well but not too viciously otherwise it will be heavy.

Getting the *Streusel* to stick on the cake has tried the ingenuity of many cooks. Some paint the dough with melted butter or cream, some with cream and beaten egg white, but Janet has devised an original glue made of six tablespoons of water, six tablespoons of sugar and six teaspoons of gelatine dissolved together over a gentle heat. Paint it on the dough and sprinkle the *Streusel* liberally on top.

Bake at 165°C for 30 minutes. Sprinkle icing sugar over the cooled cake and eat it – if you're not trampled in the rush to get to it! *Streuselkuchen* freezes well if properly wrapped.

Janet's way of making *Streuselkuchen* is efficient because of various techniques she has developed from years of experience. But it is by no means the end of the story. Variations exist on the original theme and they are as interesting as they are numerous.

The most common variation is the *Streuselkuchen* that has a layer of fruit spread between the dough and the *Streusel* before baking. It can be a layer of sliced apples, halved red plums, ripe apricots, or, best of all, a layer of fresh young sultana grapes. As far as I can tell, nowhere else in the world do cooks put fresh sultana grapes under the *Streusel*. I loved *Streuselkuchen* made this way as a child. I wish the bakeries would make it more often these days.

Streuselkuchen with a layer of Grapes, Apricots, Apples or Plums
Use fruit that is slightly tart, picked early in the season.

When the cake dough has risen for the last time, brush the top with melted butter or 1 beaten egg-white mixed with ½ cup cream. Place fresh sliced fruit in rows on the cake. Cover generously with *Streusel*. Bake at 165°C for 30 minutes. Check to see that the dough under the cake is properly cooked after that time. It may need a little more cooking.

It is revealing to look back at old hand-written Barossa recipe-books from the turn of the century to see how ingredients and methods for making the *Streuselkuchen* compare with the way it is made today.

The main difference is that hop-yeast, the kind made with potatoes and fermented in bottles, or dried as a crust, was invariably used before the introduction of compressed yeast. It is the same hop-yeast used for making bread that was described in the previous chapter. For the amount of dough in Janet's recipe, you would need about two cups of bottled hop-yeast but this is perhaps hard to tell because often the recipes just say 'and yeast' or *Hefe*. They expect you to know how much and, indeed, what to do with the ingredients.

From the very early migrations, letters back to Europe giving advice to others contemplating the journey urged that people should bring the yeast ingredients 'for baking cake' (mentioned in preference to bread). These, along with ham, wine and brandy, were considered essential for the voyage and every cook had a perfectly clear idea of how to use the yeast to make *Kuchen*.

Streuselkuchen truly was the staple of the Silesians' food culture. There are accounts of early settlers sending trays of *Streuselkuchen* to a recently docked ship to welcome the new arrivals. People ate it at weddings and christenings, at choir meetings, at *Federschleissen* (or feather-stripping parties) and at tin-kettlings, those noisy evenings before a wedding when all the young people in the neighbourhood made a din outside the bride's house and were welcomed in for wine and *Kuchen*. People ate it on feast days and ordinary days. They ate it after funerals. No other food was so well-known and so universally served.

Many variations of *Kuchen* have not been written down. They simply exist in people's memories. One is for the topping that was put on the cake when the *Streusel* ran out. When that happened, the cook made dimples all over the dough with a finger and poured sugar, cinnamon and farm cream onto the cake's surface. This sauce thickened as the cake was baking, running into the indentations and making pools of caramel. Many preferred it to the traditional *Streusel*. In areas of Germany where the yeast cake is still made, this version is called *Zuckerkuchen*, or sugar-cake.

The other ingredient that repeatedly appears in century-old recipes for *Streuselkuchen* is saffron, and there are still some local cooks who colour the cake dough with the golden stamens of this bulb.

Saffron was used to colour and flavour not only the *Kuchen* dough but other dishes as well. Over and over, I heard people reminisce about *Quarkkuchen*, a yeast cake with a saffron, cream-cheese topping – but nobody seemed to know how it was made. 'Ah, the *Quarkkuchen*,' they would say, rolling the 'r' of *Quark* in a particular way, 'Auntie Tilly used to bake it. I remember it well.' But where was a recipe?

And then one day Maggie Beer and I met Bertha Hahn and were lucky enough to spend a morning in her kitchen, learning how to make this special cake with its *Quark* or cottage-cheese topping flavoured with currants and saffron. It soon became clear that we were being taught by an expert who was making a dish long known in her family. Bertha's method began with producing the yeast itself from potatoes and hops. Let's start with compressed yeast.

Quarkkuchen

The cake tastes good without the saffron, but the saffron makes it extraordinarily good.

KUCHEN

Make half the quantity of yeast dough as for Janet Nitschke's *Streuselkuchen*, without sultanas. Use half to make one tray of *Streuselkuchen*. Pat the other half of the dough into two springform pans or onto one tray with edges 2.5 cm high lined with baking paper, sprinkle finely with flour and cover with *Quark* topping.

QUARK TOPPING

500 g *Quark* (This cottage cheese is simply made by straining sour milk through calico, a process described in the next chapter. However, commercially prepared cottage cheese makes an acceptable substitute. In this case, stir in a tablespoon of powdered milk to approximate the consistency of true *Quark*.) To this you add 1 teaspoon salt, $1^{1}/_{4}$ cups sugar, 1 whole grated nutmeg, 1 cup rich farm cream, 1 cup washed currants, 2 eggs, well-beaten, grated rind $^{1}/_{2}$ lemon (optional).

Now for the saffron. On top of the stove in a small pan with a heavy base heat about 12 strands of saffron. Be careful not to burn them. When cold, crush them to a powder with a mortar and pestle. Add 1 tablespoon of boiling water and stir. Add this to the *Quark* mixture.

Pour the *Quark* mixture over the cake. Cover loosely with a large plastic bag and leave to rise for 30 minutes. Place in the oven preheated to 200°C, turned back to 175°C, for 35 to 40 minutes. Do not open the oven door for at least 15 minutes after you have put the cakes in.

The fragrance and flavour of the *Quarkkuchen* when it finally comes out of the oven make it different from the ordinary *Streuselkuchen*. The saffron smells like sweet, cured tobacco. Combined with the sour cottage cheese and the dark flavour of currants, it produces a wonderful taste.

This cake is hardly known today, partly because saffron is expensive to procure unless you grow your own as some people still do. Nita Stiller explains that it is also hard to make today because you need to have cows to obtain the proper *Quark*:

Nobody but me would have a cow today. Different ones say, 'What? You still milk cows!' 'Yes,' I say. I love my cows, Honey and Lucy. They're lovely. Honey is a Jersey-Guernsey and she gives beautiful cream. She's a beautiful cow. You need that real cream. I use my own cows' milk – and if I've got time I make the Quark. *But the occasions are limited because I'm cooking for other people all the time.*

The *Quarkkuchen* topping in a book of recipes published by the elderly people in the Tanunda Lutheran Rest Home in 1977 claims that 'only the Wends could make this dish'. This makes me wonder whether the saffron-flavoured *Quarkkuchen* was originally a Wendish cake that was adopted by other European food cultures. Certainly all local references to it came from the northern end of the Valley, in places where the Wends had settled.

The Wends, whom I mentioned in the first chapter of this book, came with the other German-speaking people when they migrated to Australia. They settled in Victoria, as well as in the northernmost part of the Barossa district and beyond. Their names are associated with the tiny settlements of Ebenezer, St Kitts and Peter's Hill. Many were meticulous farmers; it is a delight to drive through these settlements and see the mellowed, stone buildings.

Today there are societies in Australia and Germany devoted to keeping alive the Wendish culture. If someone's family name is Noack, Pech, Doecke, Mickan, Zwar or Biele, to mention just a few, probably they are of Wendish origin.

Because the Wends were such an integral part of the Lutheran congregations, it is hard to identify aspects of the food culture that are genuinely Wendish. Everybody shared recipes with other non-Wendish members of the family. It appears that the Wends did use saffron in their cooking. Rhoda Noack remembers her Wendish grandmother making beer soup, a sweet, creamy soup flavoured with beer and spices: 'But only when she had saffron left over from making the *Quarkkuchen*.' Whether the *Quarkkuchen* is Wendish or not, it is an interesting cake and should not be allowed to disappear from the Barossa Valley food culture.

This chapter cannot end without some reference to quicker ways to make *Streuselkuchen*. Some cooks discovered that you can achieve something of the texture of the *Kuchen* yeast dough if you make an ordinary cake using potatoes or beer. Recipes for beer cake and potato cake abound in country recipe-books. These recipes are much easier to make than the yeast *Kuchen* and are delicious cakes in their own right.

Potato Cake
A useful stand-by.

CAKE
½ cup warm mashed potato ∣ 1 tbsp butter ∣ ¾ cup sugar ∣
½ cup sultanas ∣ ¾ cup milk ∣ grated rind ½ lemon ∣
2 cups self-raising flour ∣ ¼ tsp salt ∣ ½ tsp nutmeg

Beat potato and butter together. Add sugar and beat again. Add sultanas and milk. Stir in lemon rind and sifted dry ingredients. Pat into two 20 cm cake tins. Cover with *Streusel* and bake in a moderate oven (180°C) 30 minutes.

STREUSEL
1 cup plain flour ∣ pinch salt ∣ ½ cup sugar ∣ ¾ tsp cinnamon moistened with 85 g melted butter ∣ grated rind 1 lemon ∣
¾ cup slivered almonds

Knead into lumps. Spread over cake mixture and sprinkle with almonds before baking.

Bierkuchen – Beer Cake
I like the yeasty flavour of the beer.

Kuchen
2 eggs ∣ 1¾ cups full-strength beer ∣ 100 g butter ∣ 100 g sugar ∣
½ tsp cinnamon ∣ ½ tsp nutmeg ∣ 1 cup sultanas mixed with peel ∣
4 cups self-raising flour

Beat the eggs, add beer. Drink the rest of the beer in the bottle. Cream butter and sugar, add fruit, spices, and flour and egg/beer mixture alternately, ending with flour as the last addition. Line a slide with baking paper and smooth the mixture out onto the slide in a rectangle taking up most of the slide area. Spread with *Streusel* topping and bake in a moderate oven (180°C) 35 minutes or longer. Put a sheet of foil over it for the last few minutes if it is getting too brown before the centre is cooked.

STREUSEL

100 g butter │ 1½ cups plain flour │ 1 cup sugar │ ¼ tsp salt │ ½ tsp grated lemon rind │ 1 tsp vanilla essence │ ½ tsp cinnamon

Melt the butter, stir into rest of ingredients, knead until crumbly. Spread over cake mixture before baking.

Many cooks add a few handfuls of chopped almonds, including possibly one or two kernels of bitter almonds, finely chopped, to the *Streusel* in any of these recipes. This is a typical Silesian touch. The beer-cake recipe came from my grandmother's collection – and so did the instruction about drinking the left-over beer.

Nita Falkenberg, Tanunda Show, 1999

Chapter 8

The Pig

It is winter and I am waiting for a phone call. On the road I have seen pigs by the truckload being taken to market, their pink bodies swaying on tottery legs, and I know that this is the time of year when some local people still make their own wursts and sausages. When Mona Doering has the meat ready, I am going to learn how she and her family make pork smallgoods from traditional family recipes and, having tasted some of her products last year, I know these will be good.

These days trained people kill the pigs in licensed, inspected slaughterhouses but years ago the whole procedure took place on the farm. Farming families knew the techniques of pig-killing, or *Schweineschlachten*. They handed down the skills and knew how to kill in the most painless way for the pig and how to cut and hang the carcass most effectively for producing good meat.

In quite a few instances, men who had learned these methods on farms in their childhood became professional butchers when they grew up. Wally Lange was one of these men. For years he was a well-known butcher in the Barossa Valley and since his retirement he has continued to help up-and-coming young butchers with advice about traditional local smallgoods. Many of the details that come later in this chapter about actual procedures for pig-killing come from visits to Wally and his wife, Hilda, and from long conversations at their kitchen table.

On any farm long ago, the operation was a family affair. Even if the local slaughterer was hired for the day to supervise operations, every adult in the household was called out to help. Well, almost everyone: in one or two families, menstruating women were forbidden to go anywhere near the wurst-making, perhaps lest they should make the sausages go bad. Whatever the reason, those women no doubt found it a wonderful excuse to lie in bed when everyone else was being rallied to catch the pig. In some families, women in 'their time' were not allowed near the vats of fermenting wine, either. They were considered to be in an unclean state and might make the wine turn sour.

Some people had no stomach for the *Schweineschlachten*. Years later, an old lady remembering her childhood said what a terrible experience it was to have pigs on a farm: you spent all year feeding them and caring for them, learning to know them as real personalities, watching them become excited when you brought them a cartload of fallen figs – and then came the day when you killed them! This particular girl would shut herself in her bedroom and block her ears so that she couldn't hear the squeals.

Without the products from the pig, though, the local farming families would have had a much harder existence. They needed the pickled or smoked meat and the sausages as a long-lasting food that was on hand when everyone was busy. Small-goods were really the forerunners of fast foods. Country families also needed the lard to use where many other people would use butter. They sold butter from their own farm for cash and then used lard for baking, frying and in the school-children's sandwiches.

For close on six weeks before the actual slaughter day, the chosen sow was fattened on softened grain to build up the stores of lard. People would talk about the number of kerosene tins of lard that came from that pig. Farmers would brag about it, standing outside church after the Sunday service.

In the afternoon of the day appointed for the *Schweineschlachten*, the slaughterer would arrive at the farm – but they had to catch the pig first and that was not as easy as you might think. A cunning pig might get away and lead everyone on a crazy race round the farmyard.

Once the helpers had caught the pig, they tied it up by the leg out in the yard. If the pig had been running fast, they might need to wait until it had calmed down, even until the next day, before they stunned it by hitting it on the head with the back of an axe. On many farms at this moment they killed the animal by shooting it through the forehead. Then they used a long-bladed knife to 'stick' the pig by cutting the jugular vein and letting the blood drain out into a dish.

It is not often that you get a photograph of this operation but there is one taken by the Minge family in 1913 that shows the point when the pig had been shot and hoisted from the branch of a tree, just after it had been bled. The slaughterer in his butcher's apron is holding the sticking-knife and sharpening steel. One woman is holding the gun and one the dish for the blood. In the background are the bags that will be used in the next stage and by the pig stands the tin tub that will no doubt hold the hot water needed for removing the bristles.

Killing the pig, 1913

There is skill required to stick a pig correctly and many people who have learned the skill can talk about their blundering early attempts, when they pushed the knife in the wrong place or let it go in too far or at the wrong angle. The knife must go in far enough to ensure that the blood drains well lest it spoil the meat. The blood seems to drain better if the pig has not eaten the day it is killed. It also helps if someone pumps the legs of the animal to expel blood from those parts, too.

As the blood drips down, the person holding the basin has a wooden whisk or even one hand in the bowl, stirring constantly. After a while coagulated blood starts to cling to the fingers in long strings, sometimes called 'the bones'. These need to be removed from the dish of blood. As long as these strings form on the fingers, the person needs to keep stirring.

When the point is reached where no more strings form, the blood is ready. Someone covers the bowl and puts it in a cool place.

Meanwhile, water has been boiling in the copper and clean wheat bags are waiting for the next part of the process. This is when the helpers remove the hair from the pig. They lower the animal onto sheets of clean corrugated iron or clean bags on the ground or else put it in a scalding-trough.

If the pig is lying on the ground, the workers cover it with more bags and pour boiling water over the bags. This means that the boiling water has cooled a little before it reaches the skin of the pig, yet the hessian helps to keep the water hot, too. The water must not be too hot, otherwise the hair will fuse to the skin; yet it must not be too cool, either, because then the hair will not come off. Tin after tin of hot water might be up-ended onto the pig. Every so often, someone lifts the bag and checks to see if the hair is falling out. Once that happens, the workers set to and scrape the skin thoroughly before turning the pig over and repeating the procedure on the other side.

If there happens to be a scalding-trough, the job of removing the hair from the pig is a little easier. The workers lower the pig into the trough of hot water. Again the water needs to be just below boiling point in the copper and in the trough. Wally Lange says that they used to add a dipper of cold water to the trough and could tell by the feel whether it was the right temperature.

Once they lower the pig into the trough of water, the workers have to keep turning it so that the temperature of the water is evenly spread. Now the hair starts to lift from the skin and they can remove most of it by running a rope up and down the pig's back and by scraping the skin with a knife or an instrument called a 'scud'. This is a scraper with a hoe-like blade on one side and a hook on the other designed for removing the toenails from the trotters. During all this time, the helpers turn the pig until the process is completed. They insert a hook into the sinews of its hind tendons and hoist it up by the pulley. Any bits of hair still remaining on the carcass are shaved off with a sharp knife and the whole body is washed in clean water and dried thoroughly with a clean cloth.

Now the workers use a sharp knife to cut off the nipples before these go hard, open the pig and remove the innards. They cut around the rectum and anus and force them out so that the manure does not come into contact with the rest of the pig. Once again, not feeding the pig on the day of slaughter makes this process a lot easier. They remove the entrails next and put them in a bowl ready to be cleaned for sausage casings. They remove all the other organs and put them in another dish. The dishes are covered, to keep out dust and insects.

At this moment they also remove the head. The workers start by cutting at the base of the skull to sever the spinal cord. They cut all round the neck and twist the head off. When they have split the head in halves, they cut out the eyes, clean the ears and scrub and rinse inside the mouth – not the most pleasant of jobs – before putting the head into a bowl of cold water, ready to be dealt with the next day.

Then they spread the carcass of the pig wide open to allow the heat to escape. It should hang in a cool place, covered in a calico bag, free from dust and flies but well ventilated. This is why the slaughtering used to be done in the afternoon, so that the pig could hang in the cool of the day and then overnight. If the day turned out to be unseasonably warm, the pig might have to be hung in the cellar.

By the time this flurry is over, all that is left of the pig is a hanging carcass, some bowls of internal organs and the head – to be cooked and preserved in different ways – and a dish of entrails waiting to be cleaned and made into sausage casings. Years ago, this was the time for the farmer to pay the slaughterer and send him home. No money necessarily changed hands: in some cases he made the payment in wine. The children could never understand why their father paid in that way but he doubtless had his reasons, and who were they to ask?

What remains of the day has to be devoted to cleaning the runners, the entrails of the pig that will be used as casings for the wursts. Having been cut into convenient lengths, these are sitting in a bowl. Now begins the tedious process of washing and scraping. The fat on the outside of the runners needs to be removed with hot water – but not too hot to spoil the membrane. On Wally Lange's family farm, they did the scraping with the rib bone of a bullock, which had just the right curve to act as a thumb-grip. It is much simpler, though, for people just to use their fingers.

When it comes to cleaning the insides of the runners, it is fascinating to pour warm water down them through a funnel and watch the runners fill and wriggle about like snakes. To do the more serious cleaning, the runners have to be turned inside out and the implements people devised to do this were ingenious. Some farmers used small lengths of bamboo to push the casing like a sleeve being turned inside out. Others made shaped funnels out of cow-horns to be used for the same purpose.

Once the runners have begun to turn inside out, pouring more warm water down them will continue the process. With the runners turned, the washing and scraping is repeated until all the slime has been removed and they are perfectly clean. Then the workers put the runners between layers of salt in a keg where they can be kept for several weeks, if necessary, before they are filled.

After all this work, nothing could be more welcome than to climb wearily into bed and catch some sleep before beginning the making of the wursts and the curing of the meat the next day.

The scene is set for an early start. In come the helpers, pushing up their sleeves, ready to process the meat at the big butchering table in the work-room. They need to cut up the cold pig. First the backbone needs to be chopped out. Then, on a very fat pig, they remove the strip of fat each side of the bone and use it later to make *Mettwurst*. This is not necessary on a thinner pig, where the fat remains part of the bacon, the two flitches of which are now removed as whole pieces. The backbone and sawn-off trotters will go into the brine later and then be smoked to use in soup. As far back as the 1890s some families, but not all, liked to remove the eye fillet of meat from the bacon to brine and smoke as a separate cut called *Lachsschinken*.

The abdominal fat is called the 'net'. The farmer cuts this by the loins and pulls downwards, stripping it off as far as the shoulder. This fat will be minced or cut into little pieces and put in a pan over a low heat to be rendered down for lard. Other scraps of good fat trimmed off the carcass as it is being jointed will be added to the pan. For some hours the pan will sit there over the heat, being looked at occasionally to make sure that all is going well.

Then, when all the lard has seeped out of the pieces of fat cooking in the pan, it will be drained off into clean kerosene tins. The crusty remains in the bottom of the pan will be minced and used as a spread called *Grieben*. The French do the same thing and call the paste *rillons*. You can buy it in tubs from French charcuteries. The English call the same paste 'greaves'. The words are related and they apply to very similar foods. It shows that across Europe people had long ago shared a discovery that the by-products of lard-making were a delicious dish themselves and could be used in other sorts of cooking.

European settlers brought their liking for *Grieben* to the Barossa.

Bacon in the smokehouse

Many may never have seen the word written and it appears in local recipe-books in different forms: *Griven, Griefen, Grevens*. Besides spreading it on bread they made it into biscuits and tarts and used it instead of suet in boiled plum puddings.

Griefen Tarts

7 cups flour | 2 tbsp sugar | 1½ tsp bicarbonate of soda | 2½ tsp cream of tartar | pinch salt | 1 cup lard | 1½ cups *griefen* | 2 eggs | cold water to mix | jam or prepared fruit

Stir dry ingredients together in a basin. Add lard and *Griefen* in pieces. Cut in with a knife or pastry-blender or blend with fingertips. Make a well in the mixture and add beaten eggs. Blend with a fork. Add a little iced water if necessary. Knead the pastry and roll into a ball. Allow to rest 30 minutes. Roll out, cut circles, place on tart trays. Spoon in a filling of jam or prepared fruit like stewed currants or figs. Bake at 200°C for 10 minutes.

Griven Biscuits

4 eggs | 340 g sugar | 1 cup sultanas and mixed fruit | 340 g minced *Griven* | 450 g plain flour | 2 tsp cream of tartar | 1 tsp bicarbonate of soda | ½ tsp cinnamon | ½ cup milk

Beat eggs and sugar. Stir in fruit and *Griven*. Fold in sifted dry ingredients. Add a little milk if too stiff. Place spoonfuls on greased tray and bake in a moderate oven (180°C) for 15 to 20 minutes.

Some might think that the recipe for these biscuits is just a pedestrian way of using up a part of the pig that might otherwise go to waste, but this is not so. Families looked forward to the annual bake of *Griven* biscuits. They are light in texture and have a flavour that people still talk about even if they do not make the biscuits any more because they no longer kill a pig.

The next job in the pig processing is to select the larger cuts of meat that are going to be cured in a tub of brine or on a bed of dry salt, sugar and saltpetre. Some of these, like the bacon and the ham, will later be smoked. Some may become rolls of pickled pork, a favourite food among the early settlers. So now the trotters need to be cut off, the middle flaps of meat rolled and tied, the hams cut and the hambone joints broken. Those who do not make pickled pork or ham will use the flaps and leg meat in the wursts.

Families must have had countless discussions over the years about the best way to preserve a ham. You can remove the bone altogether to make the meat keep better. Some people preserve the meat near the bone by putting peppercorns into pockets cut with a sharp knife down its side. Butchers inject fresh pickling brine along the bone, especially in hot weather. However there is no need to do any of this if the ham has been thoroughly cured in pickling brine before smoking for at least four weeks.

Before the days of refrigeration, people relied heavily on their preserved meats and it was really important to make sure that the curing and smoking processes worked. Nobody then wanted to risk food poisoning any more than they do now. A critical factor in the success of curing and smoking was that the meat had to be drained of all blood. (This was another reason why farmers would not slaughter a pig that had been running hard from being chased around the yard: it would still have too much blood in its muscle tissue. For the same reason, they never killed a sow when it was on heat.)

So at this moment, the cuts of meat to be cured were often rubbed with salt, sugar and saltpetre – say five cups of salt, one cup of sugar and two teaspoons of saltpetre – and allowed to stand in the clean, dry pickle-barrel for at least a further 12 hours. This was to leach out any remaining blood. Then the pickling brine was poured over the top of the meat the next day. That could be made by mixing the same quantities of dry-salting ingredients and adding four gallons of clean, boiled water.

Making ham and corned meats seems very remote from the cooking habits of people living in cities and towns today but plenty of old recipe-books contain the ingredients for preparing the curing brine and it appears to have been a skill quite common to cooks up to the early decades of the twentieth century.

Brine for Pickling Meat

½ *kerosene bucket of water* | *4 cups salt* | *2 cups sugar* | *1 dsp saltpetre* |
1 dsp peppercorns or cloves

Bring to a boil. Place meat in the liquid and boil for ten minutes. Skim the scum. Allow to cool. Keep meat immersed. Cover well.

For all these recipes one can find countless variations and every family had a slightly different method. From about the same era is another method for curing bacon and ham taken from a hand-written letter simply signed, 'Your friend, Fritz'. Fritz, whoever he was, had obviously made many hams in his time:

Curing Bacon and Ham

Take: salt, saltpetre, peppercorns and bay leaves. Take one gallon of water and put in saltpetre – a few ounces – 6 bay leaves and a few ounces of peppercorns. And to one gallon of water take 2 lbs of honey. Add salt to bring the brine to 68 per cent strength or use a medium size potato and put it in the brine. If she is floating the brine is OK. Add salt if she still sinks to the bottom of the container. If the strength is satisfactory bring the whole to the boiling point. After boiling 5 minutes take the scum off then take off the fire and let cool off. Then take the meat which had to be brined and salt it well. Also, if you pump the meat before putting in the brine then the curing period will be only 4 weeks for a ham of about 28 lbs. (If the weight is below 28 lbs less brining time.) After curing take meat out of brine and put in warm water for 6 to 10 hours. After that put in cheese cloth. Let them dry well before smoking. Smoke meat slowly and cool only (!) for about 10–12 days and use hard wood sawdust only – oak or okatzie: Good luck whit the prosidure and I hope you have suxes [sic]. Your friend, Fritz.

This is where we pay a visit to the Doering farm at the northern end of the Barossa Valley to learn about local wurst-making, for no people are more skilled at this art than Mona Doering and her cousin-in-law, Rhoda Noack.

The solid, old, stone farmhouse sits in the crook of the northern hills. This is one of those few remaining farming enterprises that is an ecological entity. Livestock from the Doering farm has won many prizes and members of the family have won farming scholarships to study overseas, and yet their business remains a true 'mixed farm'. Free-range hens scratch about in the grass; cows graze between the vegetable garden and the wheat paddock; pigs loll in the sties or under the trees and the produce from each of these areas of the farm supports the rest in some way.

The wurst-making is an important occasion, with sons, daughters, grandchildren and friends calling in at different times during the day to help with the mixing. Rhoda and Mona have everything ready and waiting when we all arrive: the work table out on the enclosed back verandah is freshly scrubbed with knives, funnels, mincer and filling machine set out. The water is simmering in the copper outside. The onions, herbs (dried from Mona's own garden), spices, salt and pepper are lined up.

In one corner of the verandah is a huge fern basking in the sun

Mona Doering with Tim and Michael (photo: A. Heuzenroeder)

Barossa Food

coming through the north-facing windows. Like much else on the farm, the plant is a traditional touch – this variety of fern has been grown on Barossa farm verandahs for generations. Locals call the fern *Frau und Mann* (wife and husband), because one side of it always grows curly, with frilly leaves, while the other side grows straight and plain.

Mona explains that there is a set order to making the wursts:

The sausages we are going to make are Mettwurst, Knackwurst, Reiswurst, *which some people call* Blutwurst *and some call black pudding, and* Leberwurst, *which is often known as white pudding. Sometimes we make* Presswurst *as well. We usually make our white pudding first, then our black pudding, then we make the* Mettwurst *and then* Knackwurst *last of all.*

Adds Rhoda:

While you're making the Mettwurst, *you boil the rinds and that's how you work to a routine so that when you've finished your* Mettwurst *your rind is ready to make the* Knackwurst. *'Schwartenwurst' [pork-rind-sausage], I suppose you ought to call it. So now the first thing we do is simmer all the meat in the copper until it's tender.*

Some of the meat has already gone into the simmering, salted water. There is just enough water to cover the heart, kidneys, ears, the two halves of the head, and the other meats. Gently, Rhoda lowers in the livers. (They are using the meat from three pigs this time, to make a whole year's supply of sausages.) It will take about half an hour before the livers are tender and during that time we stand at the kitchen sink chopping up the twenty onions that will go into the white pudding.

Now the meats in the copper are ready. The liver comes out before the other parts, still tender and pinkish. Rhoda lifts out the pieces and drains them, then sorts them into different piles on two large plates. She ladles some of the broth into a stockpot and puts it to boil on the kitchen stove, to cook two cups of rice for the *Blutwurst*. Another lot of broth is poured over a dish of cubed bread to soak. Yet another lot of salt water is put on to boil with the rinds for half an hour ready to make this afternoon's *Knackwurst*.

The family stand around the table as the meat is minced for the *Leberwurst*. The most important moment of all is when the flavourings are added and the family shares the tasting of the mixture. As Mona sprinkles spice and thyme into the meat, fingers dip, tongues roll and eyes watch the other faces round the dish. The tasting is a

Rhoda Noack (photo: A. Heuzenroeder)

ritual that the whole family shares. Even the grandchildren's opinions are sought. How is it for you, Kylie? What do you think, Tim? When everybody is satisfied, they can proceed to filling the runners.

The casings are already rinsed of their salt and now Mona has taken a long, white, rubbery runner and attached it to the filling-machine nozzle. She eases the filling down as her son turns the handle. As the mixture is pushed down and flattened, the grey, filled runner snakes slowly across the table, pushed on by different sets of hands along the way. Up the other end, Rhoda is tying the sausage segments off with string and throwing the excess mixture back into the bowl.

At last all the mixture has been used and Rhoda takes the dish of white puddings out to the copper. She checks the fire and the temperature of the water, tosses in a dipperful of cold, then counts as she lowers the wursts into the broth. She wouldn't want to lose any, after all.

Leberwurst – White Pudding
Delicious!
Mince together the fatty meat of the pig, which might include the cheeks, the tongue, scraps from the belly and part or all of the liver plus some onions (Mona and Rhoda used about six to a pig). Crumble $1/2$ or 1 loaf of white bread and pour about $3/4$ cup broth over it to soak for 15 minutes. The amount of bread you use depends on how fatty the meat is, as the bread absorbs the fat. Add the soaked, squeezed-dry bread to the meat-and-onion mixture. Add salt, pepper, thyme and allspice to taste and work the seasonings into the mixture with the hands. Fill into runners, prick well and simmer until done (20 to 30 minutes). Lift them out, dry them and hang in an airy place.

Now Rhoda goes back to the kitchen to check the rice while Mona minces the pile of meat for the *Blutwurst*. *Blutwurst*? *Reiswurst*? Are they the same? Both seem to be very like the English and French black puddings and many local people use the three names indiscriminately for the same sort of sausage, a mixture of meat, cooked rice or groats, and about half the blood of the pig.

Some very old recipes for *Blutwurst* contain no rice and are thickened with coarse flour. On the other hand, some recipes for *Reiswurst* contain no blood. They may use the head of the pig and they produce a much lighter sausage.

Reiswurst
Adjust the amount of herbs to suit your taste.
Mince together the lean meat: the ears, kidney, spleen, heart and lights. Add salt and pepper and 3 cups of the rice that has been cooked in the broth from the cooked meats. Experiment with the taste as you add allspice and marjoram. (This last, in Rhoda's book, is written in German as *Majoran* and she pronounces it as a German word.)

Lastly, pour in about half the blood of the pig. Fill into casings, prick well and simmer 20 to 30 minutes.

When it comes to checking the seasoning, the family members once again take part in the ritual tasting. Most do it before the blood is added but the more stalwart wait until Mona has poured it in.

While the *Reiswurst* is being made, Rhoda has been keeping an eye on the time and after about twenty minutes she goes to check the copper. Presto! The white puddings, now cooked, have floated to the surface and she ladles them into a dish. We spread newspaper over the kitchen table and lay the steaming wursts in rows to dry.

If you don't have a copper to cook the wursts, says Rhoda, they can be steamed for twenty or thirty minutes, or even baked in dishes in the oven like a terrine. But however they are done, white pudding and black pudding can later be grilled or fried in slices for a most delicious breakfast, almost as delicious as fried *Presswurst*.

'We used to make what Granny called *Presswurst* with the stomach,' says Mona. 'You put your coarser cuts of meat like the tongue into the stomach of the pig. Then you boil that and press it and smoke it. It was always very nice but we haven't made it for a while.'

Presswurst

Use most of the meats that you would otherwise use for *Reiswurst*: the tongue, the ears and other meat, blood, spices to taste such as pepper, salt, allspice, cloves and a bit of cooked mince meat to bind the mixture. Cut the tongue into coarser pieces than the rest. Fill the mixture into the stomach, simmer it 1 hour. Hang to dry out the surface thoroughly and smoke it, then weigh it down and press it so that the sausage becomes a rectangular shape.

Although the local butchers still sell the other traditional wursts today, keeping alive an important tradition, it is a great pity that *Presswurst* is hard to find. You can still get it at Schulz's butcher shop in Angaston and also at Lyndoch Valley Meats, where the butcher is Christopher Flamank. Chris allowed me to watch one afternoon as he made *Presswurst* to Wally Lange's old recipe. It is really the recipe for black pudding, only it has lumps of cooked peeled tongue, both plain and pickled, mixed into it.

Chris was making 30 kilograms of *Presswurst*. He minced coarsely three-quarters of the tongues on a mincing disc and added the rest, which he cut into large chunks by hand. To this he added some coarsely minced back fat, the pickled jowels, the blood, jellied broth made from boiling the trotters, the usual seasonings for black pudding – in his case, salt, nutmeg, white pepper, thyme, pimento and ground cloves – and a setting agent. On a farm, this would be the boiled rice.

In no time, Chris had mixed the ingredients and was packing them into belly after belly of pork runners. It was a bit like filling messy Christmas stockings. Apart from the volume of meat that Chris was working, the steps were exactly the same as they would have been on a farm, and he soon had the sausages simmering in a huge tub of broth. They would stay in the water for about 1½ hours, until a thermometer inserted into the middle of the sausages measured 68°C. Chris intended to smoke them overnight and then press them squashed between two plastic tubs, the top one filled with water as a weight.

When I look at an 1834 recipe-book, poring over the instructions in Gothic German writing to see how the wursts were made by the first settlers, I notice that this book tells the cooks to make the wursts in a slightly different order. It starts with *Mettwurst*, which can be made without having to wait for the organs to cook in the copper. None of the recipes give precise amounts but then most recipes I have seen for these foods speak only in general terms. After all, every pig is a different weight and the seasonings can only be added according to taste. The other difference seems to be in the cooking and smoking times, which go on for days in this old recipe-book, whereas the local notebooks consistently give shorter times.

Now the story returns to Mona and Rhoda, cleaning and preparing the mincer and plates for making the next lot of sausage, the *Mettwursts*. But just as we are about to start, Rhoda exclaims that she has forgotten to describe the *Kehlebraten*, a kind of meat paste, that they sometimes make from the brains. It keeps quite well for about a month in the fridge or the deep freeze – if it doesn't get eaten first. It is good on bread with tomato or pickles.

Kehlebraten

When the pig's head has been cut off, cut the bloody meat from the neck. Mince it. Add to it a good lot of finely chopped onion and the skinned, deveined, sliced brains. Moisten the mixture with some of the rendered lard and add salt and pepper to taste. Fry the lot gently in a pan long enough for it to make a soft spread. Watch that the meat does not go hard. Store the dish of *Kehlebraten* in a cool place.

Now the mincer has been thoroughly washed and dried and everything is ready to make the final lot of wursts. These are the ones to be preserved in the smokehouse, although the fire will only be lit in a day or so when the hanging wursts have had a chance to dry out.

'We'll use chips with a bit of dirt from the wood heap and sawdust,' Mona says. 'It's no particular sort of wood, just the ordinary chips left over from chopping the wood. A bit of dirt scattered on it will choke the fire and just give smoke.' No doubt, though, the woodheap contains piles of mallee, blue-gum and red-gum, which most people recommend for a smokehouse fire, and if there are some almond shells handy Mona will probably use those too. The smoke of ages, clinging to the ceiling of the shed in black stalactites, gives off an aroma that makes you think all the best hams, bacons and wursts in the world are dangling in front of your nose. It is not necessary to have a special building as a smokehouse. Some butchers have a firebox on wheels. You can even smoke smallgoods in a barbecue kettle; you just need to be able to adjust the air vents and keep the smoke cool.

The most fascinating smokehouses of all are the ones built by the first settlers to the Barossa Valley. They were part of the main house; in fact, the whole house was literally built around them. You entered a front door placed centrally in the long building and found yourself right in the middle of the wurst-smoking room – the *Schwarze Küche*, or black kitchen, as it was called. There are several of these historic buildings still dotted around the Barossa. They are all planned slightly differently but the principle is the same: a centrally placed fire feeds the bake-oven and a chimney where the smoking of food was done. Sometimes, this fireplace is actually the kitchen itself and you can stand in the centre of the tiny room, look straight up the chimney and see branches spanning it all the way up, where the sausages and hams were hung on hooks to smoke.

It cannot have been long before the settlers realised that this cooking arrangement was entirely unsuitable for the Australian climate and removed the smokehouse to a room out in the yard. That must also have been when they devised those bake-ovens that projected outside the house to disperse the heat. Some families then dismantled the central chimney of the *Schwarze Küche* or covered it with a new roof and you cannot tell from outside the house that there is a black kitchen within. However some fine, unspoiled examples still remain, especially in Bethany and other tiny villages. If you drive past a long German cottage and see a centrally placed chimney, it is quite possible that you are looking at one of the early houses with a black kitchen.

In Poland today, just south of Zielona Góra, which was once Grünberg, a district from which the first settlers departed, there is a village called Ochla. In this village is a settlement of historic peasant buildings brought from different parts of the country and reconstructed as a folk museum. Most of the buildings are Polish in design and extremely charming but the very first house in the settlement, half-timbered with a thatched roof, looks much like the early houses in the Barossa – and what's more it has a black kitchen!

Mettwurst

11.5 kg pork | 4.5 kg beef | 10 tsp pepper | 2 cups sugar |
3½ handfuls salt | 1 tbsp or more of minced garlic |
¾ bottle medium to sweet sherry | 2 tsp saltpetre

Mince meats and garlic and work in the other ingredients thoroughly. Fill into the wider runners carefully. Hang to dry. Smoke until the wursts are done – about 4 to 7 days, in cool smoke.

Knackwurst or *Schwartenwurst*

Set aside some of the *Mettwurst* mixture and add to it the minced, boiled rinds called the *Schwarten*, add salt, pepper and seasonings to taste – such as thyme and caraway. Fill into the wider runners and smoke until done.

While Mona's son, Michael, is mincing the meat, we have a discussion about how much fat the mixture should contain. If you have too much, the wurst is too soft and can go rancid. With too little fat, it goes as hard as a rock. The proportion of fat would be about a fifth of the mixture, but really the best way to tell is by the look of the meat. If it looks too fatty, you need to add more meat.

There is quite an art to filling the casings. If you don't fill them firmly enough, after a while in the smoke they go grey inside because the wurst contains too much air. You have to ram the meat in so that the sausage is firm and you can soon tell by the feel. You soon

Hooks on the ceiling for the sausages

know, too, if you make one too full because it will burst. Bang, over she goes! Some, Rhoda says, she can patch up nicely but some she can't.

'A patched *Mettwurst*! What an idea! How on earth do you do that?'

'Well, it's quite simple really. You just press a patch of runner skin over the hole and it fuses to the surface beneath. It will stick and keep the wurst from drying out.'

The filled wursts are hanging now from the smokehouse ceiling by their strings. This is to dry them out a little before the smoking process. Every now and then, over the next few days, Mona will test them and when she can run her hand over the casing smoothly, the wursts will be ready to go into the smoke.

How long they will stay in the smokehouse, Mona explains, depends on the weather. In dry weather they can be smoked relatively quickly. Last year the weather was nice and dry and they had the *Mettwurst* smoked in three days. In damper weather it takes a little bit longer, sometimes even a whole week. The wursts need to be golden all over and feel quite firm. You leave them to hang until the smoke goes right through them and then you give another burst of smoke until they are done. In the days before refrigeration many people used to smoke the *Leberwursts* and *Blutwursts*, too, to make them keep longer. That gave them quite a different flavour from the fresh ones.

The same goes for ham and bacon. When the pieces have been in the pickling brine long enough, take them out, then wash and soak them in fresh water for 24 hours to remove excess salt. Dry them out thoroughly before smoking. (Keep all meat as clean and dry as possible.) The actual smoking of hams and bacon takes from two to five days, although for larger pieces it takes longer. Some people rub the skin of the smoked meat afterwards with oil to help preserve it. Hang it in an airy cellar, wrapped in calico and never in plastic.

The *Schweineschlachten*, and the activity that surrounded it, may be an almost forgotten activity these days. When you go into any of the old cottages built by the settlers, however, and see the hooks on the ceiling, it is easy to picture the hams and the sausages that once dangled there. At the end of a long day, when I leave the Doering family and their farm, I feel glad that this important part of the local food culture is still being practised and that some people are still enjoying the flavours of the home-made sausages on their own farms.

Some people may wonder why the farmers did not make the sausage called 'Fritz'. This soft, pink wurst with an orange skin was produced only commercially. Called 'Fritz' in South Australia, 'Devon' in New South Wales, and 'German sausage' in other places, it was first made in South Australia by an Adelaide butcher called Conrad, who came to South Australia from a central part of Germany, the Eichsfeld, near the Harz Mountains. In South Australia, it has always been a custom of butchers to cut off a slice of Fritz to give to young children who come into the shop. It's a custom that should not die out.

spring

Chapter 9

Noodles and Cheese

Spring has come to the Barossa Valley. Magpies are warbling and the kookaburras laughing down in the gums beyond the vines.

It is time to get out in the garden. Tugging to remove a weed, I think ruefully about an unfortunate legacy from the early settlers. The first pastor wrote back to congregations in Prussia giving lists of medicinal plant seeds that would be useful to bring to Australia. St John's wort was amongst them. It is now declared a noxious weed in some states. Other weeds, like hore-hound and fennel, have a similar history. Hore-hound, described by Noris Ioannou in his book, *Barossa Journeys*, was used by early settlers in cough medicine and in early recipes for beer. Fennel helped to settle upset stomachs. Today it rages along the roadsides and railway line, pretty but an intruder.

Now the frogs call out that it is time to plant the cucumbers and marrows and the beans for Christmas. But look to the moon. Is it waxing? As the new moon swells, plant all the vegetables that will grow above the ground. When the moon wanes again, put in the carrots, beetroots and radishes so that they will be ready for summer salads. This is how planting has been carried out in the Barossa for generations.

In poultry sheds when the morning grows late the hens squawk boastfully as they lay their eggs. Green grass will make orange egg yolks. From free-range hens there will be no such thing as anaemic scrambled eggs, and the noodles will be a good yellow colour.

Noodles have been an important food in the Barossa for as long as there have been hens here. Without noodles there would not have been the noodle soup that was the classic opening course of every Sunday meal. People made noodles as they were needed, but spring was a good time because the air was not too dry for handling the dough and yet the noodles had a good chance of drying out before being cut and put in storage tins. When families were large and hungry, cooks had to make huge quantities of noodles and the process could last all day.

Some people still make their own noodles and this is how they do it. First the table has to be scrubbed and spotless. Then they count out the eggs that the children have collected from the nests in the old egg-collecting saucepan:

Nudeln – Noodles
Freshly made noodles are worth the effort.
$1^1/_2$–$2^1/_2$ cups unbleached bread flour ❘ 1 tsp salt ❘ 3 eggs

Mix the flour and salt in the basin and make a well in the middle. Break each egg on a saucer and slip it into the well, working the flour into the egg after each addition. The cook has to tell by the feel of the dough whether it is stiff enough. It may need less flour. Roll the dough out thinly and evenly in small batches. Allow it to sit about 15 minutes until it becomes leathery. If the weather is damp, the dough may need to be draped over the oven door to reach the right consistency. Cut the dough into thin, even strips about 5 cm wide. Stack the strips on top of each other. With a sharp knife, slice the stack into fine slivers of noodles. If the noodles are not used immediately, spread them over the table to dry completely. Store in an airtight container.

Some households had a special noodle-cutting machine and the children would often join in the noodle-making, clamouring to be allowed to turn the handle. A noodle machine rolls the dough out thinly and then out come the noodles in fine threads, thicker strands or ribbons. They should go into the soup in their fresh, leathery state but can be dried completely, ready to be packed away.

Yvonne Burgemeister working the noodle machine

Today most cooks avoid all this trouble by buying the local Wiech's noodles that are made like the traditional recipe only on a much larger scale at Margaret Hale's noodle factory in Tanunda. In this family business, machines do the mixing and the noodles are laid to dry on stacks of gauze racks, but the principle of preparing the noodles is just the same as for the home-made ones and the quality is very good.

Margaret remembers well how her mother, Marie Wiech, started making noodles at home to supply to the local hotel kitchens in 1938. As a girl, Margaret rode the streets of Tanunda on her bike, delivering noodles to people who had ordered them. These days her business sends the noodles across South Australia and into the north of Australia, too.

Buttered Noodles
Use this butter–nutmeg mixture over hot beans or cauliflower as well. Nutmeg is a favourite flavouring for Barossa foods.

In a large pot of boiling salted water cook a packet of noodles until tender. Be careful not to overcook them. Meanwhile in a small saucepan gently brown 25 grams butter. Add $1/2$ teaspoon nutmeg and when it is foaming pour it over the drained noodles. This goes well with salad, roasted meats or *Hasenpfeffer*.

A few generations ago, as the days grew warmer and the egg-layers swung into full production, the farmer could anticipate a tidy profit from her hens. Once a week the grocery van would call and take the surplus eggs to be sold either in the shops to the 'townies' or to the egg merchant, who would set them down in a lime solution in vast cement tanks under his house and keep them there for months until the hens started resting up and the bakeries were anxious to buy from him again.

Of course, the cooks did not send all the eggs – they also needed them at home for cooking, baking and pickling. An English invention, hardboiled eggs pickled in vinegar with allspice and peppercorns have lent to many a Barossa food-cellar their particular savoury smell.

Pickled Hard-Boiled Eggs
Use a mild-tasting vinegar.
6 eggs I 2 cups vinegar I ¾ cup sugar I ½ cup water I 6 peppercorns I 6 whole allspice I ½ tsp salt

Hard-boil the eggs by stirring them gently in a saucepan of water until the water is boiling then letting them simmer for 10 minutes. Drain and hold them under running water until they are cool. Crack and peel the shells. Gently pack all the eggs in a tall sterilised glass jar. Mix the other ingredients in a saucepan and boil for 5 minutes. Pour the mixture over the eggs. Make sure that the solution covers them well. Put a lid tightly on the jar and keep for a week before using. Eat them as a snack or slice them to decorate hors d'oeuvres and other dishes. They last a couple of months.

Many a farmer had another arrangement to sell her eggs to the local winery, because until 1942 the fining of wines, especially of delicate white table wines, was done by mixing them with egg whites, which would sink to the bottom of the tanks taking all the impurities with them. Then, having cracked up to forty-dozen eggs and separated out the whites, the wine-makers sent the yolks to the bakers in the district, who were only too happy to use them.

Using egg whites to refine wines was later restricted because, if wine-makers did not work under hygienic conditions, bacteria might develop in the wines. Some very exclusive wines may be refined with egg whites today, but wineries do not generally use the process. By the end of the Second World War farmers were no longer sending large numbers of eggs to the wineries.

Eggs were vital to women because they meant money. Barossa farming women have often made the business decisions in the family, urging the men to invest in a certain piece of land or at the very least taking charge of the cheque-book. This financial sway is due largely to the money the women have traditionally made in their own right from butter and eggs. When the grocery van came round in the 1930s, it would pick up the butter and eggs to be sold in the towns. Even though most were totally subservient to their husbands, in many ways farming women prided themselves that they were contributing to the farm finances. They were such a driving force on the farm, with both their business acumen and manual labour, that some families had the saying: 'Father holds the lantern while Mother chops the wood.'

When my father, who had a motor garage, sold a car to a farming family in the 1950s, it was often the wife who paid the money. On one occasion, after agreeing to buy the car, the farmer's wife said, 'I can pay by the end of the month because next week I'm getting my schookie scheck.'

Dad asked what she meant. 'I mean my schookie scheck from Schmidt.'

Ah yes! The chookie cheque! But who was Schmidt? 'Schmidt! Och, you know, Elder Schmidt, the man that buys the eggs!' (Elder

Smith & Co. was the name of a stock and station firm that traded with farmers across South Australia for many years.)

Spring is a good time for letting the milk go sour and for making *Quark*, that home-made cottage cheese that was spread on home baked bread with a slice of smoked *Lachsschinken,* or used to make the topping for *Quarkkuchen.* Whether it was called *Quark* or *Schlippermilch* or some other name, it was a hugely important part of the pioneer food culture and people had plenty of it. After all, if the weather was starting to warm up, *Quark* just made itself!

Quark – Cottage Cheese
Another childhood memory. I need to stress that, for the sake of their health, people making *Quark* must be sure that the milk they use comes from a dairy where strictest principles of hygiene have been practised.

Place two litres milk, obtained freshly pasteurised from a dairy, in a covered bowl in a warm place near the stove at a temperature of around 36°C. (A little whey or crumbled *Quark* from the previous batch was sometimes added to hasten fermentation.) Allow to stand for about two days without stirring. When the curd starts to separate, the bowl can be put in a slightly warmer place, to accelerate the process. The curds should thicken and the whey become yellowish. Pour the curds into a linen or calico bag or pudding cloth or an old pillowslip that has become thin through much laundering. Suspend the bag from a tap or a branch in a cool place, away from dust and flies, until the whey has drained out, leaving the curd crumbly.

Quark can be mixed with fresh cream, salt and caraway seeds or chives to taste and eaten on bread. Without the herbs, it goes well with jam made from dark fruit, such as cherries.

These days we have developed a taste for the same sort of cottage cheese, only made from goat's milk. Dairies in Australia are making good quality goat-cheese. But they are not really starting anything new; the very early paintings of the first Prussian settlements in

South Australia and early ship records of the livestock they brought with them show that goats were very much part of the Prussian farming scene. In the old George French Angas pictures, goats seem to hang around the houses almost like pets. Or nuisances!

So it is certain that the very first Prussian settlers made their *Quark* out of goat's milk.

To see how important goats were in the early Barossa food culture, you need only to visit the first village square of Tanunda. It is a few streets west of today's main street. Here the most delightful old pug cottages, some of the first in Tanunda, with high-sloping, European-looking roofs and tiny doors and windows, surround an open space that has always been called Goat Square or, more familiarly, Billygoat Square. Even survey maps from the 1880s have a drawing of a goat in the square. This was the place of the first farm market in the district. During the Vintage Festivals, which take place straight after Easter every odd-numbered year, the picturesque original markets are recreated and, to capture the original setting, people tether goats around the area.

Thinking about this leads to other questions. If the first Barossa settlers had goats, did they pot-roast the meat in their big iron cooking-pots? And if goats were so visible in the villages, what happened to them? They are certainly not a common sight today.

As far as the first question goes, I have found no written records that talk about roasting goat meat but very few meat recipes were written down unless they were for some animal that requires special treatment, like hare. However, you may rest assured that in the Barossa nothing was ever wasted and that a goat past its time as a provider of milk would not simply be given honourable burial.

Now for the second question: what happened to the goats? Why did they disappear from the Barossa food culture?

Colin Thiele, a South Australian author who has written extensively about bygone days in the Barossa Valley, has some explanations. He believes that goats were simply too much trouble in proportion to the return they gave, 'even though they were as hardy as desert goannas'. Goats ignored fences and got stuck into the vegetable gardens, the crops and the washing on the line. They may have been containable back in Europe but not in Australia's open spaces. They were always where they were not wanted.

One family tells the tale of their forebears who settled at Siegersdorf, right in the centre of the Barossa Valley. They lived in a tent while they built themselves a cosy cottage. On the first night that they lit a fire in their new fireplace, the cottage burnt down. Rain was beginning to fall as they escaped from the burning building and so they huddled back into the tent. It seemed very crowded, with many bodies crammed against each other in the dark, until someone realised that the family goat had joined them!

Colin Thiele also suggests an economic reason for the disappearing goats. People may have had goats when they could not afford a cow, but the expense of buying a cow was amply rewarded since butter meant money. The population of the new colony was predominantly English, with English tastes in food. Customers preferred cow's milk, cream and butter to goat's milk. As Thiele points out, the steady flow of income from butter kept many nineteenth-century German families supplied with desperately needed cash. It was such an important money-maker that families would hardly use butter at all in their own kitchens. Instead they ate lard. Many children took sandwiches to school spread with lard or dripping 'because their mothers couldn't afford to "waste" butter like that'.

Goats did not bring in enough money to remain and so they just died out – or else they escaped up into the Barossa Ranges, where some survived until just a few years ago. Local children used to go up there and hunt them. Their quarry was a legacy from the early farmers.

Without having a cow to produce a supply of milk – and dishes and cloth bags of milk sitting around in various stages of fermentation – we find it hard to realise how important this food once was and how much it pervaded people's lives as recently as the 1950s. People used

The dairy was often in a cool cellar

Locally-made wooden butter churn

milk and cream, both sweet and sour, in different ways. Buttermilk, separated from the cream during butter-making, made biscuits and sour cream made fine soup in combination with vegetables like beetroot and cabbage.

It is also hard to realise what a difference farm-produced milk, cream, butter, cheese and buttermilk made to the taste of the food. You simply cannot compare those and the dairy products that have been processed in a factory. Pasteurisation has meant that people do not get some terrible diseases, but in return we have had to forego the intense flavours of raw milk foods.

On pioneer farms the dairy was often in a cellar, the coolest place. In some well-known pioneer families, the farmer had his eye on that cool cellar, eager to experiment with making wine. The first Mrs Seppelt, whose husband could see the advantages in converting the dairy to a wine cellar, finally agreed to give up her domain provided that her husband built her another and better one. That is how the illustrious Seppelt winery began. The first Henschke winery at Keyneton was also established in Mrs Henschke's dairy.

All the work in the dairy was much easier in springtime. A month or two earlier, the cream from cows that had eaten the rich winter grasses took much longer to be churned into butter. When the butter finally came, it was orange in colour, almost like marigolds.

Down in the dim light of the dairy, the milk sat in large pans. As the cream rose to the surface it was skimmed off with flat ladles before being turned in the locally made wooden butter-churn. (Hand-turned separators appeared in the 1890s.) Round and round sloshed the cream on the wooden paddles until the swishing noise changed to a thudding as it solidified into butter.

In summer this became a hellish job. If the cows had not dried off and were still being milked, people tried all sorts of tricks to keep the cream cool. The cool safe with damp bags hanging over the sides was in constant use. On a hot night, the farmer's wife might put the cream can in a big tub of water outside in the lucerne patch. The cloth draped over the cream-can would draw up the water from the tub and act like a cool safe. Then she would have to rise early to make the butter before the temperature started to mount. She would try any measure to make butter firm enough to be worked in the wooden butter-press and stamped with a seal ready for sale. Financial need kept her going and it continued to do so for farming women in the first half of the twentieth century.

To return to cheese making: the basic *Quark* can make two other sorts of cheese and the first is called *Kochkäse* or boiled cheese. It used to be on sale in local shops in paper cups. It looked like candied honey with caraway seeds stirred in.

Kochkäse – Boiled Cheese

This is a pleasant, mild-flavoured cheese spread. Maggie Beer suggests that to make a more substantial dish, it could be combined with raw green tomatoes, tossed through cooked ribbon noodles.

500 g *Quark* (the commercially-available cottage cheese made from pasteurised milk is an acceptable substitute) | 1 tsp ammonium bicarbonate, available from pharmacists, or 1 tsp bicarbonate of soda | 1 tsp butter | salt, pepper and caraway seeds to taste

Mix *Quark* and bicarbonate of soda or ammonium bicarbonate. Allow to stand overnight in a warm place. Next day, the mixture should have a yellowish, glassy appearance. You can then proceed with the next step or wait a few days to let the mixture increase in flavour. Melt the butter in the top of a double boiler placed over simmering water. Add the *Quark* mixture. Stir gently with a wooden spoon until the mixture goes creamy and smooth. Add salt and pepper to taste. Pour into bowls or jars and allow to set for a few hours. As the mixture sets and thickens, stir a pinch of caraway seeds into each container, according to taste. Wait for a day before serving, to allow the flavour of caraway to permeate the cheese. It keeps for at least a week in the refrigerator.

The other farm cheese that people remember well is aptly called *Stinkerkäse*. It's now rare in the Barossa but is still made in Germany to much the same sort of recipe and is even produced on a small commercial scale in many places there. It is a soft, translucent-looking cheese with a pungent farmyard flavour.

Stinkerkäse

This cheese tastes very good. The caraway adds to the complex flavours. Serve with crystallised figs and dark rye bread.

500 g crumbly dry *Quark* – made from freshly pasteurised milk ┃ 15 g salt ┃ 1 tsp bicarbonate of soda ┃ caraway seeds

Mix the *Quark* and other ingredients (except the caraway seeds). Knead until the mixture is able to hold its shape. If it is too damp, drain it longer through the cloth. From the kneaded *Quark* make cakes of cheese weighing about 100 g each.

To ripen, lay the cheeses in an earthenware crock or small wooden cask (according to some recipes each layer of dried cheeses is wrapped in clean cloths). Cover the container and keep at about 25°C. After 2 or 3 days the cheeses develop a surface that is at first slimy and later dry. On the third day, wash the cheeses in a 6 per cent salt solution with a paint-brush or other soft brush. Then leave the cheeses to ripen and dry out for yet another day at about 18°C. On the fifth day the cheeses can be wrapped in foil, packed tightly into a container and stored at about 8°C in the vegetable crisper of the refrigerator. The cheeses are often sprinkled with caraway seeds before being wrapped.

As with other traditional foods, many families had variations on the recipe. Some people left the balls of cheese to mature sitting on a plank in the garage. Another recipe says to leave the balls on the plank in the hot sun for about a week until they are rock-hard (not a practice encouraged by today's health authorities) then to wash them in cold water and drain and wipe them with a cloth before putting them in an earthenware jar. Repeat the washing, draining and wiping procedure for about three days. Then the recipe says to place a damp cloth over the cheeses in the jar and leave them for two weeks. At the end of the two weeks, the cheeses will be ready.

Some people wrapped the balls in outer cabbage leaves instead of the cloth before leaving them to mature in the jar. A scrubbed, ironstone weight sitting on a saucer would press down on the contents of the jar. When the cabbage looked glassy, the cheese was ready. Unwrapping the cabbage leaves revealed that the *Stinkerkäse* had developed a yellow, jelly-like coating and a mature flavour.

The question remains whether farmers were also used to making hard, rinded cheeses in their dairies. The evidence is sketchy. Ann Jacob ran a cheese factory at Jacob's Creek for many years, and exported her cheeses to Mauritius and to Western Australia. The first farms established by English settlers south of the Lyndoch Valley very quickly developed a reputation for making fine cheese, too. Presumably these were hard cheeses.

An old recipe-book at Hahndorf in the Adelaide Hills, used by people coming from the same places in Europe as Barossa Valley settlers, contains instructions for making rennet for cheese using the stomach of a young calf. This suggests that some farmers in the Barossa were also making rinded cheeses as well as the ones produced from *Quark*. Elderly people a generation ago talked about storing cheeses in the haystack, packed in with the sheaves so tightly that no mice could get at them while they were left to mature at a constant temperature. These, too, must have been hard cheeses with a protective rind.

All the indications are there that the early dairy farmers did make rinded cheese. Even a few generations ago, some were still making it. Bertha Hahn gave me her family recipe:

Hard Cheese (Historic recipe)
17.5 L new milk ❙ 2 plain junket tablets dissolved in warm water – soak the junket tablets before going off to do the milking ❙ 1 tsp cheese-colouring, obtainable from the creamery ❙ salt to taste

The milk should come straight from the cow and be at body temperature. Strain the new, warm milk into a large pan. Add the junket solution and cheese-colouring – butter colouring will not do. Stir well and leave to set about 2 hours. When the milk is set, cut it each way with a long knife in squares like a draught board. The whey oozes out. Strain it off. Warm the curd to 36°C by standing it in a large dish of hot water. This will make the whey rise and the curd sink. Pour off the whey carefully without breaking the curd. Put a colander over the whey dish as you pour, to catch any pieces of curd that fall. When all the water is off, take salt to taste. Sprinkle over the curd. Crumble the curd for three minutes only. This brings out more liquid.

Line an open-ended cylinder made from a 3.5 kg treacle tin with a muslin cloth. Put in the crumbled curd and fold in the cloth. Put a circular piece of plank on the top and bottom of the tin. Press with a 20 kg weight. Turn the cheese every day for a week. After 2 days, change the cloth. Do this every second day. Then put the cheese in a fly-proof safe and turn every day for a month. After that, you can wax the cheese by dipping it, in its cloth, in melted paraffin. Store in a cool cellar.

Even though recipes like this were used on local farms, most people were happy with soft homemade cheeses – with *Quark* and *Kochkäse* – and that is why some cooks still make those today in preference to hard, rinded cheese.

Chapter 10

Food Outdoors

The days of spring weather have become warmer and more frequent and the call of the outdoors grows stronger. Wearing thick socks and boots in case of snakes, friends and I make several hikes up into the Barossa Ranges. We've been seeking out some of the foods that people used to gather from the wild and also places where they used to eat in the open. This land was once home to the Peramangk people; we want to look at the part of the hills area that provided them, and the European settlers, with food.

We follow a creek up into the hills. The path is well-worn at first. Then the hills begin to rise steeply on either side of the creek, criss-crossed with animal tracks that must have been there since the communal herdsman of the first settlement at Bethany took livestock up there to graze all day long. At the sound of his horn as he returned in the evening, the villagers would come and collect their animals from his care. Now the tracks are clearly sculpted, way up on the steep slopes.

We come to a place where there was once a large stone flour mill, built in 1843, to which farmers carted their sacks of wheat. All that remains is a fig tree and a sunken bank of stones on one side where the wheel was turned by water racing down a wooden chute from above. Even the stones are crumbling now. Photographs of the many local picnics at this spot show how imposing the ruined mill was until a flood swept it away in 1923.

Interestingly, the cereal grain that early European settlers were bringing to mills like this to be ground for their bread was wheat rather than rye. You might expect them to have made northern European black-rye peasant bread, but this was not so. The climate here was suited to growing wheat that produced excellent flour and visitors to the district in the 1880s commented that scarcely any rye was grown.

Many local families have early pictures of people picnicking by this flour mill or in other places in the area. To be outdoors with friends, a keg of wine and baskets of food on a beautiful day was the best of fun and different groups would go off together for picnics; it might be with the choir, the school or the extended family. The hills behind Bethany echoed with German part-songs like the *'Lorelei'* and *'Heidenröslein'*.

An insight into what food might have been packed into the picnic hampers can be found in the book *Sunny South Australia* written by May Vivienne and published in 1909. This travel writer describes the Barossa and Adelaide Hills areas and in one chapter she writes about the food she ate at a large picnic hosted by Germans living in the Adelaide Hills. The German hosts were new arrivals who clearly missed dark Pumpernickel bread, for they had imported it in tins, along with Limburger cheese. (Had they known about locally-made *Stinkerkäse*, they need not have bothered to import the latter.) The cream cheese, pickled cucumbers, *Sauerkraut* and wursts on the menu bring no surprises. The pickled fish, probably roll-mops, served at the picnic were favoured and imported by other German-speaking South Australians as well. The picnickers also ate a 'noble Australian turkey stuffed with apples and raisins served with preserved strawberries ... supplemented by English roast beef, white bread and cakes for those who did not care for German cookery'. To May Vivienne, a person of English background, the distinctions between the English foods and the German that sat on the picnic table were clear, but she may not have been aware that by 1909 most Australian families of Prussian and German descent were quite used to eating both.

An unpublished story by Colin Thiele, written for Lutheran schools celebrating South Australia's 150th anniversary in 1986, describes another outing, this time a Sunday School picnic held in 1925. The setting is the clearing in the scrub near Gonunda, the fictitious town situated some short distance to the north of the Barossa that features in many of Thiele's novels. The families at the picnic are Australian farming families of European descent still speaking a mixture of German and English. In between the running races, the egg-and-spoon races and the tug-of-war, the picnickers eat ham, pork, cold sausage, honey biscuits, *Kuchen*, sour cucumbers, home-made bread and butter, cheese, preserved fruits, cream, tea, poisonous-looking cordial and, 'for the fathers', port in earthenware jars 'to help mit d' digestion'.

When railway services had come to the Barossa and districts further north after 1911, a whole town would catch the train to the seaside for an annual Town Picnic. People remember lots of singing, wine-drinking, unpacking of hampers and skylarking. Somebody might even bring along a band instrument to do a bit of warbling.

The faces of these picnickers peer out of sepia photographs in the collection at the Tanunda Museum: serious, shy, with teeth clenched from the gritty feel of wet sand in their hand-knitted bathers at the seaside; or fresh and smiling under straw boaters up at the ruined mill in the scrub – but always with a swaggering sense of celebration at being out in the open air.

By the 1940s, the style of picnic food had changed. Families intending to eat in the open put grillers and cuts of raw meat into the boots of their cars and set off to find a place suitable for the serious business of preparing a 'chop picnic'. Then the children had to search for rocks for the fireplace and the men grilled the meat and made the billy tea, periodically delving into their kitbags for another *Schluck* of wine or beer. Yet the food preparations at home beforehand were just as mammoth, and the charred meat was still supplemented with

A picnic near Tanunda, c. 1910

the kind of food mentioned in Colin Thiele's story, including, in most cases, bottles of home-made tomato sauce.

The Barossa picnic of the 1990s became a much more stylish, self-conscious affair. Picnics in the 1990s were designed as part of larger events like the Vintage Festival and the Barossa Music Festival. Recreating the lavish picnics of previous decades, these occasions let people imagine what it was like to belong to an earlier age – but with someone else to do the cooking and cleaning up. At the Jacob's Creek picnic in the Vintage Festivals of 1995, 1997 and 1999, under huge gums along the river flats, school-girls in frilled pinafores, boys in baggy short pants suspended from striped braces and maids in mob caps moved among the crowd toting giant baskets creaking from the weight of meats and salad, *Rote Grütze*, biscuits and traditional *Kuchen*, with not one piece of plastic in sight. The organisers made sure that the electrical equipment required for cooking and other activities was kept discreetly hidden from the picnickers.

From the early 1990s, people wanting food with style at their own private picnics might order a hamper packed with delicious home-made food from Joylene Seppelt's Barossa Picnic Baskets. Or, at Vintage Festival time, they have been able to buy their own selection from the two-day Yalumba Harvest Market. The only problem is choosing from the dazzling display of cheeses, fruits, sauces and sausages to go with the wonderful breads. All these foods, the very best made by small local producers, look beautiful under the striped awnings and the trees in the gardens at Yalumba Winery. You should try a slice of Joylene Seppelt's Barossa Picnic Loaf, which won a prize in 1994 as the most innovative picnic food using Barossa ingredients, and which is one of the treats packed into her Barossa Picnic Baskets (but leave room to sample her Gourmet Slice, made of glacé fruit and nuts).

Joylene Seppelt's Barossa Picnic Loaf

Take a long batch-loaf or any round crusty loaf. Cut off top and hollow out bread to leave a shell. (Reserve the crumbs for something else.) Paint the inside of loaf with a paste made of sundried tomatoes or tomato relish.

Fill the loaf with layers of the following: garlic *Mettwurst*; *Lachsschinken* (smoked pork); olives, rinsed, chopped and seeded; 1 eggplant, sliced, salted, brushed with olive oil and grilled; 3 small zucchini, sliced lengthwise and panfried or grilled; marinated artichokes; slices of goat's milk cheese (Joylene recommends Oxley Farm, a South Australian brand); rocket leaves; fresh basil or oregano; 2 grilled red capsicums.

Fill the bread completely, finishing with a layer of *Lachsschinken*. Put the lid on the loaf. Tie the loaf at intervals with string, wrap it in a tea towel and press it under a plate weighted down with a heavy tin from the pantry. Next day, slice cold or bake in the oven at 180°C for 20 minutes. Serve with a green salad.

Barossa people on outings in the nineteenth century found it easy to feel at one with the natural environment – most local families had lived off the land for centuries. It was second nature to make use of the wild foods that the outdoors had to offer. Back in Europe, they had hunted animals, fished and gathered plants for food in a land of

Joylene Seppelt prepares a picnic

lakes, woods and marshes. Here in the new land, what was there to eat?

This was a vital question for the first boatloads of settlers. Aboriginal people showed them what they could gather, what was good food. At Hahndorf, the early German settlement in the Adelaide hills, the Peramangk people taught the newcomers how to dig 'buttercup roots' and how to catch 'opossums'.

The buttercup roots were most probably the same as the yam daisy (*Microseris scapigera*), which in some Aboriginal languages was called *Murnong*. The roots were considered tasty by all who ate them, so much so that Baron von Mueller, a colonial botanist who came first to South Australia and later established the Botanic Gardens in Melbourne, recommended that they be introduced to Europe as a vegetable.

A little to the south of the Barossa, it must surely have been the Aboriginal people of the area who showed the new arrivals how to gather the wild currants that ripen around September. How else could the Europeans have realised that they were edible? The fruits look like dusty brown animal droppings growing close to the stem of a most unremarkable bush, surrounded by a skirt of dry fronds and twiglets of spiny leaves that make the berries hard to gather. To get at them, you have to force your way through prickly wattle and thorny heath. It is a mission fraught with pain.

Yet picking native currants marked an important season in the lives of generations of local people living in the Barossa district. Every family I interviewed remembered the annual spring expedition. For one day at least they found the time to pack the picnic baskets, pile up the billies and sacking and trundle off in the waggon, and later the car, to the spot in the hills where these sour berries (*Acrotriche depressa*) grow.

What was the big attraction? Was it the beauty of the undulating bushland where the berries are found? In spite of the prickly lower story, the bush certainly is lovely here and from one point the view stretches north forever. Was it the fact that the berries make

Picking native currants, 1920s

extremely good jam? It looks like cranberry jam and has the purplish taste of black currants. Being tart, the berries gel very easily. Steeped in sugar syrup and brandy, they also make an interesting liqueur and some cooks also used to make them into chutney.

Was it that an outing like this in the warm spring weather truly marked the turn of the season, a return to warmer days and life in the open air? Or was it that people of Prussian extraction simply could not decline an opportunity to gather free food from the wild, even if it involved scrambling around for hours being scratched by the shrubbery for only a few billies full at the end of it?

Probably all these motives drove them to the annual ritual. They would arrive at the favourite spot, assign different areas to different members of the party, spread the sacking under the bushes, then spend the next few hours pulling and shaking, letting the berries plop onto the bags before scooping them into the billies.

Some grew impatient with this process and, with shameful disregard of the environment, pulled up the bushes, roots and all, in order to harvest the crop more easily. The patches of bushes have shrunk over the years, not surprisingly, but some still survive. It is just as well that the passion for these prickly picnics has waned, because it may give the plants a chance to regenerate.

Back home after a tiring day, the children still had to pick the leaves out from the currants and wash the fruit. A good way to do the separating was to have a big, flat board covered with a blanket. They would tilt the board and make the berries roll to the other end, leaving the lighter bits behind. Then the cook made the jam.

Native-currant Jam

This is good jam. The tart-flavoured berries also make a good sauce for game birds. People are experimenting with the cultivation of native currant bushes for the commercial market. The quantities are adapted from a recipe supplied by Olga Lehmann.

1.8 kg native currants | 1.5 L water | 1.8 kg warmed sugar | grated rind 1 lemon (optional) | $1/2$ jar plum jam (optional)

Bring the currants and water to the boil, skimming off the final bits of dried foliage, which will rise to the surface. Boil until the berries are tender. Slowly add the warmed sugar. Boil for about 45 minutes. Test it on a saucer to see if it gels. Add plum jam and lemon rind if desired. Bottle when warm. Cover when cool. Store in a cool, dry place.

Native currants weren't the only wild foods around in springtime. As recently as the 1920s, people were gathering cress (*Lepidium ruderake*) in the creeks up in the ranges, quandongs (*Santalum acuminatum*) and native cranberries (*Astroloma humifusum*) in the sandy foothills and wild strains of domestic celery in the creek at Greenock and Tanunda. They also cooked with the bitter quandong (*Santalum murrayanum*), muntries (*Kunzea pomifera*) and the sour-bush (*Leptomeria aphylla*).

The quandongs were often stewed and baked with a *Streusel* topping, just like the one given for Janet Nitschke's *Streuselkuchen* in an earlier chapter. The native cranberries tasted rather like apples and were useful for making pies. As for the runaway celery, its flavoursome pencil-thin stems and leaves made an excellent vegetable and addition to soups and stews. An early German botanist in Australia, Otto Tepper, is said to have made marmalade from the bitter quandong, which he gathered in scrub near Sandy Creek. The muntries, which today may be bought from nurseries and cultivated in the garden, made very good pies and tarts. As for the sourbush berries, when they ripened in November and turned golden, early settlers near Nuriootpa used to gather them and make a refreshing, lemon-tasting cordial for summer.

Settlers probably gathered many other wild foods, but the one about which an actual story has been recorded is the native cherry (*Exocarpos cupressiformis*). This is a strange plant, or at least a tree with a strange-looking fruit. The tree itself has foliage that looks like strappy green twigs and it has small red fruits in springtime, each with its seed growing outside the flesh.

The story is in the papers of the Matthews family, who lived in the hills behind Angaston. One spring morning in about 1845, young Thomas, Joan and Arthur Matthews set off as usual to walk to school in Angaston. As they passed through the scrub outside the town, they saw that the wild cherries were ripe and stopped to pick them. They were busy spitting out the pips when suddenly a spear landed on the earth beside them. They looked up, startled, as some men and women, presumably of the Peramangk people, stepped out of the bushes where they had been hunting for food. The hunters were probably just as surprised as the children to see that their quarry had not, in fact, been a kangaroo. They took some trouble to assure the children that they had meant no harm and finally the children picked up their bags and continued on their way to school, running for all they were worth. The account in the family history ends very archly – 'you may be sure they were not long in getting to school!'

Thomas, Joan and Arthur were understandably startled by the spear landing near them but they were mistaken if they thought that the Aborigines were automatically hostile towards them. Mostly the Europeans and the indigenous people in this area treated each other with caution but lived peaceably side by side.

A c.1850 painting by Alexander Schramm of a Prussian farmhouse in South Australia shows Aboriginal people paying a visit and sitting by the outside fire while the farmer's wife is doing the washing and the farmer stands in the open doorway holding the baby. The facial expressions and body positions of the people in the picture seem placid and give no indication of menace.

There are several accounts of Aboriginal people giving the Prussians help and advice, especially in relation to food and places to settle. There are also reports of Europeans giving the Peramangk people bread and lard and other supplies. Many of the farmers were probably not aware of the devastating effect they were having on

A Prussian farmhouse in South Australia c. 1850

the food-lands and culture of this group of people or on those of the Ngadjuri who lived on the plains to the west of the range.

By the turn of this century and possibly even earlier, Aboriginal people were no longer in the Barossa district but we know from the presence of implements and cave paintings and from the recollections of white people of earlier generations that they had once lived well from the animals and plants along the creeks and in the hills.

My hikes into the Barossa hills brought some disappointments. On one occasion, I found a stone ruin: the stunted remains of four stone walls and a tangle of iron and splintering joists. The stone hut that had been destroyed – who knows how and by whom? – had been home at different periods to local people living off the wild in hard times. Back in the 1890s, when Australia was being squeezed by economic hardship, it was difficult for farmers to sell some of their crops but tanneries were still making leather. In order to obtain cash to pay off their debts, the men in the family would go into the hills and collect wattle bark to sell to the tanneries for tanning the hides. They would stay away for days at a time, only returning to the farm at the end of the week to sell the bark to the tannery, the wood to the baker and to replenish their supplies.

Much of their food came from the land itself and often it was rabbits, which had well and truly taken over the southern Australian countryside by then. 'Underground mutton' was invariably on the menu.

The best time for wattle-barking was spring, when the early wattles had finished flowering, and it is at just this time that rabbits are producing their kittens. Kitten rabbits are the best rabbits and you cook them whole. You only cook them for about six minutes and they are so tender that they melt as you sink your teeth into them. So those poverty-stricken wattle-barkers and land-clearers lived well.

People used the hut and continued wattle-barking over the years. In the 1920s and 1930s, the person who spent most time in the hut on the hill was Ben Dost. He had a bed, a table and a fireplace in there.

He had salt and pepper and a tea billy and tea. He would leave all these in the hut for the times when he'd go trapping, for he was trying to earn a living by selling rabbits to households in the towns. He would go trapping and take a two-gallon jar of wine with him. When that was empty, he'd go down the hill to Falkenberg's winery, get the jar filled and go back into the hills with his dog to check his traps. He had no trouble catching rabbits – the place was infested with them. Just in the stretch of a mile along the creek, he could catch more than 80 rabbits, many more than he could sell. So he spent most of his time up in the hills living off the rabbits (his diet possibly varied by wild duck and stubble quail) as well as making damper and drinking water from the creek.

Down in the streets of the town, Ben would knock on the doors of the houses and offer his rabbits for sale. Thrifty cooks bought them often, for they were cheap and there was not much money around. Proof of the number of times people made a meal of rabbit lies in the numerous recipes for rabbit pie or curried rabbit that appear in the second and third editions of the *Barossa Cookery Book*.

Rabbit Pies

A delicious adaptation of several recipes in the *Barossa Cookery Book*. You may prefer to make your favourite short-crust pastry with butter, instead of the lard pastry. It is easier to serve in ramekins: you will need six.

RABBIT FILLING

3 rabbits ❙ 2 L stock or water ❙ 1 stick celery with its end leaves, chopped ❙ $1/2$ peeled carrot, chopped ❙ 1 onion, peeled and quartered ❙
1 bouquet garni of parsley, thyme and a fresh bay leaf ❙ finely peeled rind $1/2$ lemon in one piece ❙ pepper and salt to taste ❙ 3 hard-boiled eggs ❙
3 slices ham ❙ pepper

FORCEMEAT

1 onion finely chopped ❙ livers and hearts of the rabbits blended in the food processor ❙ 5 or 6 small sprigs fresh thyme ❙ 2 cups fresh white breadcrumbs ❙ 2 tsp lemon zest ❙ pepper ❙ salt ❙ nutmeg

GRAVY

2 tbsp flour ❙ 2 tbsp butter ❙ 3 cups rabbit stock ❙ salt and pepper

PASTRY

2 cups flour ❙ 1 tsp baking powder ❙ 1 tsp salt ❙ $1/2$ cup lard ❙ juice $1/2$ lemon ❙ $1/2$ cup iced water

Remove livers and hearts from rabbits, blend and set aside. Cut off the front and back legs to use for the pie. (Use the saddles and fillets for another dish requiring less cooking time.) Place legs in a pot with the stock, vegetables, bouquet garni, lemon rind and seasonings. Simmer gently until the meat is tender, about 1 hour, but start testing earlier than this. Allow to cool in the stock. Remove the meat from the bones, and break it into pieces. Arrange in six deep ramekin bowls, with the quartered hard-boiled eggs and broken bits of sliced ham.

Make forcemeat balls by frying onion and pureed liver and hearts in butter and combining with thyme, breadcrumbs, lemon zest, pepper, salt and nutmeg. Form into balls and add to the ramekins.

In a saucepan, melt the butter for the gravy and add flour. Cook for a minute, remove from the heat and gradually blend in the stock. Return to the heat and bring to the boil so that the sauce thickens. Add salt and pepper to taste. Spoon gravy over the meat in the ramekins.

While it is cooling, make the pastry. Mix flour, baking powder and salt. Cut in the lard with a knife or pastry blender. Add lemon juice and iced water. Blend with a fork. Knead until the pastry becomes a smooth ball. Chill in the refrigerator for 20 minutes.

Roll out and cut out rounds to hang over the sides of the ramekins. Press firmly around the edges. Glaze with beaten egg. Cut slits to allow the steam to escape. Cook at 220° C for 15 minutes, then turn the heat back to 180° C for another 15 minutes.

Chapter 11

Grand Entertainment

The Barossa is so beautiful in spring that in the 1990s visitors poured into the valley for two spring events: the Gourmet Weekend at the very start of the season and the Barossa Music Festival in October.

Often the Gourmet Weekend scored some of the first of the warm spring weather. In early spring the grass along the roadsides is tender and green under the sun. For the first time in months the sky is intensely blue. The vines are scarcely in bud but along the edges of the vineyards the almond trees are still in blossom and have a strong perfume of honey.

Against this backdrop, visitors to the Gourmet Weekend were able to follow their programs and choose to visit wineries offering the food, music and wine that best suited their tastes: a chamber orchestra, chargrilled tuna and chenin blanc at one winery; an Irish jig, kangaroo satays and basket-press shiraz at another.

Later, in October, flowers are out along the roadsides. White irises, which children call 'flags', scatterings of red sparaxis, paddocks of purple Salvation Jane and yellow soursobs cover the countryside with vibrant colours – joyful decorations for the Music Festival.

The success of this festival of chamber music has come from its blend of performances, settings (in historic local churches and rich-smelling wine cellars) and accompanying serves of food and wine. With Maggie Beer overseeing the presentation of food during her years on the Music Festival Board, the standards became high. Once I walked in to one of the luncheon sites and felt as if I was stepping into a still-life painting featuring huge panniers of breads, fruits, cheeses, hams and pots of pickles and sauces.

In *Maggie's Orchard* you can read about the elaborate feast that was dreamed up to complement the baroque music of Purcell's *Indian Queen*, performed one year as an opera in the stone storage sheds at Yalumba winery. As Maggie says, her accompanying baroque banquet was a feat of orchestration in itself. It had to be assembled in silence while the opera was in progress in the next room. After the performance, the diners entered the room lit solely by candle light and feasted on asparagus, beetroot, game pies and caramel floating island desserts all carefully researched as being true to the period of the music they had just heard.

The people of the Barossa are renowned for providing festive foods for large numbers. Over the years, on many grand occasions, they have fed hundreds and sometimes thousands of guests. The nature of the catering may have changed or become more sophisticated (and, in the best instances, more exacting) but there was never a time when someone wasn't devising an ambitious plan to cater for a crowd.

In the 1950s, it was the Vintage Dinners that required masterly organisation to put elegant food on the table for over 1000 people. Teams of volunteer workers, directed by Mrs Laurel Hoffmann (a legendary community worker from a local wine-making family) took sections of the street plan of Tanunda and knocked on all the doors. They asked if the housewife at each address would kindly cook a chicken to provide meat for the table. They delivered the chicken on the morning of the dinner with instructions about how to broil it and collected it later in the day to be cut up and put on platters. As a reward, the cook was allowed to keep the broth! Many of the women who had spent all day making tiny hors d'oeuvres and icing petits fours down at the dining hall would race home to change into their formal ball-gowns, complete with long, white, kid gloves, and return

Grand Entertainment

to the dinner looking as though they had never cooked a meal in their lives.

The Vintage Festivals, too, from the time they first began, have always included major events requiring large-scale food preparations by local people. Again, teams of volunteer workers have spent hours preparing cheese and *Mettwurst* rolls or serving potato salad or washing stacks of dishes in a system that enables them to raise money for their local committees: the school, the bowling club or the church auxiliary. While crowds dance at the carnival on the oval, or stroll among the children bowling hoops at the old-fashioned picnic down by the river, people behind the scenes are chopping and slicing, putting food on plates or setting tables. It's all part of the life of the community that brings together people of all persuasions for a common cause.

Over the years, people providing food for such vast numbers have learned how best to do so from all the previous experience but not every ambitious catering project has been a total success along the way. People still remember the time when three large bullocks were roasted whole for the 1949 Vintage Festival. The local newspaper ran a breathless story before the event saying that 60 loaves of bread and two bags of onions would be needed to make the stuffing for each of the three bullocks. It was going to take 38 hours to roast them for the barbecue at Tanunda and workers would have to take shifts during the night to watch over the cooking meat.

As the end of the 38 hours approached, the sour smell alone was enough to tell everyone that the stuffing inside the carcasses had fermented and that the bullocks were unfit to eat. People turned away in disgust. Ah well! Plenty of stupendous events since have made up for that day of disaster.

If you look back into the Barossa's past you can see how the people of the area came to take large-scale catering for festivals in their stride.

Families last century were mainly large. Some may have lived in tiny cottages, but when everyone sat down to each meal at least 14 people might be at the table, counting the hired help in the house and on the farm. So peeling a whole bucket of potatoes at one sitting or making stacks of noodles was just part of the normal food production.

On plenty of occasions people met to celebrate a special event: big families meant large Sunday afternoon visits, big Christmas gatherings, huge funerals with food to follow, more weddings and more tinkettlings or *Polterabende*. No wonder the cooks made *Streuselkuchen* in bulk. No wonder the recipes for honey biscuits were designed to make 'a good lot'. No wonder Annie Heinrich's recipe for melon jam required 45 pounds of pie-melon and 35 pounds of sugar!

Perhaps the one surprising exception was people's birthdays, which many families did not always celebrate. 'Och, we were too busy working to think of birthdays,' one woman told me. 'There was no such thing as a birthday cake.'

It was a different matter in other families, where life was not shaped by hard work on the farm. Anna Ey, the wife of a Lutheran pastor who was in the Barossa at different periods from about 1860 to 1907, mentioned people's birthdays several times in her diary. On one occasion her brother gave her money to buy herself a birthday present. Later, in 1903, by then a widow of 75, she was treated to a birthday surprise while she was visiting her son's family who had gone to live in Minyip, Victoria:

When I got up in the morning, the table was nicely set with a bunch of flowers, a lovely cake, a bottle of wine and a pair of warm slippers. Then all came and congratulated me.

In some families, a birthday treat might be waffles for afternoon tea. The recipe listed on the lid of the old waffle iron in the Historical Museum at Tanunda obviously catered for a large crowd, for it required '2 lbs flour, 6–8 eggs, ½ gallon milk, ¾ lb butter [and] 1 spoonful of yeast'.

In other families, the treat was often a batch of *Berliner Pfannkuchen*, or Berlin buns, whipped up from the dough of the rising *Kuchen*, filled with raspberry jam, fried in lard in a saucepan and then rolled in sugar like a doughnut. Modern bakers still make these buns and – whisper it – embellish them with mock cream.

Berliner Pfannkuchen – Berlin Buns

These are still a treat. Make them quite small and serve them soon after they have been cooked. There are two methods described here; each makes about 16 small buns. These are also known as sugar buns or Kitchener buns.

(A) 15 g compressed yeast | $1/3$ cup warmed milk | 1 tsp sugar
(B) $1/3$ cup milk | $1/3$ cup plain flour | 1 dsp sugar
(C) 55 g butter or lard | $2^{1}/4$ cups bread flour | $1/3$ cup sugar | $1/4$ tsp salt | 1 egg | $1/4$ cup milk | 3 tsp rum | 1 tsp vanilla essence or grated rind 1 lemon | $1/2$ jar firm dark jam | a little milk | caster sugar to coat the buns

In a warm saucepan, mix ingredients in (A). Keep in a warm place 5 to 10 minutes. In a bigger saucepan, mix the ingredients in (B) and add mixture of (A). Again, put the lid on the saucepan and keep in a warm place 10 to 15 minutes.

Melt butter or lard. Into a large, warm dish, sift flour, sugar and salt. In a smaller dish, beat egg, milk, rum and vanilla or lemon rind and add melted fat.

Combine the flour mixture, the egg mixture and the yeast mixture, and stir well. Knead 10 minutes. Put dough in a greased 2 litre plastic container with the lid on in a warm place. Let it rise 1 hour.

METHOD 1 FOR MAKING BUNS

Roll dough out 1 cm thick. Divide rolled-out dough in half. Make ring marks on one sheet of dough with a glass and put a spoonful of jam in the centre of each ring. Using a pastry brush, paint the ring outlines lightly with milk to help them to seal. Lay the other sheet of dough over the top, noting where the jam and rings are. Using the glass, cut out the pastry covered rings.

METHOD 2 FOR MAKING BUNS

Make the dough into a long roll and cut off round slices about 12 mm thick. Put a dob of stiff, tart jam on one, place another on top and seal the edges. Continue to make round buns in this way until the dough is used up.

Cover the buns with a greased plastic bag or a tea-towel and allow them to rise again for another half an hour. Deep fry in at least 4 cm lard in a saucepan. First fry the bottom side until brown (45 seconds) then the top side (35 seconds). Drain them on kitchen paper. Roll them in caster sugar.

Perhaps the most momentous celebration was the wedding feast. In families where relatives were scattered and rarely saw each other these could go on for days. It was a joyful time for young and old alike. Practically the whole settlement was invited to attend, including the pastor and the school-teacher.

The preparations began just as early as they do for large weddings today. The parents needed to get in brandy, wine and beer. All the farm workers and family members helped. They would give the German waggons, which were to be the wedding conveyances, a new coat of paint: shiny blue sides and bright red wheels. The horses and harness would be brushed and rubbed to a high sheen. The men painted the house with a fresh coating of white lime wash, with the interior walls sometimes tinted pale blue from the addition of a blue-bag to the mixture. The barn was cleaned out thoroughly because that was where the feasting would take place, and so were the farm outhouses, where visitors might sleep.

Several weeks beforehand, the family would kill a pig to be made into wursts and bacon for the wedding. Friends and neighbours would help by killing a fat calf as well as geese, ducks and hens. In the kitchen, the girls had to make great stacks of bread and German cake the day before the wedding, and cut up the wursts, salads, pickled cucumbers and other vegetables that were generally part of a festive meal.

They set aside some of the *Streuselkuchen* for the tin-kettling or *Polter Abend*. This originally took place at the bride's house the night before the wedding (although in later years it took place at the newly-weds' house when the honeymoon was over). That night, young people lay in ambush around the house and the terrific din that they made with tin trays and shotguns and horns stopped only when the bride and groom-to-be invited them inside for wine, cake and coffee.

At last the wedding day dawned and everyone rose and washed and put on their finery. As many as six young couples could be in the wedding party. When the groomsmen arrived at the bride's house they would all be jostling for space in front of the mirrors to do their hair or adjust their collars and the ribbons and myrtle or roses in their lapels. Punctually at ten the waggons pulled up at the door, decorated with red, white and blue rosettes. A ribbon floated from the top of the driver's whip.

Out walked the bride in her veil, wreath of myrtle and black or navy-blue gown, hitching it up carefully above her black, buttoned boots as she swung up onto the footplate of the waggon. The groom, with his tall top-hat, climbed in beside her. The other members of the wedding party settled themselves in the rest of the waggons. Then the driver gave the command – *'Vorwärts, marsch!'* – and the horses moved off at a trot.

Along the road to the church people gathered to cheer and carry out a Barossa custom that is still practised to this day. Every so often, a group of young bystanders would stretch a rope across the road, with flags or old clothes hanging from it, forcing the waggons to stop. This was the signal for the groom and bride to lean down and hand out slices of *Kuchen*, conversation lollies or bottles of wine. (I think that for our own wedding, it was mostly the wine they were after! We handed out bottles of it through the car window after the wedding ceremony was over.) The bride and groom couldn't help noticing that each time the waggon stopped the same faces were in the crowd waiting for their reward before racing on ahead to another vantage point. And so in fits and starts and with much amusement the wedding party made its way to the church.

The service began with the bride and groom walking together up the aisle followed by the couples in their wedding party. A hymn would follow, usually *Jesus lead Thou on*. I remember years ago hearing someone exclaiming what a mournful hymn this was for a wedding and wondering why it was always chosen. Just read the second verse:

If the way be drear,
If the foe be near,
Let not faithless fears o'ertake us
Let not faith and hope forsake us,
For, through many a woe
To our home we go.

And in case all that was a little too optimistic, the congregation then listened to what has been described euphemistically as 'a powerful sermon', during which the bride and groom sat solemnly on matching wedding chairs, often made especially for the occasion and symbolically tied together with satin bows.

After the service was over the wedding party handed wine and *Kuchen* to people standing outside the church. Then the horses were harnessed back into the waggons and soon the party left, bumping over the stony track. They made their way back to the house, stopping when the rope was stretched across the road and well-wishers held them up demanding food and wine.

At the bride's home the barn had been decorated with fern fronds and white flowers twined into garlands and looped over the doors and rafters. The meal started with noodle and fowl soup with giblets, followed by the mountains of food that had been prepared in the days beforehand. For the sake of logistics, because the guests were often fed in a couple of sittings, the meats were mostly cold ('cold collations' were at one stage the universal Barossa wedding breakfast.) Yet some people speak of elaborate hot meals being dished up and of weddings in Tanunda around the end of the nineteenth century where at each guest's place was arranged a *Streuselkuchen* baked in the shape of a woolly lamb. A whimsical touch which, like some European plaited breads, may have had religious significance.

In the kitchen the children would polish off the leftovers and then rush to play on the haystacks while the merry-making, joke-telling and poetry-recitations continued inside. Occasionally some of the adult guests would slip away to have a break, too. My mother, who was then five, recalls a wedding at Point Pass, to the north of the Barossa, in 1911: the women congregated in the bedroom to try on the hat of a particularly elegant guest from overseas – until the lady in question walked in at the critical moment.

Whether the wedding was English or German, someone was bound to play music (although in many congregations dancing was not permitted). The diary of Ann Jacob, who lived at Jacob's Creek, describes a wedding she attended at a neighbouring farm in 1842 where the music was most indifferent, because it consisted of someone playing a violin with no great skill, accompanied by Mr Menge on a gum leaf. At other weddings the guests sang together around the table as they ate and drank. At midnight, the bride removed her veil and the groom the flowers and ribbons from his buttonhole, a symbolic declaration that they were now a regular married couple.

The food on the second and third days of the wedding celebrations followed much the same pattern as the first wedding feast, with breakfast and an evening meal included in the daily fare as well. The guests would spend the afternoons hiking and picnicking in the scrub or taking excursions in the horse-drawn waggons. They returned to the wedding house to more eating, drinking, music and singing.

This is how Australian–German farming communities organised weddings in the 1870s, and the pattern continued until the 1920s in some places (although by 1910 most brides had abandoned dark-coloured wedding dresses in favour of white). When you count up the number of times food was handed around during those three-day wedding celebrations, and think of the number of people waiting round to eat it, you get an inkling of the number of trays of cake that the cooks needed to bake and the number of slices of meat that needed to be carved.

It was handy to have recipes giving the quantities required for satisfying large numbers of people. The recipe below for making large batches of cream puffs was used for Barossa weddings in the 1920s. Cream puffs were probably at the height of their popularity in that decade and were a new, fancy delicacy for many local people. This

Wedding preparations – 1960s (photo: Peter Wells)

is interesting because cream puffs are claimed by Germans to be a traditional German food: *Windbeutel* or 'windbags' they call them. Yet most Barossa people did not know about them until the early 1920s.

Windbeutel – Cream Puffs
This makes about 300

1.5 kg butter (with a little salt added if butter is unsalted) | 12 cups water | 10 cups flour | about 36 large eggs (the exact number depends on the size), beaten | 3600 ml cream, whipped and slightly sweetened with icing sugar and vanilla

Bring the butter and water to a rolling boil in a large pan. Add the sifted flour all at once. Stir until blended. Add beaten eggs in batches. Beat until smooth and shiny. (Test the viscosity of the mixture as you add the eggs by pinching a piece of the dough between thumb and forefinger. If the mixture forms an unbroken string between the thumb and forefinger as you pull them apart, you have enough eggs in the mixture. If the dough breaks, you need to add more eggs.) Place spoonfuls on greased slides. Sprinkle lightly with a fine spray of water. Bake in a hot oven (220°C) for 5 minutes then reduce the heat to moderate (180°C) for a further 15 minutes. Fill cases with whipped cream.

Large families and large celebrations may have led to the huge dinners and feasts that happened decades later, but these would never have been as ambitious without the influence of the wine-making families.

Take the Seppelt family as an example. The enormous winery with its distillery and vinegar house that Benno Seppelt established at Seppeltsfield was famous for its catering. I can imagine what it was like, that day in 1877, when buggies carrying local identities and a trainload of Adelaide dignitaries from the terminus at Gawler came to the opening of the great stone cellars. They sipped wine and nibbled biscuits under the arbor and then, to the cheerful tones of the local brass band, made short work of the lunch provided by Sophie Seppelt in the cellars themselves.

From then on Mrs Seppelt and her helpers dished up lunches to an endless line of visitors who called at Seppeltsfield from across the world to see this progressive winery. They went away raving not only about the wine but also about the food, especially the bacon; it was made from pigs that had eaten fermented grape skins left from the crush and it had a much sought-after, delicate flavour. You could buy Seppeltsfield bacon in shops, too, but you had to pay high prices.

How did Mrs Seppelt cope with organising so much food? Besides providing the meals for visitors, she raised nine sons and four daughters and fed the winery workers as well, all 70 of them. (In fact by the start of the twentieth century the numbers had grown to around 100.) That meant a cooked breakfast and a cooked midday meal for 100 people every day during vintage.

The cellar hands would arrive from neighbouring towns and farms for their porridge at seven and at midday they were back in the Seppeltsfield dining-room (which is still used for various functions today) for their mutton and freshly baked bread. The kitchen hands baked sixty loaves and cooked six sheep every day to satisfy the hungry workers.

Much of the food used to feed the workers and guests came from the Seppelt gardens, grown under the supervision of Sophie Seppelt herself. She had fruit trees, vegetables, flowers for the house and table, orpington hens, bees in hives ... Visitors remarked how fresh and clean everything looked when they were taken on a conducted tour.

This seems an extraordinary story and it is certainly not the kind of benefit that workers expect from their employers any more. But most of the families connected with the larger wineries have been keenly interested in food and catering. Somehow it seems that whenever anyone is preparing good food for numbers of people, the winery families are involved in some way.

The Seppelt family, the Gramp family of Orlando, the Hill-Smith and Wark families of Yalumba, Grant and Helen Burge, Laurel and Erwin Hoffmann, Peter and Margaret Lehmann: these and other families in the mid to late twentieth century have worked to bring wine and food together for large numbers of people. They have served on committees organising wine and food events in the Vintage Festivals. They have held galas and feasts to raise money for local charities. They have supported the local Bacchus Club for wine and food connoisseurs.

In 1953 the Adelaide Bacchus Club, a group that fostered members' interest in fine food and wine appreciation, suggested that people in the Barossa should start a similar club. The founders, Colin Gramp, Max Hackett, Rudi Kronberger and Alf Wark, all associated with wineries, had no difficulty in persuading people to become members. Who, after all, can resist a good nosh-up among friends? Largely because the founding committee was keen to set an excellent standard, the Bacchus Club had a big influence on Barossa Valley life. It meant that people from different towns, who previously did not know each other (coming from 'foreign parts' as they did), became a friendly and outward-looking group. And because Bacchus Club meals explored food from different countries, it meant that men – and women twice a year – learned to be adventurous. Not that the food was always international: Alf Wark once prepared a family dish of smoked cod simmered slowly in milk with bay leaf and pepper as a hot entrée. Colin Gramp remembers using his mother's recipe for herring salad for a Christmas barbecue.

All the wine-making families have stories to tell about serving food and wine to large numbers of people. But I'd like to tell you about Helen Hill-Smith, whose catering and hospitality have been closely associated with Yalumba Winery and influenced other people in a far-reaching way.

Helen began by working for the Angaston Hospital Auxiliary, which made jams and mended sheets and catered for small events. When the hospital needed large sums of money spent on it, the small catering projects of the Auxiliary grew larger. Yalumba, the family winery, supported the group by using the caterers for all their entertaining. So did other wineries and businesses in the district. In the

1960s, the catering grew bigger and bigger. The Auxiliary catered for lunches, afternoon teas, receptions and dinners; they entertained cricket heroes, royalty and arts celebrities. The caterers divided the work so that each member made a portion of a course. Their teamwork was so good that they could feed 22 or 402 with style. (The latter number is how many they had to feed at the dinners of the Barons of the Barossa, a group of local identities honoured for their contribution to the wine industry.)

Part of their skill was working in places where there were no amenities for serving food. They became used to converting empty wine-storage sheds by having electricity and water brought in and installing huge gas coppers for cooking soup: lettuce soup and walnut soup and potage St Germain. They cooked pigeons with brandied cherries, roast duck and barons of beef. For lunches they made great salvers of salad and trenchers of meat. They placed the serving dishes in huge sheep-troughs of ice decorated with vine leaves. It was tiring but supremely successful and it raised enough money to provide operating theatres for the hospital.

Pigeons with Brandied Cherries

This recipe is supplied by Helen Hill-Smith from the Pre-auction Vintage Dinner of 1971. It is adapted to serve eight people. The Hospital Auxiliary caterers each made at least one batch of the recipe, thus achieving the amount needed for the crowd at the dinner.

110 g bacon, diced ı 55 g butter ı 4 pigeons ı 4 medium onions, chopped ı 4 medium carrots, chopped ı 1 bay leaf ı 2 tbsp chopped parsley including stalks ı $1/4$ tsp dried thyme ı $1/2$ tsp salt ı $1/4$ tsp pepper ı 30 g flour ı 400 ml chicken stock ı 2 sherry glasses red wine ı $1/2$ cup brandied cherries

Fry diced bacon in a thick saucepan for 2 minutes, add butter and pigeons and brown quickly on all sides. Remove pigeons and bacon and add chopped vegetables, herbs, salt, pepper and flour – mix well and cook lightly. Drain off excess fat, replace birds and bacon, pour on stock and wine. Bring to boil and simmer gently for $1 1/2$ hours or until birds are tender. Garnish with brandied cherries and serve with red currant jelly. A little cream may be added to gravy.

The story does not end there. Helen Hill-Smith was also part of a group who opened Angaston Cottage Industries, a shop where local people could sell their homemade jams, pickles and crafts. She saw it as a way of using surplus fruit and vegetables and enabling people to make money from their skills.

The catering style that Helen and her co-workers adopted has become part of the hospitality style of wineries throughout the Barossa. And at Yalumba itself, the Hill-Smith family has continued to promote food as well as wine, especially since they began the Yalumba Harvest Markets at the Vintage Festivals. As for the cottage industry shop, it is just the first of many business ventures where local people are turning their favourite recipes into preserves, biscuits and pickles for a larger market. The brand-names of some, like Farm Follies, are known in many states of Australia.

In the mid-1960s, when Australians were becoming more wine-minded and starting to appreciate food with wine, some people saw that there were very few places in the Barossa Valley where visitors could try food and wine from the local region. Apart from the Angaston Hotel, site of many a Bacchus Club dinner, the scene was bleak.

The first restaurants set up in the early 1970s to change this situation were the Weinstube, built strategically between Tanunda and Nuriootpa, and the Gramp family's Weinkeller Restaurant at Jacob's Creek, followed by Die Gallerie in Tanunda. It was a risky business, especially persuading the licensing board that the district could support as many as three eating-places with wine licences!

This is how Colin Gramp described the first menu of his restaurant (which has now become the Grant Burge Winery):

We selected a menu that used quite a few of the old dishes brought out by our forebears. For example, the Herringssalat.

We put in yabbies in memory of my youth, when I used to catch yabbies down from the North Para cellars. In the Christmas holidays I had made quite a bit of money catching and cooking yabbies and piling them into the small Black and Croswell anchovy jars, which I sold for 3d a jar. (When I think about that today, they were getting yabbies at a very reasonable price!) So we served garlic yabbies on the menu.

Grandfather and William Jacob were great friends. Every time Grandfather visited William Jacob, they had steak-and-kidney pie. On the return visit they had Kassler *and* Sauerkraut. *So we put those on the menu, too.*

Yet another recipe was the gazpacho that I enjoyed on the Mediterranean coast, just down from Xeres. The temperature was 108°F that day. The restaurateur gave us the recipe because we enjoyed it so much. Yes, we took some risks but had some popular successes.

Colin Gramp's Garlic Yabbies
When using live yabbies, always numb them in the freezer before taking the tails. The Weinkeller's recipe has here been reduced to serve 4.
250 g butter | 1 tsp crushed garlic | juice of ½ lemon | 24 large yabby tails, preferably uncooked, removed from their shells

Melt butter in a pan then add garlic and lemon juice and stir well. When butter is nearly boiling add the tails, stir and simmer until white. Do not heat cooked tails too long, just enough to serve them hot. Serve in small, heated, deep bowls with lemon wedges and garnish with parsley or finely chopped chives with a touch of ground pepper. Serve with fresh, crusty pretzel sticks or bread, accompanied by a riesling or unwooded chardonnay.

William Jacob's Steak-and-kidney Pie

Preparing this recipe from the Gramp Family Weinkeller Restaurant brings back nostalgic memories. It makes between 12 and 25 individual pies, depending how large the ramekins are that contain them.

FILLING

6 kg stewing or blade steak, cubed ¦ 1.5 kg ox or calf kidney, cubed ¦ 6 onions, chopped ¦ 1 cup oil ¦ beef stock ¦ 2 cups red wine ¦ 1 cup water ¦ 2 cups plain flour ¦ salt and ground pepper to taste

PASTRY

$2^{1}/_{2}$ kg plain flour ¦ salt to taste ¦ 1.2 kg butter ¦ 600 ml iced water

Fry steak, kidney and onion in oil until juice comes out of meat. Stir occasionally, then add enough beef stock to cover the meat. Continue stirring and cook slowly for $^{3}/_{4}$ hour. Finally thicken with a mixture of red wine, water and flour. Cook for another 15 minutes, adding salt and pepper to taste. Place in bowls about $^{3}/_{4}$ full. Cool

To make the pastry, sift flour and salt. Rub in butter. Add iced water, kneading into a ball. Rest pastry in refrigerator 30 minutes. Roll out on a floured board. (Do not have it too dry, otherwise it will crumble.)

Cut pastry into rounds and press them over the bowls of meat. Glaze with egg yolk. Cut slits to allow the steam to escape. Decorate centre of each with a rosette of pastry. Bake at 200°C for 10 minutes then lower the heat to 180°C for a further 15 to 20 minutes. Put a sheet of foil over the pies if they are becoming too brown.

It was precisely because the early restaurateurs took risks that the restaurant scene in the Barossa is successful today. We now have several restaurants that have won prestigious awards for excellent food. Barossa people who would never have dreamed of eating in public places before the 1970s are now familiar with them all.

summer

Chapter 12

Hives of Activity

Angry bee weather. The overcast sky is like a brass lid clamped tightly over the earth. Maggie Beer and I confront the glare of the summer light as we drive towards the tiny village of Moculta, on the north-eastern rim of the Barossa. We are on our way to look at the historic apiary on the Rosenzweig farm.

Will the heat and clouds disturb the bees? Mark Rosenzweig, speaking on the phone to arrange this visit, warned that it might. But we are curious to see these beehives, which have been here for over a century. This time of year, when the gums are flowering, is the best to see the bees working and to watch the honey being extracted – and this is the time of year to buy honey for making traditional Christmas honey biscuits.

Along the creek at the roadside, red- and blue-gums dangle their bundles of cream flowers. The farm house, sheds and windmill sit on the slope leading to the scribble of peppermint-gum scrub at the top of the hill. All around, undulating paddocks of wheat, oats and barley offer their gold. The harvest is well under way.

Over behind the old almond trees, a figure is bending towards a cluster of boxes. The air is moving and humming. The shrouded grey figure turns towards us. 'Don't come any closer,' it warns. 'I'll walk over to you and take you to the honey room.'

The smell inside the tiny room is a heady combination of honey and smoke. There are four of us in there now, as well as some sluggish

Mark Rosenzweig and the historic beehives

bees that have arrived on the frame of honeycomb from the hive. A few squirts from the smoker nozzle send these crawling towards the window. Off comes the beekeeper's veiled hat to reveal Gloria Rosenzweig underneath. 'The bees are not too happy today,' she says, 'but you'll be quite safe from them inside the suits.'

So we take turns to don the extra beekeeper's outfit and follow Mark back to the hives. Gloria and Mark make sure that we are wearing the gloves correctly and that the tapes on the suit are tightly tied so that no bee can find an opening. I wonder what will happen if my nose starts to itch under the helmet and think that astronauts must have the same problem.

These hives are different from the ones dotted around in other parts of the district. For one thing, they have a home of their own, a long, narrow, corrugated-iron shed built like a right-angled cloister. The roof and the weather-side outer edge of the right angle are covered in iron but the inner edge is open.

Through the open side it is easy to see how the hive boxes are stored. They sit on planks suspended by metal rods from the old roof timbers. With each rod passing through a pot of oil, the hives on the planks are impervious to marauding ants. Anyone paying a visit to these bees first makes an inspection of the hive occupants through the glass window inside the door of the hive. The window is a feature of these Upper Silesian-designed Berlepsch-Dzierzon hives, with their back-opening doors – most of the portable hives that you see out in the paddocks open at the top. Through the door can be seen the hexagonal patterns on the first plane of honeycomb parallel to the window.

Here are the bees. They crowd onto the inspection window as it swings out and Mark subdues them with another puff of smoke. Carefully he slides out the first frame of honeycomb, disengaging the bees as he does so. Already oozing, it goes into the bucket. More frames follow.

Mark reaches deeper and deeper into the hive, removing each successive frame until he comes to the one that contains the brood cells where the eggs are stored. These he leaves, although it is

Mark extracts the honey

possible to extract honey from the cells all around the brood on the frame if he is careful. He closes the hive door and we take the bucket back to the honey room.

That's quite a load of honey sitting there in the bucket. When we have removed our outlandish gear we take turns to assess the weight of the frames. They must each weigh between four and five kilos, easily.

Gloria flicks off a few groggy bees with a turkey feather. She has been heating a hand-forged capping knife in a pot of water over a kerosene primus stove. Now she uses it to slice off the wax capping over the cells on the first frame. Gleaming dark honey sits in the cells beneath. Gloria puts the wax capping, dripping with honey, into a dish and lifts up the open frame of honey for us to see. The shadings of gold are like a stained-glass window.

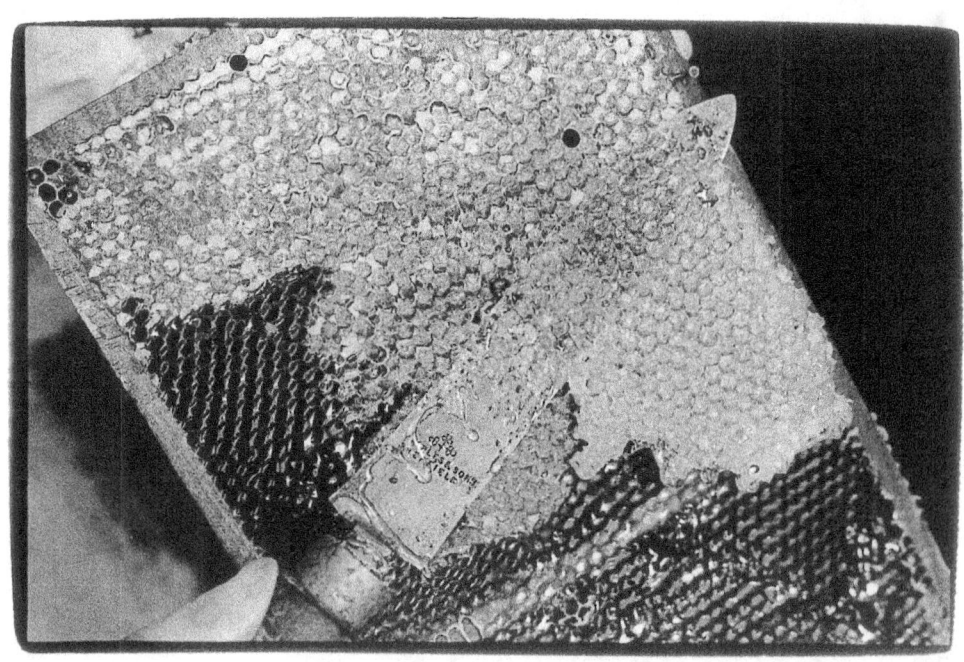

Next to the fireplace is a steel drum with an ornate cast-metal handle on top: the honey extractor. Some years ago it won a prize at an apiarists' congress as an unusual historic piece of equipment still in regular use. Now Gloria loads the first frame of honeycomb. It starts to spin as she turns the handle and tracers of light show the honey flicking onto the inside wall of the drum, where it runs down to the bottom.

While Gloria extracts the honey, Mark talks about the bees and the historic hive. Just how the Berlepsch-Dzierzon hives came to be used here in Australia is not certain, as there are no apiary records dating from before the turn of the century. He does not know much about the bee-keeping traditions of his family, either, although back in 1844 there was a Rosenzweig who was a confectioner. Maybe he needed the honey!

When the honey extraction is completed, we go back to the farm house for a cup of tea and for a honey-tasting.

It is particularly interesting to taste the honey that is extracted from the wax capping on a frame of honeycomb. This honey is much darker and tastes much stronger than the honey from the main cells. In years past, the family always gave it away to the local churches so that the guild women could use it to make *Honigkuchen*, or honey biscuits, for Lutheran institutions like boarding schools and missions. It so happens that the flavour of this brown honey made the best biscuits of all. Those are the honey biscuits that I want to make this year.

Gloria brings out some of her own honey biscuits, not too sweet, soft – as they are supposed to be – and full of flavour. Honey biscuits like these are the major part of the baking in the weeks leading up to Christmas in the Barossa. They really are a traditional Barossa food. There are dozens of different recipes for them in local cookery books. Some of these contain no fat.

Honigkuchen – Honey Biscuits
This is Gloria Rosenzweig's recipe. The biscuits are soft, moist and delicious. You could try the other spices mentioned below.

1 cup honey and 1 cup sugar (or you can use all honey) | 1 tbsp butter | ½ cup cold water | 1½ tsp bicarbonate of soda | 1 egg, well beaten | 1 tsp ground cloves | 1 tsp cinnamon | 2 cups self-raising flour | 2 cups plain flour | extra flour for rolling out

Heat the oven to 180°C. Put honey and sugar in a large saucepan with butter and stir over a gentle heat until the butter and sugar are dissolved. Remove from heat. Add water and bicarbonate of soda. Let stand until lukewarm then add the well-beaten egg, cloves, cinnamon, and flours, until the mixture becomes a soft dough. Chill in a basin with a cloth over it at least overnight. Next day, roll out on a floured board and cut shapes with biscuit-cutters. Arrange on trays that are coated with melted butter and cornflour or lined with baking paper. Bake in a moderate oven for 7 minutes or until golden brown.

Note: the dough is difficult to handle because it is soft – over-mixing will make it even softer – and there is a danger of adding too much flour, making the biscuits rather dry. A good way to avoid this is to let the mixture sit in the refrigerator, which will keep it firm. This is not, of course, a century-old tradition, but it works. Otherwise, choose a cool run of days to bake and keep the mixture in the cellar until the last minute. If the biscuits turn out to be hard and brittle, a piece of fresh bread stored with them in the biscuit tin will soften them within a day.

Barossa honey biscuits are not the same as gingerbread, which is generally made with treacle, not honey, and which tastes, logically enough, of ginger. What is more, they seem to be much simpler than most of the *Lebkuchen* or *Pfeffernüsse* that are made traditionally in Germany for Christmas. The predominant taste is of honey, with a background taste of spice. The spices that feature in most local recipes are ground cloves, cinnamon and sometimes ginger or allspice.

The spices in traditional German recipes and in the German commercial packs of spice prepared especially for Christmas biscuits may

Margaret Lehmann makes honey biscuits

include cinnamon, cloves and pimento and also cardamom, nutmeg, lemon peel, mace, aniseed and coriander. These biscuits taste strongly of spice and less of honey. Many regional German recipes also have ground almonds mixed with the flour. Early European Christmas baking symbolically contained seven spices and the nuts in the biscuits also had religious significance.

Even the icing can look and taste different on the local biscuits. The European ones are often dipped in thin white icing or in chocolate. This is not done with the local biscuits. If they are iced in fancy patterns, it can be with European-style royal icing, made of icing sugar, egg-white and lemon juice, which flows smoothly but dries very hard; or the icing can be made with icing sugar, milk, a little melted butter and vanilla, producing a less controllable but much softer icing mixture.

People who do not like the sweet taste of icing may prefer to decorate their honey biscuits in the way that is used at Linke's Bakery at Nuriootpa, which sells honey biscuits that are soft and un-iced. Chris

Linke has a few tips to give about making them. At the bakery the mixture is made the night before baking. The Linke bakers are careful not to over-mix the dough. They roll it out, squirt it with a mist of water, sprinkle it with hundreds and thousands – an Australian innovation – and then cut it into rectangular shapes. They prefer to under-bake the biscuits, then leave them on the tray until they are cool. This finishes the baking without letting the biscuits become too hard.

Why did the traditional recipes changed their taste, appearance and ingredients when they were brought to Australia? Some people have suggested that what we have here remains from the very simple lifestyle of the peasant people who came in the nineteenth century. Even though the published recipe-books they brought with them did in fact contain the ancient elaborate recipes, those early immigrants may not have had access to the ingredients when they were still living in Prussia. The other possibility, of course, is that a long time elapsed before such spices as cardamom and aniseed were imported to rural South Australia and so the cooks were forced to simplify the recipes. Either way, the honey biscuits known traditionally in the Barossa are not quite the same as the ones that have been made in Europe for centuries.

In the weeks before Christmas, chemists in the local pharmacies spend a fair amount of time weighing out small amounts of powdered ammonium bicarbonate for customers who are preparing to bake another of the local Christmas specialities: ammonia biscuits. The demand, say the chemists, is not as strong as it was years ago but it is still there.

Barossa cooks still make these white, lemony shapes that remind them of the times when Mother would take down the glass jar on the sideboard, remove the stopper (which had to be airtight, otherwise the paper bag inside would contain nothing but wind) and take out the rock ammonia called *Hirschhornsalz*, which she ground to a fine powder. Her eyes smarted and everyone in the room complained about the smell. The ordeal continued as the dough was mixed. The fumes shrieked out if the oven door was opened during the baking. Yet when the biscuits had finished cooking, all traces of ammonia had disappeared, leaving delicate treats that had been cut in the shapes of birds, bells and stars, to be iced and hung on the Christmas tree.

Recipes for ammonia biscuits appear frequently in the hand-written recipe-books from the early twentieth century and are called *Weihnachtskuchen* (Christmas cakes). In the first edition of the *Barossa Cookery Book*, published in 1917 (when such a foreign name as *Weihnachtskuchen* would identify food from the Enemy), they are called Kilbourne biscuits but everyone who still knows them today simply refers to them as ammonia biscuits.

This recipe for ammonia biscuits is adapted from a hand-written recipe-book dated 1898. It was written in both German and English in the book, but the German version used the English word 'ammonia' instead of the German word *Hirschhornsalz*. (Meaning 'salts of hart's horn', H*irschhornsalz* was centuries ago made from ground antlers of deer.) People's language was changing! I decided to make half quantity. Most old recipes flavoured the biscuits with lemon essence, but I used grated lemon rind and preferred the flavour. The unbaked mixture freezes well.

Weihnachtskuchen – Ammonia Biscuits

Similar recipes can be found in German cookbooks under the names *Warmbrünnergebäck* and *Danziger Weihnachtsbrot*. Instead of icing the biscuits with lemon icing, some cooks pressed chopped almonds on the dough before baking.

2 cups flour | ¾ cup sugar | ½ cup butter | grated rind 1 lemon |
1 tsp ammonium bicarbonate | 2 eggs | ¼ cup milk

Put dry ingredients and butter in food processor and blend until the mass resembles fine breadcrumbs. Add eggs and milk and blend again. Roll out very thin and cut into fancy shapes with biscuit cutters. Bake in a moderate oven, 180°C, 7–8 minutes.

When a recipe for 'wurst-machine biscuits' kept appearing in old cooking notebooks, I thought at first that early Barossa cooks had found an ingenious use for their smallgoods and sausages. Not so. At Christmas, the mincer machine that had been pressed into use during winter wurst-making now had a different nozzle attached to produced long, thin buttery biscuits for filling up the Christmas visitors. In German recipe-books they are called *Spritzgebäck*.

Spritzgebäck – Machine Biscuits

The mixture has to be quite stiff for the biscuits to keep their shape during baking. Excellent biscuits.

DOUGH

230 g butter | 230 g sugar | 1 egg | 1 tsp vanilla or lemon essence | 500–505 g self-raising flour | 1 tsp salt

ICING

1 cup icing sugar | juice and rind ½ small lemon | 1 dsp melted butter

Cream butter and sugar in the food processor, add egg and essence. Stir in sifted flour and salt. Set up the mincer with the star nozzle, or the flat nozzle with the 'pinked' edge. Keep forcing the dough as you turn the handle, cutting fingers of biscuits about 4 cm long. Arrange on slides that are greased and floured or lined with baking paper. Bake 7 minutes in moderate oven (180°C). Join pairs of biscuits with icing.

Biscuits called almond fingers seem to have become very popular in the 1920s. They are extremely easy to make. Where they came from is not clear but there are floods of recipes for them printed in local cookery books of the time under various titles. For many local families they are a traditional part of Christmas.

Almond Fingers
A great favourite in my family. Best when very fresh.
110 g butter ∣ 30 g sugar ∣ 1 egg, separated ∣ 2 tbsp milk ∣
230 g plain flour ∣ pinch of salt ∣ 1 tsp baking powder ∣
115 g icing sugar, sifted ∣ almond essence ∣ 70 g chopped almonds

Cream butter and sugar and add yolk of egg beaten with milk. Sift flour, salt and baking powder and work into mixture (this can all be done in the food processor). Knead well and roll out ½ cm thick. Beat white of egg lightly, add sifted icing sugar and almond essence, spread over mixture and sprinkle with chopped almonds. Cut in fingers. Place on lightly-greased tray, or line tray with baking paper. Bake at 185° C for 8 minutes or until pale golden-brown.

The final batch here were made especially to go on the Christmas tree. Called *Schaumkuchen*, they are simply meringues coloured and flavoured in different ways and piped into scrolls and other fancy shapes.

Schaumkuchen – Meringues
Make them after all your other baking, then leave them in the oven to cool down overnight when they have finished cooking.
3 egg-whites ∣ pinch salt ∣ ¾ cup caster sugar ∣ 2 tsp cornflour ∣
1 tsp vinegar ∣ food colourings ∣ lemon and vanilla flavouring essences

Beat egg-whites and salt until firm peaks form. Add caster sugar gradually, beating well until sugar is completely dissolved. Stir in cornflour and vinegar. Divide mixture into 2 or 3 portions. Colour and flavour each of the portions with different colours and flavourings. Cover a baking tray with baking paper. Using a piping bag with a nozzle about 1 cm wide, pipe meringue scrolls, rosettes and other shapes on the paper. Sprinkle the shapes with coloured sugar crystals made by letting a quantity of sugar soak up food colouring in a glass jar. Bake them in a slow oven (100°C) for about an hour. Allow to cool in the oven. Store in a biscuit tin for a week or so. Hang them on the Christmas tree.

It is easy to imagine how important it was for European Australian families of the nineteenth century to keep Christmas customs alive. There must have been aching hearts come December, with people remembering their old homes and family. As the years rolled on some of the early food traditions were abandoned, yet others remained.

Here in the Barossa, elderly people can remember some of the old foods still prepared by their grandparents at Christmas time before the First World War, foods that must have reminded the cooks of their own grandparents back in Europe.

Those whose memories were of Silesia continued to make a special meal on Christmas Eve, to be eaten late at night. There was always a salad containing imported salted herrings that were bought from the grocer in wooden kegs.

Heringssalat – Herring Salad

This recipe comes from Colin Gramp. Rather than going to all the trouble of preparing salted herring, use a jar of Matjes herring instead.
12 new small potatoes | 1½ medium-sized onions | a little vegetable oil | 1 cup mayonnaise | 1 tbsp sugar | 2 tbsp wine vinegar | mustard powder to taste | tabasco to flavour | salt and pepper to taste | 6 fillets Matjes herring (or 3 whole salted herring filleted and marinated) | 2 hard-boiled eggs

Thoroughly wash potatoes then boil in their skin in slightly salted water, taking care not to overcook them. Plunge into iced water so that they retain their firmness. Cut potatoes into halves then into 5 mm slices. Place in refrigerator. While the potatoes are cooking, finely chop onions then fry in a little vegetable oil until they turn translucent. Remove from oil and cool in refrigerator. Pour 1 cup mayonnaise into mixing bowl and add the vinegar, sugar, mustard, tabasco, salt and pepper to flavour. Mix thoroughly and refrigerate.

Cut chilled herring into 1 cm squares. In a large bowl mix all the prepared ingredients, taking care not to break up potatoes, then place in a closed container and refrigerate for at least 12 hours before serving. Sprinkle servings with finely chopped chilled hard-boiled egg together with a segment of lemon on the side. An aged riesling (2 or 3 years) together with slices of dill cucumber are ideal complements.

My mother and aunt can remember a pudding made from ground poppy seeds in their grandmother's household. This pudding was the domain of the adults, particularly the men. Children were never allowed to eat it and they certainly did not want to do so, for to them it looked like a grey sludge. Great-grandmother made it for the men, though, at other times of the year as well for their card-evening suppers, when cigars and poppyseed pudding were brought out together.

Sometimes my aunt (now in her eighties but then a golden-haired cherub of four) and my mother would hang about hoping for some supper. Although they might cram themselves with so much *Streuselkuchen* that they would call out later in bed for *Boonekamp* (a commercially prepared medicinal spirit and herb drink) to settle their stomachs, they were never allowed the poppyseed pudding. 'You realise why, don't you?' said an elderly woman I was interviewing in Tanunda:

The seed originally used came from opium poppies and those particular seeds have not been officially available since their importation was banned by the government [in 1905]. People still used to grow them, though, for a while afterwards, just as they had done in Europe. I remember once seeing some on the other side of a fence in Nuriootpa [long after the regulations had gone through]. I said, 'Look at all the opium poppies!' and the next day every single one had disappeared.

Mohnklöße – Poppyseed Pudding

Literally: poppyseed dumplings, which is a misnomer but perhaps they do look like dumplings when dolloped out with a spoon. The dish is rich and a little goes a long way.

½ L milk | 4 tbsp sugar | 250 g ground poppy seed | 40 g raisins, sultanas or currants | 40 g chopped almonds | 12 or 16 slices of white bread or *Zwieback* rusks

Heat half the milk, sweeten to taste with sugar, and pour over the poppyseed, making consistency of porridge. Add the dried fruit (some recipes say these may be soaked in rum), and then the almonds. Heat the other half of the milk and sweeten to taste (some recipes include 1 teaspoon cinnamon). Brush it over the bread slices or rusks – they should become soft but not soggy. Assemble the pudding in a greased mould. Start with a layer of poppy seed, then a layer of bread and so on. Cover and store in a cool place to allow the flavours to permeate the pudding. To serve, tip the pudding onto a plate.

This chapter ends with a mystery and some thoughts about the Christmas foods brought from the old world. The mystery is this: why did the local settlers bring some traditional food recipes with them and continue to make them, even in a slightly altered form, and yet discard others?

For example, many families living in the Barossa district have ancestors who came from a region in Prussia around Liegnitz (which today is in Poland and called Legnica). Liegnitz is famed for a special Christmas sweet called *Liegnitzer Bombe*, a pudding containing honey, spices, dried fruits and chocolate that is baked in a large, spherical form or in several smaller balls. Now, some of the Barossa families came from villages just a handful of kilometres away from Liegnitz, and yet the sweet is unknown to their descendants and they do not possess any molds that might have been used to make it. Was it a question of poverty? Did someone invent *Liegnitzer Bombe* only after the emigrants had departed?

A question also hovers over the Christmas *Stollen* that originated in Dresden in Saxony and was said to represent the shawl used to wrap the infant Jesus. Regional recipe-books produced in Germany sometimes claim that this *Stollen*, a yeast dough filled with fruit, spices and butter, was also a favourite with Silesians who lived just north east of Dresden. Yet nobody in the Barossa can remember their grandparents making the Christmas *Stollen* and there are no old hand-written recipes for it in any of the books I have seen.

To say that it was once again a question of economy – the *Stollen* was made with and then smothered in scads of butter – still begs the question, because some of the families coming from *Stollen* regions built substantial farms with large, comfortable farmhouses here in Australia. They, at least, could surely afford to make *Stollen* with butter; and yet family recipes indicate that they did not. Was the religious symbolism more associated with Catholic families in Europe than with Lutheran? The question must remain unanswered.

Chapter 13
Christmas Celebrations

Hier steht ein schöner Weihnachtsbaum
Mit vielen Lichtlein dran
   ('Here stands a lovely Christmas tree/decked with many
   little lights' – children's Christmas song)

In the first weeks of December, with all the baking and food preparation going on in the house, the younger children could not fail to sense that something important was about to happen. But apart from the cooking, they could see no other visible signs that it would soon be Christmas. From the nineteenth century until well after the Second World War, it simply was not the way among Barossa families to put up the Christmas tree or any decorations before 24 December.

Certainly the children could see the great pine wreath on the pedestal in the church on which yet another candle was lit during each of the four Advent Sundays leading up to Christmas – but still no tree. At home, except for a few whispered conversations between Mother and Father (which stopped as soon as the children appeared) nothing but the cooking suggested that Christmas was at hand.

Then, mysterious happenings started on Christmas Eve, when the door of the sitting-room was locked early in the morning and all through the day sounds of stealthy rustling came from inside. What was happening? Trails of pine needles and a few carelessly dropped scraps of tinsel lay on the matting. What did it mean?

The sitting-room door-handle was securely tied with string and rattling it brought nobody to the door. 'Come away from there,' the elder sisters would say. 'Father Christmas might be inside.'

Father Christmas! If only they could see! All day the young ones hung about hoping for something more. But now it was time to prepare for the evening church service, to wash and scrub at the basin, to put on the best dress or serge pants. They had no time to try to get into the room. Everything was hidden and confused!

So when did the moment for celebrations finally arrive? It must surely have been that moment when the family arrived at church for the evening service.

The doors would be wide open for the warm summer night; the windows blazed in the dark as the family joined the throng following the strains of the organ into the church. A wonderful sight awaited them. To one side of the altar the Christmas tree rose right up to the ceiling, glimmering with candles and decorations. To the other was a Nativity scene, a thatched, wooden stable with carved animals, shepherds, shepherdesses and the three Magi. All were gazing at the family by the manger.

The sweet perfume of the pine tree and the Christmas lilies near the altar, the warm air and candle light, the strains of the old songs, interlaced with words of calm, brightness and radiance: these were the heralds of the Christmas season.

Outside, after the service, the children dug their fingers into the paper-bags of lollies that had been handed out with the Sunday School prizes. They did not notice elder brothers and sisters sneaking away into the darkness but they, too, became eager to return to the house, and waited impatiently for their parents.

Paper lanterns bobbing above the verandah, each with a candle glowing inside, welcomed their return. Was it time to go in to the big room? Yes, to come and see if Father Christmas had been!

That moment when the children stepped into the room and saw their family Christmas tree for the first time gave them their most ardent and firmly fixed memories of Christmas. Far more important than the chairs heaped with presents – or the bowls of nuts, sweets and cherries – was the tree slowly revolving on its pedestal to the sound of the tinkling music-box. Candles glimmered and burned – now softly, now brightly – as the tree turned and the silver and white decorations and the *Schaumkuchen*, *Weihnachtskuchen* and *Honigkuchen* swung slowly around.

Everyone knew that this would be the only night when the candles could be lit: the pine tree dried off quickly in the Australian heat, whether it was standing in a pot of water or on a music-box pedestal. Even now, one of the aunts or uncles stood by with a bucket or hose, just in case the tree should catch fire. The moment for the Christmas tree was really that fleeting minute when everyone stood in the doorway and saw it for the first time.

Families develop their own Christmas traditions. After the presents had been unwrapped on Christmas Eve some families sang carols around the piano, some sang while walking in a circle with joined hands around the Christmas tree, some just talked, joked and swapped yarns as the children played with their toys. Whatever they did, they handed around *Streuselkuchen*, honey biscuits and all the rest in the happy atmosphere of a warm summer night.

The real eating took place on Christmas Day. The huge midday meal with the roast poultry, ham and plum pudding very soon came to resemble the traditional English Christmas dinner, complete with threepences and brandy sauce and a kitchen that steamed up in the heat like a Turkish bath.

Still, some ways of preparing the foods set on the table seem to have been part of the Prussian-based Barossa tradition and it is worth making a journey around the plate of Christmas dinner just to see what these customs were.

First of all, the bird. While for some this meant the fowl or the turkey, for many Barossa families the dinner would not be the same without the Christmas goose. Geese were once a common farmyard sight. I once heard an apocryphal story about the time during the First World

War when the German-speaking people of the Barossa Valley were under suspicion and soldiers carried out surprise searches on houses and farms. 'Where are the guns!' demanded one soldier of a grandmother who was at home alone when they arrived. In her confusion, hampered by her limited understanding of the language, the old lady meekly led them down to the fowlyard, where her beloved goose, the *Gans*, was pecking away at the scraps, fattening up for Christmas.

Some Barossa families still eat goose for Christmas. Peter Lehmann is a man whose skills at cooking a Christmas goose almost match his wine-making abilities. Peter has a few jealously guarded sources of locally grown geese. Each year he waits for the call some days before Christmas telling him to come and collect his two specially fattened, freshly killed geese together with their giblets including feet, neck and stomach, as well as the livers and heart.

Peter Lehmann's Roast Goose

STUFFING

2 or 3 tbsp butter | 2 onions, chopped | 2 or 3 rashers double-smoked Schulz's Barossa bacon, diced | 1 loaf stale white bread | 1 bunch parsley, chopped | 1 handful fresh sage, chopped | salt and pepper

In the butter, sauté onions and bacon. Make breadcrumbs from a loaf of bread. Add chopped parsley and sage. Add a good covering of freshly ground black pepper and a little salt.

COOKING THE GOOSE

1 goose | 2 or 3 tsp lard or ghee | 2 tbsp plain flour

Goose is notoriously fatty just under the skin so prick the skin all over with a skewer to let the fat ooze out during cooking. Stuff and truss the bird. Put a few spoonfuls of lard or ghee into the baking dish and place the dish in an oven pre-heated to 250° C until the fat smokes and melts. Place the goose in the dish and baste it with the smoking fat. Leave on the high temperature for about 15 minutes to crisp the skin, then turn down heat to around 180° C for

remainder of roasting, basting every 10 minutes or so. The roasting takes about 1½ hours. Test with a skewer in the breast – the juices will run clear. Put in a warm place to rest for half an hour if possible before serving.

GRAVY
Drain the fat. Scrape up the pan juices, sprinkle these with plain flour and brown. Add goose stock made from boiling the giblets and some sweetening agent. A good dollop of quince jelly is best, otherwise red currant jelly. Serve with apple-sauce.

If the poultry is fowl or turkey, not goose, next to it on the plate will be the ham. The Barossa Valley is fortunate to have several butchers who make very fine ham and so these days there is an array to choose from, provided your order is placed in good time.

What about the vegetables? Back in the spring, when the frogs were starting to call out in the creek, gardeners put in their beans and cucumbers in time to have them ready for Christmas. Tomatoes went in too. Now comes their moment of glory. Alongside the roast potatoes will be some of the following vegetables.

Glazed Beans and Carrots
Don't use too much flour. You just need a fine coating to make a glaze. Many cooks in the Barossa glaze and flavour their vegetables like this.
300 g carrots | 300 g beans | boiling salted water just to cover | 2 tbsp vegetable stock reserved from the cooking | ½ tsp black pepper | ½ tsp sugar | 1 dsp vinegar | a knob of butter | scant tsp cornflour blended with a little water

Slice the vegetables finely or cut them into strips of similar size and shape. Simmer in boiling salted water until tender but not over- or under-cooked. Drain thoroughly. Use most of the stock for making gravy for the meat but return 2 tablespoons stock to the pan with the vegetables. Add the other ingredients. The liquid will thicken slightly and just glaze the vegetables. Add a handful of chopped fresh parsley and serve. The same method is often used with a combination of peas and carrots.

Baked layers of tomatoes and seasoning are certainly not the legacy of the early German-speaking settlers. The German encyclopedia of cooking dated 1909 stated that Germans were just beginning to enjoy this fruit so popular amongst Southern European, American and English people. Yet, tomatoes had been in the Barossa in 1842, when Ann Jacob mentioned them in her diary. They were first on sale in the Adelaide markets in 1854. Tomato pie appears in the 1917 edition of the *Barossa Cookery Book*.

Tomato Pie (Scalloped Tomatoes)
This is good made with spring onions and crumbs of very light bread.
In a buttered casserole place layers of sliced tomato, finely sliced brown onion rings and crumbled, soft, white breadcrumbs. (Season the tomato layer with pepper, salt, a pinch of sugar and a pinch of very finely chopped fresh thyme.) Repeat the layers a few times. The top should be breadcrumbs. Dot with butter and place in a moderate oven for about 15 minutes.

Gurkensalat – Cucumber Salad
It simply would not be Christmas without this salad. It is to be found in recipe-books of typical Silesian food. Make it with apple cucumbers, although most cucumber varieties (even Lebanese cucumbers) can be used.
Peel and slice two cucumbers into paper-thin slices (some cooks grate them but this makes them very sloppy). Spread on a flat plate and sprinkle with salt. Allow to stand for half an hour, then drain the cucumbers and pat them dry with a clean towel. Add a little finely chopped onion (optional). Sprinkle over them a tablespoon or two of white wine vinegar, then pepper to taste and a pinch of sugar. Allow the cucumbers to macerate in this dressing in a cool place. Just before serving, stir in a tablespoon or two of farm cream or crème fraîche. Serve immediately.

Lettuce Salad

This is a recipe from Peter Lehmann's family. It is typically German in that it uses farm cream rather than oil as a base for the dressing. Before the 1940s, cos lettuce would probably have been used.

Finely shred an iceberg lettuce. Put it in a bowl and add lemon juice. Sprinkle generously with sugar and at the last moment before serving toss with cream. This also makes a good sandwich filling, combined with hot poultry and stuffing.

The only thing to do when the meal is over, when the last of the plum pudding has been offered around and refused from sheer lack of staying power, is to find the coolest spot in the house to stretch out and sleep. I remember from my childhood the corpulent forms of uncles and fathers stretched out along the passage and on the sitting-room carpet while mothers, aunts and sisters got on with the washing-up and prepared the evening meal.

They set out cold poultry and ham, sliced mettwurst and brawn on plates next to salads in crystal bowls equipped with the best silver salad-servers. These salads were bound to include tomatoes, cucumbers, beans, beetroot and Barossa potato salad. Ways to make these salads varied in each family, and you can read other versions of them in the *Barossa Cookery Book*.

Tomato And Cucumber Salad

An old family favourite.

Place layers of finely sliced tomato, cucumber and onions in a bowl and season with salt, ground black pepper and a little sugar. Then sprinkle a few tablespoons of red wine vinegar and let the salad stand for a while.

Bean Salad

2 cups cooked green beans at room temperature ׀ 1 onion, finely sliced ׀ $\frac{1}{2}$ tsp salt ׀ $\frac{1}{2}$ tsp pepper ׀ pinch sugar ׀ 2 tbsp vinegar

Season green beans and finely sliced onions with salt, pepper, sugar and a sprinkling of vinegar.

Rote Rüben – Spiced Beetroot

This way of making beetroot salad was given by Prue Henschke, whose work managing the family vineyards for Henschke Wines plays a crucial role in the success of the famous winery. The recipe came from some of the Henschke great-aunts in Keyneton; they had a reputation for being fine cooks.

2 bunches of baby beetroot | water to cover | 60 ml aged red wine vinegar | ½ tsp caraway seeds | 1 tsp sugar | salt and pepper to taste

Trim the leaves off the beetroot without breaking the skin. Place in a saucepan and add enough water just to cover them. Cover and boil gently for 30 to 40 minutes. Drain. Save some of the cooking liquid as a dressing and peel the beetroot (leave the tails on). Place in a serving dish. Season with vinegar, caraway seeds, sugar, salt and pepper.

Kartoffelsalat – Warm Potato Salad

A legendary dish! Any left-overs (which are rare) make delicious fried hash the next day.

6 medium-sized old potatoes (or a variety of potato that holds its shape when cooked) | water for simmering | 3 or 4 tbsp wine vinegar | salt and white pepper to taste

Gently simmer potatoes in a pan with salted water to cover for about 15 minutes or until the potatoes are nearly tender. Remove from heat and allow potatoes to sit in the water to cool a little – this continues the cooking without breaking up the potatoes. Skin the hot potatoes and cut them into cubes. Place them in a glass dish.

While they are still hot, sprinkle over them the vinegar, pepper and salt. (The crisp fried bacon may be added here instead of later.)

SAUCE VERSION 1

knob of butter | 1 small onion, finely chopped | 3 rashers bacon, finely chopped | ¾ cup cream

In a small frying pan, melt butter and gently fry onion and bacon until cooked. Stir in cream to warm through. Fold warm cream mixture into the potatoes gently so that they do not break. Check seasoning. Sprinkle with parsley to serve.

SAUCE VERSION 2
This version has a creamier texture.
1 knob butter | 1 small onion, finely chopped | 3 rashers bacon, finely chopped | 2 tbsp flour | $1/2$ tsp salt | $1/4$ tsp pepper | $1/4$ cup white wine vinegar | $1/4$ cup water | $3/4$ cup cream

In a small frying pan, melt butter and gently fry onion and bacon until cooked. In a cup, mix flour, salt, pepper, vinegar and water. Pour onto onions and bacon and stir until it thickens. Stir in cream. Continue cooking until sauce thickens. Fold mixture into potatoes. Check seasoning.

Christmas Brawn
Brawn was a dish that appealed to both English and German tastes and was known to early settlers from both cultures. Possibly the Germans favoured it more, for *Mrs Beeton's Cookery Book* of 1862 gives one brawn recipe, whereas the 1834 *Bremisches Kochbuch* gives seven or eight.

2 pig's hocks, 1 pickled and 1 plain | 2 or 3 slices of veal knuckle (or shin of beef) | 1 pickled ox tongue or 4 pickled sheep tongues | 2 bay leaves | $1/2$ tsp nutmeg | 6 peppercorns | $1/2$ tsp allspice | $1/4$ cup vinegar | pepper and salt | zest of a lemon

Halve trotters and roughly slice meat, put in a saucepan, just cover with water. Bring to simmering point. If pickled meats are very salty, renew the water and bring to simmering point again. Repeat if necessary. Add bay leaves, nutmeg, peppercorns and allspice. Simmer on a very low heat 4 hours. The meat should be very tender. When cooked, take out meat, removing all bones, skin the tongue and chop meat into pieces. Strain stock and bring to boil with vinegar. Reduce by half. Add seasonings to taste. Add meat. Bring to simmering point for a few minutes. Pour into 1 or 2 basins to set. Scrape off fat before turning out onto a plate. Do not freeze.

The evening meal is over. After Christmas cake, biscuits and *Kuchen* for dessert, everyone is ready to burst and so it is nearly time to close this chapter. However there is a curious observation to be made first, about the kinds of foods Barossa people ate traditionally on Christmas Day.

Critics are often amazed and amused that settlers coming from the northern hemisphere to Australia, in observing what had previously been a winter festival and was now a festival celebrated in the extreme heat of summer, persisted in serving the same heavy pudding and the same hot meat dishes. Here is an example, they say, of a culture imposed on an environment with which it bears no relationship at all and is therefore ridiculous.

If they look closely at the menu, they may be persuaded to change their minds. Salted herring dishes and poppyseed-bread pudding from the central European Christmas table were foods that could be prepared at a time when few fresh vegetables were available. They had some competition in the early part of the twentieth century from roast poultry and plum pudding, foods that – admittedly – had to be cooked in often unbearably hot conditions. Yet the bulk of the Christmas dinner consisted of an array of accompanying vegetables and salads, made with ingredients that were fresh and abundant in the Australian summer season. The food customs indeed had responded to the enormous change in the climate and season of Christmas – and were not so ridiculous after all.

Chapter 14

Summer Fruits

After Christmas, the deluge. Here come torrents of tomatoes and avalanches of apricots! Just as everyone is drying the last dishes from Christmas Day, the pickers bring in the fruit. Kitchens hardly have time to cool down before the next lot of activity begins. The pungency of pickles spreads into every room. The smell of simmering fruit rolls up to greet you as you come in the front door.

These days people think of the Barossa as a place where most farmers grow grapes for wine, but if they had visited the district in the 1950s they would have seen fruit trees jostling vineyards everywhere. Back at the turn of the twentieth century, fruit-preserving canneries and jam factories were as important as wineries. Today large orchards still produce commercially at Angaston and this is a good time of the year for school children in the district to earn money picking and cutting fruit.

One owner of fruit-sheds who employed local children in the 1950s was Roy Ellis. People around the district used to sell him their fruit and ask him to spray their trees. The horse that pulled his spray-cart was blue from the copper and lime spray. Roy's hair had a bluish tinge to it, too. There was no mistaking him as he and his mates disappeared into a winery for a couple of *Schlucks* after a busy morning spraying.

Often Roy and his friends would travel to other parts of the state, selling fruit and pickled cucumbers and trying out the pubs along the way, where they got to know the drinkers and a great deal of local history. History was one of Roy's passionate interests. He knew who was buried in the cemeteries from Bute to Blinman and he knew all about the farming families from Yunta to Yarcowie.

Being a kind-hearted man, Roy would do anything to oblige the people he met. If a latecomer to the pub was disappointed because Roy's supplies of fruit had run out, the following week Roy would travel all the way back, hundreds of kilometres, with a bag of dried pears or apricots.

The pubs were the important part of the trips, of course. One morning when Roy was on his way to Melbourne with a group of cronies, they stopped to quench their thirst in a pub at Greenock, just on the edge of the Barossa. It was a beautiful day and the hospitality at the Greenock pub was somehow especially welcoming. The travellers seemed inclined to linger through a companionable afternoon and years later some of them would laugh to think that they had spent the first night of their long journey in a hotel so close to home.

Good old Roy! In his love of drinking and company and local food he resembled many hospitable people in the Barossa way back to that time in 1850 when 'Old Colonist' was welcomed by Fiedler on his farm amidst all the fruit trees and sat down for a chat over a glass of wine. Even though the sulphuring process employed by Roy was a later development, Roy's drying sheds, too, were part of a long tradition amongst country people that food must not be wasted and that any excess should be preserved in some way.

In fact, wasting food was almost a sin and nobody would ever throw out stale bread or fallen fruit. Bread was one of the sacred fundamentals of life. For people whose forebears had crossed to the other side of the earth partly to escape hunger and poverty, that is an entirely understandable attitude; but it can also be fanatical and irksome. I remember talking some years ago to an elderly woman who had come as a young bride from Adelaide to marry a local man.

Even after all those years of marriage, she was still indignant because her new parents-in-law had found the effrontery to examine her bucket of kitchen scraps, her 'chookie bin', in case she was wasting food on the fowls that might have been used for the table.

All the summer season's fruit and vegetables flooding into the house are a challenge to anybody who does not want to waste food and this must have been so from the time the first settlers planted watermelons and fruit trees and marvelled at the huge crops.

They ate much of the produce fresh, of course, and people still do. In fact it was not so long ago, in about the 1950s, that a completely new variety of table pear was developed in the Barossa. This was the Corella Pear, a pretty little fruit with a red blush that ripens just after summer. A plate of them really do look like a cluster of corella parrots sitting together. They were developed on the property of Cecil Robins, who happened to find a tree growing in his orchard that produced pears of a particular rosy colour. When he was satisfied that he had developed a consistent variety, he kept the tree buds a closely guarded secret. These days, though, the present owners of the orchard have released the buds to other districts and demand for the Corella Pear is spreading in Australia's eastern states.

Much of the avalanche of fruit was stewed and eaten as a dessert. The 1834 *Bremisches Kochbuch* has recipes for compotes of fruits. It says that apricots should be peeled and then stewed for three quarters of an hour! This *Bremisches Kochbuch* recipe for apricots is interesting because farming families from Posen, Brandenburg and Silesia probably did not see apricots growing in the land they came from. It is quite likely that the book they bought in Bremen as they were leaving for Australia was written for people far wealthier than they: people who could afford to let their cooks buy fruit imported from the Mediterranean. What good luck that they came to a land where apricots grew easily! Both the English and the Prussians discovered this in the very early years of the colony and planted apricot tree cuttings (possibly from New South Wales, or from Cape Town like the grape vines) almost as soon as they arrived. Gardening notes in the colony's early newspapers like the *South Australian Register* of 1847 say that the apricot 'flourishes everywhere and bears most abundantly'.

In the Barossa, there are also some traditional family recipes for cooking with fresh fruit, like this recipe for fruit tart. It was known as a pear cake in the Traeger family but it was made with apricots in other families. You can also use fresh plums or peaches sprinkled with cinnamon. Any soft fruit that cooks without turning bitter will do but with pears or apricots it is especially delicious.

Apricot Tart
This is a very good tart, especially if the fruit layer is generous.

BASE
115 g butter | 100 g sugar | 1 egg | 60 g plain flour | 180 g self-raising flour | freshly grated nutmeg or cinnamon

FILLING
2 or 3 cups sliced fresh fruit | 1 or 2 tbsp caster sugar | $1/2$ cup cream

Cream butter and sugar, add egg and sifted flour (this can all be done in a food processor). Make a fairly soft dough. Chill 10 minutes. Knead a little on a lightly floured board with lightly floured hands. Press into a flan dish or lamington tin. Allow the dough on the dish to rest about 30 minutes. Cover with a generous layer of sliced or diced juicy pears or newly ripened apricots. Sprinkle with a little caster sugar and pour cream over the fruit ($1/2$ cup of cream for pears or 4 tablespoons for the apricots). Be careful not to use too much cream. Sprinkle with nutmeg or cinnamon. Bake in a moderate oven (180°C) 20 to 30 minutes. Serve hot or cold.

Jam-making was next on the agenda when people a few generations ago turned their attention to dealing with all the fresh fruit. A good line-up of jars of apricot jam on the kitchen table was a familiar summer sight and they often had blanched apricot kernels stirred in – until someone pointed out that the kernels contained cyanide and that this addition was probably not a good idea.

In the very early days of Barossa farming, were cooks able to obtain the large amounts of sugar needed to make jam? In Europe, the Prussians would have used sugar made from sugar beet. Beet-processing factories had been set up in Silesia from 1802 onwards to counteract a shortage of cane sugar caused by trade embargoes during the Napoleonic Wars. Sugar was still a precious commodity. In an English colony like South Australia, the first settlers would have obtained sugar refined in Sydney from cane brought to Australia from other British colonies. Only in the 1860s was sugar cane grown commercially on a large scale in Australia. Does this mean that jam was a luxury before the 1860s?

It is very hard to say, except by looking at circumstantial evidence. For example, a ship bringing immigrants to South Australia from Prussia, like the *Zebra*, typically carried five barrels of sugar. Other shipping supply lists mention enough sugar to give each passenger a ration of about 120 grams per week. That's just the amount for passengers to put sugar in their tea or coffee, morning and night every day. No jam was mentioned in the ship's menus, only syrup to go on the prunes and cereal.

The noted botanist J.G.O. Tepper, whose papers are in the Mortlock Library of South Australia, remembers Barossa people ritually gathering native currants as early as 1856 and says that the berries were 'bottled like other preserves'. He does not mention specifically that they were made into jam.

In South Australia in the years before 1850, the geologist Menge was said to have been fond of jam but, as a guest at colonists' tables, when he helped himself too liberally to jams and jellies, people commented on it. They even wrote about it! Clearly the first settlers had jam, but it seems it was indeed a luxury; in that era people didn't 'fill up on bread and jam' the way they did some generations later.

It is also fairly certain that the kinds of jams made by the German-speaking settlers traditionally did not contain as much sugar as English jams. The old German recipes for apricot jam state that a quantity of apricots requires three-quarters of its weight in sugar. The apricots are boiled with a little water first, until the pectin is released, and the sugar is added towards the end. The English way, on the other hand, has even amounts of fruit and sugar and the fruit is steeped in sugar to release the juices before the mixture is put on the stove. Here is my English grandmother's recipe:

Mrs Jansen's English Apricot Jam
This jam is a good colour but very sweet so add some lemon juice at the end. The blanched almonds in it are good. Do not refrigerate the fruit. This recipe makes about 16 jars.
6 kg apricots, firm but ripe | 6 kg sugar

Stone and quarter the apricots. Put them into a well-greased preserving pan with half the sugar and stir to mix, without scraping the bottom of the pan with the wooden spoon. Allow to stand overnight. Next morning, bring to the boil slowly. Boil $1/2$ hour or so. Add the remaining sugar. Boil again about $3/4$ hour. Skim the scum. Five to 10 minutes before the end, add a handful of blanched almonds. Fill the jam into jars while it is still hot. Use a little jug to top the jam right up in the jars. Seal with metal lids while warm. If the jars have plastic lids, seal first with cellophane dipped in vinegar, held in place with a rubber band.

There are, in fact, two German words for jam-like preparations: *Marmelade* and *Mus*. The German *Universal-Lexikon der Kochkunst*, or encyclopedia of cooking, from 1909, describes and gives recipes for both. It seems that for *Marmelade*, the fruit is cooked and sieved first then the sugar added. A *Mus* is more likely to be a reduction of fruit over a gentle heat, with a much smaller amount of sugar added towards the end of cooking time. This is the kind of preparation that is mentioned in mid-nineteenth-century cookbooks and I am guessing that it was probably made by early Prussian settlers more commonly than jam. The most usual *Mus* was from plums. Making and tasting it was a delight for me; the kitchen was filled with the smell of fresh fruit and the final paste, which looked like plum jam, tasted more tart, more like the fruit itself than jam does. The recipe is adapted from a book on Mecklenburger cooking and is similar to one in a Silesian cookbook.

Pflaumenmus – Plum Conserve

This delicious fruit makes a wonderful accompaniment for breakfast yoghurt. It would also go well with cheese. Use it in the centre of *Berliner Pfannkuchen*, too.

1 kg very ripe dark red plums | 250 g sugar

Halve and stone the plums. Place in a stainless-steel pan with a heavy bottom over a very low heat. Stir until the juices start to run, then keep stirring from time to time during the next 3 or 4 hours. As the mixture thickens towards the end, gradually add the sugar in batches, allowing each batch to thicken and dissolve. Stir and watch carefully in case the fruit burns. From this point, some recipes finish the cooking in the oven at 150°C. The *Mus* is done when the spoon can stand straight up in it and when a furrow drawn through it remains. Put in hot jars (over 100°C) and seal tightly. Refrigerate after opening. Adding more sugar will make it keep longer.

As the years rolled into the twentieth century, sugar was plentiful and cooks made masses of jam. All those lovely hand-written recipe-books dating from before the First World War have variations on jam recipes that go on forever. Cooks made jam in preserving pans and laundry coppers; they used huge wooden jam-stirring spoons as big as canoe paddles.

In the Barossa, congregations of women banded together to make jam for the Lutheran boarding schools and outback missions. After a day of cutting and boiling, they would pour the jam into clean kerosene tins. The pastor took the sealed tins to be weighed on the scales at the flour-mill. Along he came, in his fine black suit and clerical collar, lugging the tins onto the big, black scales used for weighing the sacks of flour. On one occasion a splash of sticky jam landed down the back of his shiny dark trousers. The miller, trying to help, picked up a flour-bag to wipe off the jam but the white flour on the bag stuck to the jam and the pastor went off down the street looking as if he had been daubed for some sort of corroboree.

You won't find exotic jam recipes in the pages of old local recipe-books. The favourite kinds were melon jam in all sorts of combinations; apricot, of course; marmalade from different sorts of citrus fruits; jams and jellies made from quinces. The only real surprise was tomato jam. Recipes for these fruits appear over and over again.

A recipe for gooseberry jam comes from the notebook of Frau Pastor Stolz. It is a reminder of a fruit that was much more popular at the end of the nineteenth century than it is in Australia now. Gooseberries still grow everywhere today in the parts of Poland and Germany from which the first European settlers departed.

Gooseberry Jam

Boil 1 lb gooseberries in 3 pints water until tender, add 2 lb sugar and boil again. (Very nice).

The old recipe notebooks show that around the turn of the century people were also preserving fruit in syrup and sterilising Agee bottles in the oven. They did so until they became the fortunate owners of a Fowler's Vacola Bottling Outfit with Built-In Thermometer for using on the hot plates of the stove. The Fowler's Units were popular in the 1950s, but they were relegated to the shed in the 1970s, when people used freezers to preserve excess food.

It is hardly surprising that bottled fruits have become popular to make once again: those tall, glass preserving-jars containing symmetrical stacks of fruit glowing deep red, amber and gold look very beautiful on the shelves of a dresser. At shows they are displayed like an artform, with the colours in the jars balanced in the overall arrangement. The fruits behind the glass are cut in fancy shapes with inlays of pieces of a different colour, like the tessellations on an old stone floor. It can take half a day to assemble the pattern of fruit in just one jar. You wouldn't want to eat it too quickly afterwards! Bottled fruits are a form of folk art.

If sugar was not plentiful in the early days of the colony, the first white settlers in the Barossa dealt with surplus summer fruits principally by drying them. This is obvious from the kinds of recipes they were used to and the kinds of foods they were served on the voyage out. On Saturdays on some ships they had peeled grain with prunes and syrup, and on Sundays they had meat, dumplings, pudding and dried fruit. The Sunday dish sounds suspiciously like *Schlesisches Himmelreich*, the traditional dish in the areas near central Europe from which they came.

A few generations later the descendants of those early families were still drying their fruit as they had done in Europe and calling it *Backobst*. They simply cut the fruits in halves and laid them out on wooden trays to dry in the sun for several days. They might even squash the fruit to dry it in a slab.

It was best to get the trays out into the garden in the early morning so that the fruits would develop a 'skin' over the cut surface before the sun grew too warm. Otherwise the bees would be attracted and eat half-way into the fruits. And it was important not to let rain fall on them, otherwise they would go mouldy. The fruit was ready when it did not bend easily or give off juice when crushed.

Local gardeners began dipping fruit in preservatives or curing it in sulphur boxes only around 1900. Before that time, they had dipped apples in brine before drying them. The new processes helped the fruits to keep their colour. One solution for dipping fruits came from the Schrapel family living in Bethany.

Fruit-dipping Solution

200 g sodium metabisulphite, bought from a chemist 1.5 kg sugar
10 L water

Pit half a case of stone-fruits and soak them in this solution for several hours, up to a whole day for peaches. Dry on trays in the sun. You can even leave them out at night unless it looks like rain.

Simple *Backobst* of an earlier generation may not have looked as appetising as the fruits later treated in this way but the taste was fine. The *Backobst* apricots might look quite black and the pears a dark brown but even after two years you could soak the slab of fruit in water to reconstitute it and make some popular dishes.

Here, for example, is a recipe for everybody's favourite pudding:

Backobst with a Champagne Crust
A delectable hot pudding. Hot stewed fresh fruit is often used rather than soaked dried fruits.

FRUIT
400 g whole mixed dried fruits: apricots, peaches, pears, prunes and apples | 500 ml boiling water | pinch bicarbonate of soda | 1 dsp sugar | juice ½ lemon

Cover fruits with boiling water to which a pinch of bicarbonate of soda has been added. Soak for several hours. The fruits should soften and be surrounded with a watery syrup. Add sugar and lemon juice to taste. Pour this mixture into a pie dish and place in a moderate oven until the fruit mixture starts to boil. *It must boil.*

CHAMPAGNE CRUST
1 egg | ½ cup sugar | ½ cup milk | 1 cup self-raising flour | 2 tbsp melted butter | a little vanilla essence or lemon rind

Beat egg and sugar. Add milk, flour and melted butter and flavouring. Pour over boiling fruit. Bake 25 to 30 minutes in a moderate oven (180°C).

Either reconstituted *Backobst* apricots or a layer of fresh fruit could also be used beneath the *Streusel* topping on yeast *Kuchen*, or later, in the 1920s and 1930s, on afternoon tea cakes like this one:

Apricot Afternoon-tea Cake

My aunt used to take this to functions when the invitation said, 'Will all ladies please bring a plate.' The recipe makes two cakes.

CAKE BASE
3 tbsp melted butter | $1/2$ cup sugar | 2 eggs | $1/3$ cup milk | 1 tsp vanilla essence | 2 cups sifted plain flour | 2 tsp baking powder | $1/2$ tsp salt

Beat melted butter and sugar together, add eggs, milk and vanilla. Beat well. Add to sifted flour, baking powder and salt, and mix. Pat mixture into two 20 cm pans lined with baking paper or else greased well and floured.

FRUIT LAYER
$1\,1/2$ cups chopped dried apricots that have been soaked several hours in warm water; or grated apple or diced fresh plums or even strawberries or diced, cooked quinces

Spread fruit on top of cakes.

STREUSEL
$1/2$ cup sugar | 1 heaped cup plain flour | $1/2$ cup softened butter | a little vanilla essence | $1/2$ cup slivered almonds (blanched or plain) | $1/2$ tsp cinnamon

Mix first four ingredients and work with your fingers until crumbly. Cover fruit layer. Sprinkle with cinnamon and chopped almonds. Bake in a moderate oven (180°C) for about 25 minutes.

Apricot butter, described as a cake filling in the *Barossa Cookery Book* of about 1920, is another versatile dish using dried apricots. Various families used to make apricot butter, which is really an apricot version of lemon cheese or lemon curd.

Apricot Butter

This very rich paste is extremely good. Serve on a soft meringue and pile on it some tart summer fruits like raspberries.

110 g dried apricots | 1 tbsp sugar | 110 g butter | 4 eggs, well-beaten | juice and grated rind 1 lemon

Cook dried apricots in a little water until tender. Pass through a sieve or blend in food processor. Cool and add sugar, butter, eggs and lemon juice and rind. Mix all together, stand in a basin over a saucepan of just simmering water and cook, stirring with a wooden spoon, until it is thick.

No table set for Christmas dinner was complete without bowls of almonds and raisins made from muscatel grapes. The raisins were made back in the fruit-drying season. They looked pretty sitting in clusters with their stalks intact. Some people used a machine a bit like a mincer to remove the seeds from the raisins, but many families left the seeds, believing that if you chewed them well they were good for your health.

As with prunes, some families still dry muscatels by first putting them in a caustic dip. In times past, the dipping was done in the copper (on a day other than Monday washing-day!).

The bunches of muscatels or the prune plums were placed in a billy perforated with holes that fitted into the copper to be submerged in the water. The copper was three-quarters full of water. Taking care to protect their faces, hands and clothes, the cooks added an amount of caustic soda, which fizzed up and simmered a while. Then they poured a tablespoonful of olive oil on the water to give the finished fruit a shiny appearance.

While the caustic water was simmering, they dunked the billy under the surface. They would bring it out after a few seconds and allow it to drain, then spread the fruit on the wooden trays until it had dried. In warm weather, this took less than a week.

Finally, they needed to put the raisins into the oven to kill the moth eggs still hidden in the berries. Years ago, this meant lighting a fire in the bake-oven and allowing it to turn to ashes, or using the bake-oven after a day's bread or *Kuchen* had been made. A tray of raisins could stay in the still-warm oven overnight and be packed away in the morning. If the raisins did not go into the oven like this, there would be grubs and moths crawling through them by Christmas. Nothing was more certain.

A most effective way to avoid all this trouble with drying fruit is to visit the Angas Park Fruit Company and the South Australian Company Store in Angaston, where you can buy delectable fruits, dried, glacé or prepared in various other ways. These are the shops for the last two fruit-processing works remaining from the time when the Barossa abounded in jam factories, canneries and packing-sheds. When you go inside the stores, all the coloured fruits displayed in tubs glow like the jewels in Aladdin's cave.

As they say in the travel guides, they are worth a visit.

Chapter 15

Yabbies, Pickles and Sauces

The heat of midsummer rises, wavers and rises again. Just as each wave grows hard to bear, the cool change comes in and we move easily once more. Fresh gully winds blow into the house in the evening, making sleep possible, and sometimes the cool change brings rain.

This year the summer has been dry but there are some seasons when summer thunderstorms pour water out of the sky and people go to watch torrents surging down the creeks, awed at the force of the current. When the water subsides, the pools in the creek are deep. Yabbies stir: time to get out the traps.

Everyone who has been yabbying has a favourite way of catching these small fresh-water crustaceans. Some dangle a string with a piece of meat or soap on the end and pull it up quickly at a tug on the line; others construct various geometrical wire-shapes covered in chicken netting or sacking, designed to scoop and hold a yabby while it is attacking the bait.

The one favoured by local children is a circle made of netting or hessian, with long strings to pull it out of the water. The bait is a quarter of a sheep's head wired to the net. Many years ago they preferred to use a dead parrot, but today's yabby-catchers head for the butcher rather than the bush when searching for bait. The children submerge this contraption in the creek and check every now and again to see whether the yabbies have succumbed to the lure.

Extracting the yabbies and putting them in the bucket needs

nimble fingers, for there are always a few that cling desperately to the netting sides and need to be prised off. You grab them by their backs away from the pincers, the way you do with crabs. Kids have been doing this for generations. They know what to do.

Years ago farm-children would bring the yabbies to Mum, who had salted water boiling in the wash-house copper or in a four-gallon honey-tin out in the yard. They would tip the bucket of yabbies into a netting basket and Mum would lower it into the boiling water for two minutes, then raise the basket and let it drain.

There is a protocol to eating yabbies. You must have the kitchen table spread with newspaper. You have salt, pepper and stacks of slices of fresh bread spread with butter at the ready. Some people have a saucer of vinegar or lemons as well. You have plates, but because of the newspaper you need no dish for the shells. And that's all, really, before you sink your fingernails into the tail shells and your teeth into the hot, sweet flesh, dropping the shells onto the newspaper.

It is a kind of eating that requires a real love affair with the whole process of food-gathering and it is one that traditionally attracts men as well as women and children. In some families years ago it may have been the mother who had the copper going ready for the yabbies, but in others cooking yabbies, or any kind of shellfish, was often done by the males.

That is why the crabbing trips to Port Parham on the coast or fishing expeditions to places along the River Murray in the first half of the twentieth century were often just for parties of men. Occasionally women did go, too, and sometimes even the children were brought along to camp in big canvas tents; but most commonly the crabbing and fishing expeditions were labelled strictly 'Men Only'. It was the time when the lads could be let off the hook, so to speak, without having to worry about the demands of polite society.

The part men played in preparing food is a very interesting aspect of the Barossa food culture. To begin with, the mere fact that men have always taken an interest in the gathering and preparation of food is

Michael and Annie Lehmann catching yabbies

remarkable in itself. Women who come to the Barossa to marry local men have commented on their first impressions of Barossa life. Some are amazed to see men in the butcher's shop buying the weekly meat for their families, inspecting different cuts, comparing prices and making choices.

Men talk about ways of preparing food in their conversations with other men. Some may not have actually done the cooking for themselves, but they might talk about it together. My own father once made me laugh because he gave me detailed directions for cooking roast pork: he who had never opened the door of an oven in his life knew all about basting and the temperatures needed to produce perfect crackling. He had learned these secrets from his mates over a drink and a game of cards.

I often wonder how it happened that some of these occasions for gathering or consuming food turned out to be all-male affairs. Was it simply that hunting, shooting and fishing have been male activities from earliest times and just continued to be so? In the Barossa, was this exaggerated by the fact that men and women were often separated in organised activities, for example in early church services, where the men sat on one side of the church and the women and children on the other? Or was the situation just the same as in other parts of Australia where men and women have notoriously tended to separate into segregated groups at social functions?

Whatever the reason, many outings were for men only, even in situations where the 'gentler sex' would have been perfectly at ease. A photograph given to me by my uncle, taken around 1920, shows his father having a picnic in the Adelaide Hills with his friends: men, of course, sitting by the side of the car, sedately having afternoon tea with not a woman in sight.

Some foods men willingly prepared in the early twentieth century and others they would not touch, because that was 'women's work'. Drying fruits by dipping them in caustic soda was acceptable, but making jam was a different story, although there were exceptions.

Men's picnic c. 1920

Sir Hans Heysen, the artist, enjoyed cutting up fruit with his family to make jam. But then he lived further south, in the Adelaide Hills, not in the Barossa Valley, so he came from 'foreign parts'!

Men would pickle cucumbers and possibly *Sauerkraut* or onions but not make sauce or chutney. Men would barbecue meat over a makeshift fire in a kerosene tin at a 'chop picnic' but few would handle the roast over the fire in the kitchen stove. Men would slaughter the pig for making the sausages, but the gathering of the blood and the mixing of the filling they mostly left to the women. And, of course, men caught fish and crabs, and cooked and ate them, on the beach or by the river or back home in the kitchen.

So mostly it was men who went on the fishing trips to Port Parham. At any time of the year, but especially at Christmas or Easter, they might pack all their gear into the old truck, including the tents, the primus stove and the fishing net. That was in the days before you needed a licence for a net and long before people were prevented by law from going out in the summer when the crabs are breeding.

Off they would go: Traugott, Soccer, Schneider, Bailiff, Cocky – they all had fanciful nicknames and goodness knows how they came by them – some sitting in the cabin and some bouncing around in the back of the truck. By the creek running into the sea they would set up camp, filling sacks with dry seaweed for their mattresses and pitching the big canvas tent. At two in the morning they would go out with the net, dragging it for what seemed like miles in the shallow water that was still only up to their thighs.

They would return home to the Barossa with fabulous stories of huge hauls of whiting, garfish and flounder – if not with the fish themselves. There was always some reason why the catch they brought home was very small. Sometimes there had been so many fish that they had sold them or given them all away. Once they caught an enormous fish but it jumped out of the bag while they all fell about laughing. Once, after a fishing trip on New Year's Eve, they headed home with a bag filled to the brim but by the time they reached the Barossa all the fish had gone off and they ended up dumping them in the local creek.

But even if they were left with precious few fish for their families, the men were bound to have a good time away on these trips. As long as there were cards to play euchre or five hundred, as long as there was enough port or beer buried in the seaweed to keep cool, and as long as the crabs kept running, they were set. (One night the fishermen cooked nineteen buckets of crabs!) The only true disaster happened if they ran out of beer, or lost it, as they did on one occasion when a huge tide washed away all the bottles they had stowed in the seaweed.

When the men arrived home, they were probably greeted by the smell of sauce and pickles. Tomatoes, beans and other vegetables were all ripening straight after Christmas and needed to be preserved. That is probably another reason why women did not often accompany men on the fishing trips; they were too busy in the kitchen coping with the garden produce and delving into recipe-books.

It was a surprise for me, turning the pages of one of the old recipe notebooks from the Light Pass area, dated 1914, to discover a pencilled recipe for 'Mrs Jansen's Onion Pickles' that came from my own grandmother. She must have passed it on in conversation; a perfectly simple recipe, which needed more specific measurements added to make it work, for the original recipe was charmingly vague. People were expected to *know* how much of each ingredient to use!

Mrs Jansen's Onion Pickles
These are very good, crisp and just sweet enough. Makes about 3 jars.
1.5 kg small, sweet, early-season's white pickling onions | 225 g salt |
2 L water | 1 L vinegar | 2 tsp allspice | 2 tsp black peppercorns |
3 tbsp golden syrup

Peel the onions and soak them in strong brine made from the salt and water for 2 or 3 days. Strain them and bring them just to boil in the remaining ingredients in a stainless steel saucepan. Remove from the heat and allow to stand until cold before packing the onions into clean jars and covering them with the cooked liquid. Seal the jars. Wait at least a fortnight before using them.

Barossa Pickled Onions

Some recipes contained no sugar at all, or just a little sugar like this one. The quantities and number of spices varied. Serve these onions with jellied meat. I can imagine a whole brawn turned out on a plate, decorated with clusters of pickled onions and radishes. Makes 6 jars.

2 kg pickling onions | 5 cups boiling water | ½ cup salt |
2 L mild vinegar | 1 cup water | ¾–1 cup sugar | 2 tbsp bruised, chopped ginger root | 2 tsp whole allspice | 6 single cloves |
2 tsp black peppercorns | half a nutmeg (optional)

Use small, hard onions. Pour boiling water over them. Wait a few minutes, drain and remove the skins. Sprinkle with salt and let stand until the next day. Rinse, dry and pack into sterilised jars. Place the other ingredients in a stainless steel or enamel pan, boil 30 minutes. Strain the liquor, pour it over the onions while hot. Wait a day and then seal. The liquor must cover the onions. Leave a fortnight before using.

One acquires much wisdom judging the pickled onions at the local show. 'Mum always said to get your pickled onions done before February,' said one onlooker (male, incidentally), 'otherwise you might as well forget it!' I pass on this advice. If you pickle onions later in the season, they do not taste as tender and sweet as the earlier ones. In fact, their flavour is acidic and they discolour quickly.

My collection of hand-written recipe-books from the early twentieth century gives a good idea of what was happening in kitchens across the district at different times of the year. For example, the recipe that follows for pickled plums, which came from a notebook started by Wanda Grosser of Tanunda in 1914, is repeated in other notebooks as well.

Pickled Plums

Serve with pickled pork, pâtés and terrines. Use them to decorate a whole baked leg ham.

1 kg plums with red flesh (not too ripe) | ½ cup vinegar | ½ cup water | 450 g sugar | 3 cloves | 1 dsp ground cinnamon

Prick plums all over and pack in a large jar or earthenware crock. Boil the vinegar, water, sugar and spices in a stainless steel saucepan, pour over the fruit and let it stand for 3 days. The juice is drawn out of the plums. Tip plums and juice into a stainless-steel pan. Bring to the boil and simmer slowly another 10 minutes. Strain off the cloves and bottle the plums in their juice. If the jars are covered with cellophane, over the years the juice will thicken and the plums become luscious.

Just about every private Barossa recipe-book from the early twentieth century has recipes for plum sauce and apricot chutney. Both seem to be twentieth century inventions for they appear in neither my English nor my German encyclopedic recipe collections published before 1910.

Plum Sauce

At Maggie Beer's suggestion, this recipe has been modified to move away from the outdated taste for excessive sugar and heavy use of cloves.

750 g dark, tart plums | 110 g sliced onions | 275 ml vinegar | 250 g sugar | 1½ level tsp salt | ¼ tsp cayenne pepper |
muslin bag containing 1 tsp black peppercorns, 3 cloves, 1 tbsp bruised ginger, 2 cloves bruised garlic

Boil all together gently in stainless steel or enamel pan, lid half on, stirring occasionally until the stones separate from the fruit – about 1 hour. Strain through a sieve. Bring back to the boil and bottle in sterilised bottles.

Apricot Chutney

Use freshly picked apricots that are just ripe. A similar recipe was used for nectarines and peaches, as well. Serve it at a party with a whole cold roast of pork. Makes four jars.

1 kg apricots washed, stoned and cut up roughly | 175 g brown sugar | $3/4$ cup vinegar | 300 g raisins or sultanas | 680 g onions, chopped | $1/4$ tsp cayenne pepper | 2 tsp salt | $1/2$ tsp ground cloves | $1 1/2$ tsp ground ginger | 1 tsp very finely chopped garlic (optional) | 1 tsp finely chopped chilli, or 1 whole chilli to be removed after cooking (optional)

Place all ingredients in an enamel or stainless steel saucepan, bring slowly to the boil and cook over a very gentle heat, stirring every so often with a wooden spoon, for $3/4$–1 hour. Put in heated jars and seal. Some recipes say to wait three months before using but I like the freshly made mixture.

Sometimes local mysteries arise in these Barossa recipe notebooks. Two women who lived in the same tiny village had almost identical recipes for bean chutney. There's nothing so odd about that. But in this village – so small that it does not even have a store – are two separate Lutheran churches, each with a very strong congregation. Each was so involved, long ago, in doctrinal differences that members of the separate congregations hardly even knew each other. So how did two women, living so close together, whose lives were yet such poles apart, manage to share the same recipe? We'll never know.

Bean Chutney

500 g beans | 2 medium onions | 500 ml vinegar | 1 dsp salt | $1/4$ tsp cayenne pepper | 120 g sugar | 1 dsp mustard | 1 dsp flour | 1 tsp turmeric

Cut and slice the beans and onions. Blanch in boiling salted water for a few minutes. Boil vinegar, cayenne and sugar together, then add beans and onions. Boil until soft. Mix mustard, flour and turmeric together with a little water and add to the bean mixture and simmer 7 minutes. Adjust the seasoning. Seal in sterilised jars. Use this for cauliflower, too.

The next recipe, for pickled nasturtiums, is a very old one. It appeared in the *Bremisches Kochbuch* of 1834. There were also written notes about pickling nasturtiums in the notebook of Fraupastor Stolz of Light Pass. *Mrs Beeton* of 1901 also has a version.

Nasturtiums were for generations a common sight in Barossa vegetable gardens and they had many different uses. Not only were they decorative and edible – both the buds and the leaves could be used in salads and on bread and butter – but they helped the other plants to bear. They flowered profusely in spring and summer, attracting the bees to the spring-flowering bushes of tomatoes and to the cucumber vines.

Many nasturtium buds and green seed pods found their way into a pickle bottle, to be used later like capers in salads and sauces.

Pickled Nasturtium Buds

Wash the young buds of nasturtium flowers and bring them just to the boil in mild vinegar. Drain. When the buds have cooled, fill them into glass jars and pour wine vinegar over them. Or, they can be salted a little and then laid in vinegar when the brine has been drained off. Wait a few months before eating them.

In each of these hand-written notebooks there is at least one recipe for tomato sauce, one for tomato chutney or relish, and often one for green tomato pickle. In the *Barossa Cookery Book* from the same period, there are dozens.

Yet although it had been in the colony for some years, the tomato did not rate highly as a food forty years earlier. In the *Farm and Garden* newspaper of 1859 a person writing under the name 'An Old Adelaide Housekeeper' urged everybody to consider eating tomatoes because they were such a cheap, easy-to-grow and versatile summer food. Why, oh why was there no section for tomatoes in the recent Horticultural Exhibition held in Adelaide? Surely this would be one way of bringing the tomato to more general notice.

Some weeks later, Old Adelaide Housekeeper was in print again, giving recipes for cooking 'this valuable fruit'. This time, the correspondent was recommending tomatoes mainly for making delicious jam 'possessing a flavour entirely unique'. Tomato jam was apparently not known for sale in the shops. This disappointed Old Adelaide Housekeeper, who liked using it in jam tarts or on bread with cream.

As for tomato sauce, Old Adelaide Housekeeper recommended it as well, to be eaten with steak and cold meat, as a condiment like Worcestershire sauce. It appears that in 1859 this was not yet a widespread practice. Only small quantities of imported tomato sauce could be bought, but now Old Adelaide Housekeeper was reassuring people that home-made tomato sauce could be produced with a colour just as bright as the commercial version 'by the addition of vermilion, red lead ... or any similar drug according to fancy'.

People must have taken notice of Old Adelaide Housekeeper's letters because by 1861 the *Farm and Garden* was advertising a tomato section in the entries for the horticultural exhibition to be held in the Adelaide Parklands and in 1867 Sir D. Daly won first prize.

Fortunately, no such ingredients as red lead appear in the sauce recipes followed by Barossa housewives forty or fifty years later, although the *Barossa Cookery Book* has pages of recipes for tomato jam. Here is a recipe for tomato sauce from Anna Geier's notebook – she acknowledges that it came from her mother. Anna wrote down other sauce recipes first in German and then later in the book she wrote this one in English. What a topsy-turvy way of doing things, for both English and German recipe-books acknowledge that the English had the recipe first!

Anna Geier's Tomato Sauce
I have halved the amounts in Anna's recipe to make about 3 litres.
'From Mother: Good!' writes Anna.

4.5 kg tomatoes | 680 g onions | 2 tbsp finely chopped garlic | 1 tsp cayenne pepper | 2 tbsp salt | 2 tsp ground ginger | 500 ml vinegar | 650 g sugar | muslin bag containing 20 whole peppercorns and 20 whole allspice | 200 ml spiced vinegar

Cut up tomatoes, onions and garlic. Gently boil tomatoes and onions together in an enamel or stainless steel saucepan for 45 minutes with the lid off. Add the garlic and boil another half hour. Add the next 6 ingredients and boil until soft, with the lid off, stirring often. Strain through a sieve or a mouli. Return puree to the heat and bring to the boil again with spiced vinegar until thick while the bottles are being sterilised in the oven. Fill bottles and seal while hot.

As the 1901 edition of Mrs Beeton says, green tomatoes make the very best sort of pickle, and that is because the acid in them balances the textures and flavours of the other ingredients. Long slow cooking of green tomatoes helps them to release their pectin, which gives a pleasant mouth-feel to green tomato pickle.

Green Tomato Pickles
Very good if you use a mild, vinegar. Makes three or four jars.
2.275 kg green tomatoes ▮ $1/2$ cup salt ▮ 1.1 L mild vinegar ▮ 230 g sliced onions ▮ $1/2$ tsp cayenne pepper ▮ muslin bag containing 4 cloves, 1 stick cinnamon, 1 dsp peppercorns ▮ 2 tbsp brown sugar for each cup of pickle

Slice the tomatoes and place in the dish. Sprinkle well with salt. Let stand overnight. Drain thoroughly. In stainless steel or enamel pan, uncovered, simmer all ingredients except brown sugar slowly until mixture thickens and becomes tender (about 1 hour). Stir occasionally with wooden spoon. Add 2 tablespoons brown sugar to each cup of pickle when the cooking is done. Put into hot jars and seal well. Wait a few weeks before using.

Tomato Relish
A mild-flavoured relish, which will soon be eaten. Makes two 375 g jars.
1.3 kg tomatoes, not too ripe ▮ 1 large onion, finely sliced ▮ $1/4$ cup salt ▮ muslin bag containing 25 g whole bruised ginger and 4 cloves ▮ $1/4$ tsp cayenne pepper ▮ $1/4$ tsp curry powder (optional) ▮ $1 1/4$ cups vinegar ▮ 170 g white sugar

Skin tomatoes in the evening by putting them in boiling water first, slice them and put them in a dish with onion. Sprinkle salt over. Drain off well in the morning. Simmer slowly with the spices in stainless steel or enamel pan, lid half on, stirring with a wooden spoon for 1 hour. Add vinegar and sugar and simmer uncovered another 20 to 30 minutes. Pour into hot jars and seal. Refrigerate after opening.

This seems to be the moment to stop and make some comments about where these pickles fit in the Barossa food picture. The fact is that many, particularly the chutneys and tomato sauce, belong more to English culture than to Prussian. German-speaking colonists tended to preserve their foods by methods that used much less sugar and that often relied on fermentation processes to cure the food.

A telling comment is contained in some of the papers of the botanist J.G.O. Tepper, who lived as a child in the Barossa Valley in the 1850s. Among the documents filed under his name in the Mortlock Library in South Australia is a handwritten book of recipes for pickles, condiments and drinks. It was clearly written by an English person, perhaps one of Tepper's colleagues. The point is that the last recipe is for *Sauerkraut* and it is given with this comment: 'The Sauer Kraut is used by the Germans ... like our pickled cabbage but more extensively.' This throw-away remark seems to show a whole difference between English preserving methods and European ones. The English were using the sugar and spices coming from their own colonies: those are the ingredients given in the pickled cabbage recipe in the manuscript. The Prussians had long ago devised other ways of coping with vast quantities of food.

Here in the Barossa, as the nineteenth century became the twentieth, the two cultures were becoming well and truly combined and it shows in the recipes to be found in the recipe notebooks of the day. German-speaking housewives were adopting with alacrity recipes from the English tradition. In their own notebooks they might sometimes write the recipes in German and sometimes in English, and sometimes in a mixture of the two.

As they talked with people in the street, they probably slipped from one language into another. Except in some very closed Lutheran communities, they were meeting more of the people of English origin who had been living in the Barossa for just as long as the Prussians themselves. They were gaining new friends, and marriages between Prussian and English families increased. These intermarriages were not always easy and sometimes it took a long while before people came to a mutual acceptance of each other's differences. Nevertheless, they were coming together and so much of the food culture in the Barossa has distinctly English influences. It is the mingling of the two that gives the Barossa a great deal of its character.

Chapter 16

Mulberries, Drinks, Apples and Cucumbers

Towards the end of summer, still thinking about the English flavours in Barossa food, Maggie Beer and I set off on another visit. This time the car is heading towards Keyneton, a small village lying a little to the south of the farm where we saw the beehives just before Christmas.

Again the morning is warm. Beyond Angaston, we travel through undulating paddocks of dry grass held fast with enormous, weighty gum trees. This is beautiful farming country and we pass some properties that have been established since the early days of European settlement.

Through the trees we catch a glimpse of Lindsay Park homestead, once the home of George Fife Angas, a founder of the early colony of South Australia. These days it presides over the white-fenced training tracks of the horseracing stud. Out in the paddocks, hollow, burnt-out girths of some of the huge old gum trees must also have been comfortable dwellings for Aboriginal people long before colonists put down the foundations for their own houses and took over the land.

Where are we going today? To see Bill Evans, great, great-grandson of George Fife Angas. Bill lives in what was once the winery of Henry Evans, George Fife's son-in-law. Bill's farm, Waterways, is well known today to conservationists because of his land-care projects and experiments with tree-planting. In Bill's great-grandparents' day the property was famous for its nursery, which sold plants to orchards and vegetable gardens all around and so had a significant impact on the landscape of the colony.

In front of the old winery and apple-processing buildings, which are now Bill's work-base, we stop and look. Half-hidden behind elms and oaks, the walls with their arched doors and windows framed by pale pink stone quoins have a soft, weathered patina. Even before there were buildings on the property Europeans admired the beauty of this place. When Henry Evans arrived in the area in 1842, he wrote back to George Fife Angas in England: 'Every mile was more and more beautiful, and the loveliness and richness of both soil and scenery increased till we reached the termination of our journey.'

No wonder Henry and his wife, Sarah, saw the land as a huge garden and planted it with vines and fruit trees. Today the early vines are gone and only one old, gnarled apple tree remains of the orchard, but in the 1860s Evandale wines had a high reputation in England, cases upon cases of apples went to market and the nursery was selling a vast range of plants.

Bill shows us the ledger in which Henry Evans kept his accounts from 1857 to 1861. It records sales of apples, apricots, quinces, carrots, strawberries, almonds, figs, currants, orange trees, shiraz cuttings, asparagus, plums, pears, onions, roses, privet for hedges, peas, tulips, rhubarb, cabbages, radishes, turnips and bulbs. The list gives a picture of the way the landscape of South Australia was by the 1850s becoming a mirror of the different home countries, with a few exotic plants from warmer climates thrown in for good measure.

We walk next to an old channel dug years ago to drain off the heavy rains. Lined with weathered, lichen-covered flagstones, it looks 1000 years old. Alongside, old fig and quince trees nudge the edges, waiting for rain. Tufts of asparagus have sprung from the cracks between the stones. This is heritage asparagus, descended from the plants in the early nursery.

At one end of the channel stand two of the most enormous mulberry trees we have ever seen. In mulberry fashion, the trunks have divided and spread out and you would think that each was a cluster of five separate trees. And the flavour of the berries! Rich, purple and sweet, the taste of the juice lingers like the stains on our clothes.

How important these trees were to the early settlers in South Australia! The oldest standing exotic-fruit tree in this state is a mulberry, planted on Kangaroo Island by settlers from Prussia in the very first days of the colony. Many old farm gardens have at least one mulberry tree and elderly people today can remember gorging themselves in the summers of their childhood.

Advisers like Menge encouraged early settlers to plant mulberry trees not so much because of the fruit, but because the leaves might be useful to feed silkworms and form the basis of a silk industry. It is easy to imagine how people must have set their minds to thinking of ways the new colony might earn money. Enthusiasms ran high for all sorts of ventures in the nineteenth century but in the case of the mulberries no silk industry ever did thrive. Perhaps people found the task of gathering the silk from the cocoons too discouraging. At least they could console themselves by eating the trees' delicious fruits.

The mulberry needed no embellishment. What could be a more perfect end to a meal than a dish of the fresh berries by themselves? And it was rare to have a surplus when a host of birds could pick them all off the tree in one sitting. Yet the farmers' wives used mulberries to make mulberry vinegar, and the residue could make a tart, refreshing drink for summer days. The thrifty cook, in this case from the Semler family, would never waste the mulberries after the vinegar had been drained from them. A bit like using teabags twice!

Mulberry Vinegar

Put 6 lb ripe mulberries into an earthenware pan and pour over them vinegar to cover. When they have soaked for 24 hours, bruise them and mix well. Add more vinegar until nearly a gallon has been poured on them. Stir with a wooden spoon every day and keep them covered with a cloth. At the end of a week, strain off the vinegar. To every pint vinegar add 1 lb loaf sugar and boil and skim for nearly an hour. To be used like raspberry vinegar.

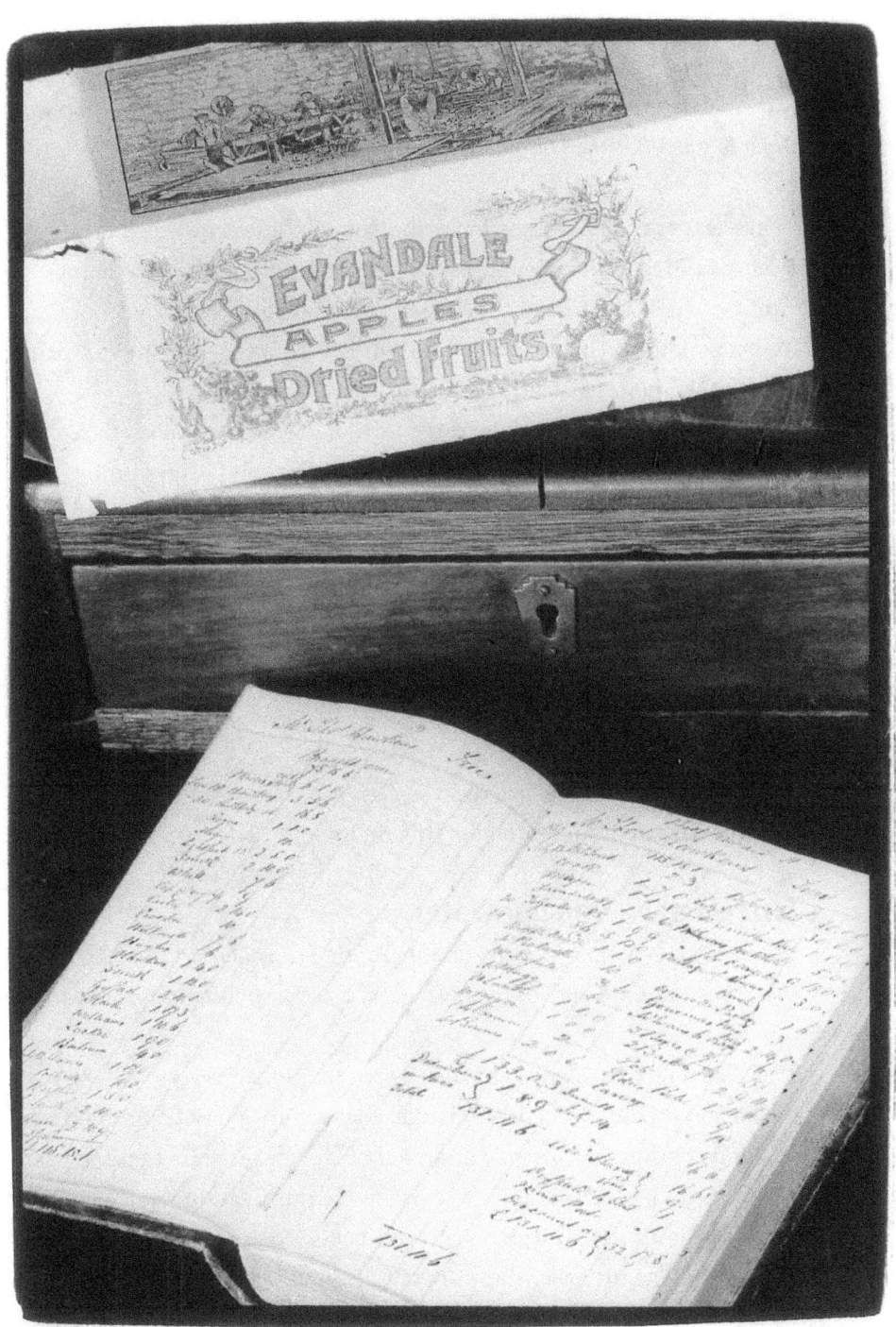

The Evandale ledger, 1857–1861

Mulberry Syrup

Take all the mulberries from the mulberry vinegar and put in a pan. Pour on water and let it boil for a while then strain. Put the juice back into the pan with sugar to taste. Boil then bottle. To be used as a summer drink.

There are so many recipes for cool drinks in old recipe-books that you cannot help feeling how oppressive early settlers must have found the summer heat. Certainly their heavy, formal clothes did not help and many people did not seem to be able to relax their rules of dress even in the hottest weather.

Well into the twentieth century, formal dress was expected, regardless of the temperature. Old photographs of grape-pickers and winery workers show them dressed in waistcoats to handle grapes, often in the hot sun. Around 1916, some lads in the Barossa set out to ride their bicycles to Port Broughton, a full day's journey. In tremendous heat in the middle of the day, they stopped on the side of the road for a discussion about whether it would be acceptable to remove their coats before continuing on the road through the deserted wheat paddocks.

A simple drink for hot days was *Essigwasser*, or vinegar water. Jan Kohlhagen gave the recipe for this drink.

Essigwasser – Vinegar Water

Dissolve ½ cup sugar in ½ cup hot water, add ½ cup plain vinegar. Add 5 pints cold rainwater. Cool. Suck through a piece of grass or straw found in the garden.

The sharp flavour of vinegar does seem to quench thirst. Whenever I walked past the Vinegar House at the winery at Seppeltsfield and smelled the barrels, I was reminded of the sweet-sour taste of raspberry cordial, which is part of everyone's childhood memories in the Barossa Valley. Who did not attend school picnics where Seppelt's raspberry was an essential part of the day? The children would line up for the races and, when the whistle blew, go pounding through the tussocks towards the rope stretched out at the other end of the grass.

Their reward was a drink of raspberry dippered out of an enamel bucket into tin pannikins. It slipped down their throats, tart and sweet, and the children lay back panting on the grass, too puffed to talk, wiping the huge red moustache stains around their lips on the backs of their hands.

In summer, people also brewed ginger beer and home-made hop beer, which they stored in the cellar. When the ginger beer was bottled, they had to be careful to tie down the corks, or they would be woken by disastrous explosions in the middle of the night.

Ginger Beer Plant

To start the plant put in a jar 2 teaspoons ground ginger, 1 tablespoon sugar, 4 or 5 raisins or sultanas with the bloom on them, 3 dessertspoons of water and stir well. Next day and each of five following days, add 1 level teaspoon ginger and 1 teaspoon sugar. On seventh day tip contents of jar into a clean cloth and tie up. Put into a pan with 40 cups water, $2^1/_2$ lb sugar, and the juice of 3 or 4 lemons. Leave plant in water $1^1/_2$ hours. Squeeze hard and take out. Bottle the liquid. Seal firmly. Ready in 7 days. Halve plant in jar. Add 3 dessertspoons of ginger beer. Continue as before omitting raisins. Plant improves with use.

Similar catastrophes could occur with hop beer. Anna Geier's recipe uses horehound, the bitter-tasting imported plant that later became a virulent weed.

Home-made Beer

Put 10 gallons water on to boil. Put 12 saucers of barley, 2 handfuls of hops and a few sprigs of horehound in a muslin bag. Put this in the boiling water and boil for 30 minutes. In a separate pan, dissolve $3^1/_2$ lb sugar in a little of the water. Let it boil without stirring until it turns brown. Add to the boiling hop mixture. Add $3^1/_2$ lb extra sugar and let it boil again. Fill it into a cask and let stand for 3 days. Skim the scum that has risen to the top. The white of an egg will help it to clear before bottling.

The old winery built by Henry Evans in the 1850s

At the end of our walk along the channel at Waterways, Bill shows us where the vineyards used to grow and we go into the building that was once part of the winery, famous for its shiraz. Red wine is not what you'd call a summer drink although it is surprising the number of local farmers who keep a bottle in the fridge to pour out on a summer's day. 'Would you like a wine?' they ask. They serve sherry this way, too, regardless of the soaring heat outside.

The wine they pour will not have come from the Evandale winery, for that establishment was closed down after 1868 when Henry Evans died. His widow, Sarah, was a devout supporter of the Temperance Movement, which was growing in the Keyneton district. When her husband died, Sarah had some of the vines ripped from the Evandale vineyard and the others grafted to currants. To think – she had kept her counsel all those years! Now she made up for it by establishing a Temperance hotel in the village and buying the land on both sides of the road so that no rival hotel could be set up to sell alcoholic drinks. She was a woman of conviction.

She also cared genuinely for the people in the community, many of whom she employed in the apple-processing plants at Evandale; now that the winery had ceased, the production of dried apples became an important substitute.

Bill shows us one of the old packets in which the slabs of dried apples used to be sold. It is a charming white box with dark blue pictures printed on the sides, as well as some recipes from Sarah for using the dried apples. And there in the pictures are the workers, packing apples in crates and spreading apple slices on racks to dry. Their hats and coats are hung neatly on the wall and they present a picture of sobriety. The next two recipes come from the side of the packet.

Evandale Apple Pie

Place 1 lb dried apples in a saucepan, covering them with water, let them gently boil for twenty minutes. When quite soft, put into pie dishes with about 3 tablespoons sugar; spice and cloves to taste. When cool, put your crust on the same as for fresh fruit. Always remember to put an egg cup bottom upwards in the centre of your pie-dish before putting in the fruit, to prevent overflow of juice. Dried apricots may be used in the same way.

Evandale Mince Pie Meat

½ lb dried apples boiled with a little water ❙ ½ lb beef well minced ❙ ½ lb suet ❙ 1 lb moist sugar ❙ 1 lb currants ❙ 1 lb stoned raisins ❙ a little lemon peel

When cool, mash finely with a fork, add beef, suet, sugar, currants, raisins, and lemon peel. Mix well together and use. In cooking dried fruits always supply the place of the evaporated material with water.

Evandale Apple Chutney

This has a pleasant, mild flavour. It is adapted from the Evans family notebook.

2 kg apples ❙ 1 kg white sugar ❙ 1 kg onions ❙ 1 kg sultanas ❙ 250 g whole ginger bruised and put into a muslin bag ❙ 1 tsp cayenne pepper ❙ 125 g salt ❙ about 1.5 L vinegar

Mince apples and onions. Boil apples, onions and vinegar together until tender and then add the other ingredients. Boil ½ hour together.

Many of the families from the Keyneton district supported King's College, a Congregational and Baptist church school in Adelaide. The mothers sent their sons off to school dressed in green and gold blazers and they helped raise money for the school by giving recipes for *The Green and Gold Cookery Book*, which was published from 1923 onwards. *The Green and Gold Cookery Book* sold countless thousands of copies and provided many amenities for the school. The recipes, often very basic, are reliable and simple to follow.

The Evandale recipe is for Apple Sago. It consists of peeled, cored apples separated in the dish by slices of lemon and teaspoons of sago, dotted with butter. The apples are nearly covered with water and the dish is baked in the oven for an hour. So it seems that in 1923 apples were still an important part of the image of Evandale. They were to remain so until the family stopped the apple-processing works in 1929.

Why did it close? One generation of family members, who had put their creative abilities into running an up-to-date, well-equipped business, handed over to the next, who went on to direct their energy elsewhere. They had so much plant and machinery, like the three-storey-high dehydration plant, that it took a three-day clearing sale to dispose of it all. Had they chosen to continue, though, a slump in world markets would have beaten them anyway.

What happened when closing day came? As the work was seasonal, the workers mostly went back to whatever occupied them for the rest of the year and no doubt regretted the loss of extra income when apple season came round. Looking at the picture of the workers on the side of the packet, I think that they would have missed each other's company, working in that lovely stone barn with the light coming through the doorway and the exquisite scent of freshly picked apples. Many people must have been sad to take their hats and coats off the pegs for the last time.

After our own leave-taking, Maggie and I drive back through the Valley on the main highway and everywhere along the sides of the road in this late summer season we see homemade signs outside farms and houses, advertising the sale of pickled dill cucumbers.

No food is more closely associated with the Barossa than the dills. These are not spiced, vinegarish cucumbers like the *Polskie Ogorki*. They are salty and sour and any vinegar taste is just a hint, a balance of flavour. Since the arrival of the early settlers, local people at this time of the year have been preparing the brine, the jars and the tins to make their favourite delicacies.

The main flavours come from the layers of dried dill weed and vine leaves into which they are packed. Those layers and the fermentation that goes on during the period when the cucumbers are set to pickle mean that when the cucumbers are ready they have acquired their golden-green colour and an almost translucent quality. For those who have a taste for them, they are very good eaten with bread, wursts, cold meats or cheese.

One of the many experts at making dill cucumbers is Colin Gramp, who learned the skill from earlier generations of his family. Colin can recall having to pick the vine leaves at cucumber time and watching the fierce rivalry between his uncle and his father. Who was the better *Saure Gurken*-maker? The whole family waited on tenterhooks for the cucumbers to be ready and joined in the tastings and discussions that ensued.

Colin has been making his own pickled cucumbers for many years, trying additions to the basic recipe. (One of his latest experiments is to put two bay leaves with each layer of vine leaves.) For many years, too, Colin convened the cucumber championships at the Tanunda Show. I wonder if his enjoyment of the competition was engendered by the rivalry between his father, Hugo, and Uncle Fred.

Colin Gramp's *Saure Gurken*

Use 4 L gherkin cucumbers around 10 cm long. Leave a short stalk on each one. Start with a large clean stone jar. Place finely cut dried dill at the bottom and then a layer of grenache vine leaves with a few of the green tendrils. A fine grenache is the best leaf because of its acidity. On this layer put a layer of cucumbers, a few leaves of dill and then cover again with a layer of leaves and so on until the jar is filled, ending with a layer of vine leaves. Then place a small saucer and a nice clean stone on top and cover it with the following brine.

Into every 4.5 L of water dissolve 200 g salt, 2 tablespoons vinegar and 2 tablespoons sugar (the sugar helps the fermentation). Fermentation takes 2 to 3 weeks, depending on the weather. The first jar is always the hardest to get going because the yeast cells are not in the air, but once you have started and have a good fermentation it is easy to make the cucumbers in the following jars ferment. You simply add a little of the juice from the first jar to the new brine.

It is not hard to see why Colin, a wine-maker, likens the pickling of dill cucumbers to the making of wine. As he says, this is fermentation, albeit lactic fermentation.

The Gramp family pickle jar

When many different families make the same traditional recipe, they each add their own embellishments, which then become family custom. Some families place a clean white cloth over the top vine leaves before putting on the plate and the weights. This means that when the cloth is removed, it takes with it the white fermented scum that has developed on top and leaves clean cucumbers underneath.

Other families put a few leaves of sour cherries with the vine leaves, and this is a tradition that their forebears brought with them from Prussia. The recipe for *Salzgurken* in the *Bremisches Kochbuch* of 1834, given below, requires sour cherry leaves. Other old German recipes for *Salzgurken* have cherry leaves in with the vine leaves, too.

Since dill cucumbers remain edible only for a few months, people have always tried different methods to increase the time they last. Some people drain the liquor when the cucumbers are ready and either replace it with an entirely new brine or else boil the old brine, let it cool and return it to the jar. If you do this, says Colin, and then store the cucumbers in the fridge, they can last nearly a year. You can also get out the Fowler's Vacola and preserve them after pickling them. (I mention this for any of the addicts who need to have dill cucumbers all year round.)

Even if you do not have earthenware jars or scales for accurate measurement, you can still produce successful *Saure Gurken*. You can use suitable plastic or glass jars. Every farm used to have a ready supply of rectangular kerosene tins to use for a thousand different purposes. Cleaned thoroughly, they make ideal cucumber tins – if they are not being used as buckets for bringing the fire-kindling vine sticks from the woodshed, or flattened out to form makeshift fences and shed walls. It is easy, too, to make the brine without weighing the salt. You just keep adding salt until the water is dense enough for an egg to float on it.

Such varied methods and outcomes! So much of the success of dill cucumbers depends on having the temperature and ambient conditions to keep the fermentation going at the right pace and it is no wonder locals love comparing different people's products. That is why the district show societies offer prizes and run championships for the best pickled dills. In doing so, they keep alive a culture that would otherwise disappear in a world where we tend to make meals on the go. Pickling cucumbers could hardly be called a fast-food!

This next recipe shows just how many of the local techniques for pickling cucumbers date back at least to the early part of the nineteenth century.

A Recipe for *Salzgurken* from 1834

Wash medium-sized cucumbers and pack them in layers in a cask with black pepper, a little salt or saltpetre, horseradish, unripe grapes, dill, bay leaves, and leaves from a sour cherry tree. Close down the lid. Make a brine thick enough to float an egg and pour it in through the bung-hole. Pour in enough pickling brine right up to the top so that the cucumbers are covered. When this is done, put the cask in a warm, partly sunny place, so that the cucumbers can sour easily. (The bunghole must remain open all the time.) When the liquor has fermented, pour it out of the cask, bring it to the boil and while it is still hot pour it over the cucumbers again. When the brew is cold, close the cask, put it in the cellar and turn it twice a day. If you do this, the cucumbers will keep for a whole year. If you want to keep them longer, you need to boil the liquor and repeat the procedure two more times.

For those who have not acquired the taste for *Saure Gurken*, here are some other recipes for using cucumbers. The first is adapted from one in the *Seppelts Wine Vinegar Recipe Book*, published in the 1940s, a book much thumbed by local cooks of the day.

Apple Cucumber Chutney
I have seen notes for using this with minced turkey as a sandwich filling. Makes three jars.
8 apple cucumbers, unpeeled | 2 small cooking apples, unpeeled | 350 g dates | 100 g sultanas | 1 onion | 15 g garlic | 1 small red chilli | 15 g salt | 40 g preserved ginger | 1 tsp mustard | 1 tsp mixed spice | 350 ml wine vinegar | 120 g brown sugar

Put all fruits, onion and ginger through mincer or food processor. Finely chop garlic and chilli (reserve chilli seeds to put in at the end if you like hot food). Boil all ingredients, except the sugar, with half the vinegar for 45 minutes over a very gentle heat, stirring often. Add sugar and rest of vinegar, stirring well until the consistency of jam. (The original recipe said 2 to 3 hours, but it will need only about 30 minutes.) Put hot mixture into hot jars and screw down lids.

Bread-and-butter Cucumbers
I reduced the sugar from the original recipe because I like tart flavours, but you could add more to suit your own taste. The recipe makes two jars.
500 g thinly sliced small, thin green cucumbers | 1 large onion, finely sliced | 1½ tbsp salt | 1 cup vinegar | ⅔ cup sugar | 1 dsp white mustard seeds | 1 tsp turmeric | 1 or 2 tsp celery seed

Put the cucumber and onion slices in a bowl, stir through the salt, cover and leave overnight. Drain well. In a saucepan bring to the boil all the other ingredients. Remove from heat, allow to sit for 15 minutes. Add drained cucumber and onion mixture. Stir. Return to the heat. Heat through but do not boil. Put in hot jars and seal. Ready in 2 days.

I think that the last word should come from Annie Heinrich, writing in 1914. Here is her recipe for sweet gherkins. We'll give it first in translation but this chapter should end with the original, which shows again just how easily people slipped from one language to another in the early twentieth century.

Sweet-and-sour Cucumbers

The cucumbers are cut into 1 inch pieces with the skin left on, then sprinkled with salt and let stand for a day. Dry thoroughly with a cloth. Boil vinegar with whole mustard seeds, and let cool. Pour over cucumbers and let stand for 8 days. Pour off vinegar and boil it again with $1\frac{1}{2}$ lb sugar per bottle of vinegar. Let cool. Pour over cucumbers and bottle.

Zuckergurken

Die Gurken werden mit Schale in 1 Zoll lange Stücke geschnitten dann mit Salz bestreut 1 Tag zugedeckt stehen lassen, dann mit einem Tuch sorgäfltig abtrocknen, dann Essig mit ganzen Senfkörnern kochen und kalt werden lassen und dann kalt auf die Gurken giessen dann 8 Tagen stehen lassen dann den Essig abgiessen und zum 2 ten Mal kochen und auf jede Flasche Essig ein $\frac{1}{2}$ lb loafsugar mitkochen und wieder kalt werden lassen und dann kalt auf die Gurken giessen in Flaschen tun und dann when they are good eat them you know. Annie.

autumn

Chapter 17

Grapes and Wine

The first signs of autumn are the birds wheeling in the sky, their wings casting a net over the sea of vineyards.

The next signs of autumn used to be stains of grape juice on the roads leading to the wineries. The sticky, sweet-smelling trails oozed from the backs of trucks as the heavy grapes began their first pressing on the way to the crushers. Drivers of cars behind the trucks had an eye-level view of the cascading drops as they crawled along. They would console themselves: this is vintage, this is part of life in the Barossa.

Tractors and trucks are still out on the roads during vintage, of course, but the grapes now mostly travel in metal bins on trailers, and the juice no longer drips in such volume. A pity, really. I used to like a sticky start to autumn.

The community used to be in upheaval when vintage began because so many people went 'grapes-picking'. It was a source of income for women and men in the district, but also a back-aching job to be endured in all extremes of weather. They put up with blasting heat or bursts of rain, snakes curled up under the leaves, and other trials. They also had the company of other pickers, the gossipy banter: some salty stories flowed. Secateurs thrust and bunches fell into the buckets; and pickers enjoyed the lively parties when the vintage was finished.

Pickers still go out in the autumn vineyards but they are not nearly as numerous as they used to be because mostly the grapes are now picked by mechanical harvesters. The headlights move up and down the rows of vines and sometimes they crawl along the roads in the dark: behemoths moving purposefully on their mission to harvest grapes in the cool of night.

In spite of the machines, vintage is still an exciting time, especially when the growers arrive at the winery weighbridge with their loads. They stand around talking with a drink and perhaps eating a slice from the huge *Mettwurst* kept behind the office door (if Peter Lehmann is at the weighbridge) while the forklifts unload the grapes into the crusher. All daily activities in the Valley are directed to the vintage and everyone's livelihood is connected with this moment in some way or another.

Just looking at the areas on the map of central and northern Europe where many of the first Barossa settlers came from, I find it hard to believe that they knew much about growing grapes and making wine before they arrived in South Australia and joined the wine-making enthusiasts from England. And yet vines had been growing in Prussia since the twelfth century. The climate may have been a little cool, but make wine they did. It must have been a very dry style of wine and the worst years produced the sourest, most unpalatable wine you could ever imagine.

Some of those years were the 1880s, as these verses from the poem 'The Wines of '88' by Johannes Trojan will show. Each verse describes in acid tones the wine from a different region in Prussia. In the last three verses Trojan speaks of areas from which settlers came to Australia. Their wine was the worst of all! The poem has been translated by David Schubert and the last three verses are printed here with his kind permission.

But the Grünberg wine is much worse yet.
Do not choose this wine!
Compared to this, the Saale wine is sweeter than sugar.

Vintage Festival scarecrow

This one is for puritans,
for the worst of poets and similar riffraff.
It makes your face fall, your cheeks grow pale,
and your nose turn as green as grass.
A cold shiver runs through anyone who drinks it,
and those who have drunk it are filled with regret.
There is something so sour about it
that nothing can soften its sharpness
and it's almost impossible
to portray it in words or pictures.

But the Züllichau wine is a dozen times sourer
than the Grünberg wine, which is a dwarf in acidity
compared to the wine from Züllichau.
In relation to the Silesian wine,
this is like a bristly wild hog compared to a gentle dove.
It's frightful; it's terrible and horrible;
it's dreadful beyond description.
It's fit only to be served at the benches of bandits;
it should be offered only to the worst of criminals;
don't insult honest boozers with this wine.

If you should come to Bomst this winter
to extend your experience,
and if, to be hospitable, they set before you this year's Bomst wine,
then I must warn you:
Take care not to spill any over your clothes;
it will eat holes in your garments
and even bite through your boots.
For the acidity of this wine is so awful
that compared to it sulphuric acid
is like the milk enjoyed by tender infants.
If even a drop should fall on the table,
it will sink straight through with a loud hiss.

Grapes and Wine

It corrodes iron like cottonwool,
it slips through steel like butter;
it is the mother of all acidity.
Walls and castles cannot withstand it.
Granite and bricks dissolve in this caustic Bomst wine.
Diamonds turn to dust in it,
and it makes platinum into dough.
Remember this, if you should happen
to come to Bomst this winter.

At least this poem answers some questions that have puzzled people thinking about Barossa food and where it came from: we now know that Silesians did have a source of vine leaves to make their *Saure Gurken* and that they also had some experience in making wine and tending vineyards. Today, in Zielona Góra in Poland, which used to be the Grünberg mentioned in the poem (a district that has given its name to part of the Barossa district, too), a vineyard still exists. The vines have to be pruned right back to the level of the earth so that they can survive the cold winters but people made champagne at the winery on the site before the Second World War.

Many of the first settlers to the Barossa would have known how to make wine. What is more, it appears that the education system in Prussia had a curriculum that included basic gardening and pruning for all students. In the new land, gardening, grapes and wine-making became important – and successful – on their farms.

Considering this, it is a wonder that grapes did not feature more in the household menu. After all, so many cooks looked out of the kitchen window at grapevines in all directions. Yet it is only fairly recently that people have been adventurous in using grapes as a cooking ingredient. A resourceful book called *Riches From the Vine*, compiled by Soroptimist International of the Barossa Valley in 1994, brings together recipes covering courses and meals using grapes and vine leaves. The recipes come from many traditions but they include detailed instructions for making the *Streuselkuchen* with grapes under the topping that is truly a local speciality.

Another local grape recipe given in this book is *Rote Grütze*, a dessert that has been made in the Barossa for some generations and has a very interesting history. In Germany, *Rote Grütze* is a well-known dish. It originated in the north, near Denmark, a long time ago. For hundreds of years groats, or *Grutt*, were a staple of peasant diet, a wooden bowl of crushed grains, either oats, wheat or maize that was placed in the middle of the table and into which the family dipped their spoons. It was a communal porridge. *Rodegrutt* was the red version, made with the juice of red berries gathered in the woods. *Rote Grütze*, made widely in Germany today – and very popular – follows the same principle: red berries of different kinds, or occasionally rhubarb or gooseberries, cooked and thickened with some sort of cereal. These days it's not groats but most often sago or tapioca. (This is an example of the way nineteenth-century colonialism was able to change part of a food culture: substituting sago for heavier grains transformed an entire dish.)

Now, here is the important bit: nowhere in Germany, as far as I can discover, is *Rote Grütze* made with grapes. This seems to be a particular Barossa development.

I wonder who thought of it first. Elderly people remember *Rote Grütze* as part of their childhood but none of the hand-written recipe-books mentions it. Neither does any edition of the *Barossa Cookery Book*. One recipe-book, however, in the cramped style of German handwriting that suggests that it was written before 1910, gives a recipe for *Stachelbeer Grütze* – made with gooseberries. This is almost certainly a handed-down recipe forming a link with the family's place of origin in Brandenburg. Some families made the dish with mulberries, too. The next step was to substitute grapes. Considering that the dish is not mentioned anywhere in early recipe-books, it may have happened as late as the 1920s.

The recipe for grape *Rote Grütze* in this book came from the hamlet of Vine Vale. Like most versions, it specifies that the grapes

Rote Grütze

must be mataro, presumably because these give a good, rich colour. Maggie Beer and I tried both mataro and late-picked shiraz grapes, however, and the shiraz won by a mile. ('So it ought to,' growled Peter Lehmann, 'with shiraz grapes at the price they are.')

Rote Grütze
This shiraz version is the best *Rote Grütze*. Delicious!
Pull berries from washed bunches of late-picked shiraz grapes. Boil the grapes for 10 minutes with cinnamon bark, a few slices of lemon and a little water. Let it sit for a while so that the colour comes out of the skins. Strain through a sieve, squeezing out as much of the juice as possible. At this point you can freeze the juice, ready for future batches of *Rote Grütze*. Or proceed as follows: to each two cups of juice add 1 cup water, and sugar to taste (about 1 dessertspoonful). Measure the warm liquid into a saucepan and for each 500 ml liquid, sprinkle on 2 tablespoons sago. Allow to soak overnight. Next morning, simmer until sago is clear, about 15 minutes. Keep cooking time to a minimum to preserve the purple colour. Chill. It will keep for several days in the refrigerator, and the consistency will improve. Serve cold with runny cream.

Once the making of *Rote Grütze* from grapes became such a success, the recipe spread to many local families and these days people offer it wherever they want to publicise a truly Barossa food. Anyone wanting to try this sweet will find it at one of the events of the Barossa Vintage Festival. You need only to wander through the *Ziegenmarkt* (the market re-enacted in the old town square in Tanunda), or visit one of the street-fairs in any of the towns to find a stall where *Rote Grütze* made from grapes is being served. But the home-produced versions are still the best.

Since *Rote Grütze* is not mentioned in the 1920s *Barossa Cookery Book*, I decided to see just how many recipes that book does contain using fresh grapes. The main ones turn out to be pickled grapes and grape sauce. The following versions are from my own collection of notebooks.

Pickled Grapes

Make sure that the liquid in the jars completely covers the grapes. This is a good pickle but be sparing with the cinnamon.

2½ cups seedless dark grapes like red globe or ladyfingers ∣ 500 ml mild vinegar ∣ 125 g sugar ∣ ½ stick cinnamon ∣ 3 whole allspice

Boil together ingredients except grapes. While boiling, pour over the grapes in a large sterilised jar. Seal tightly with a screw-top lid. Refrigerate after opening.

Grape Sauce

The aim with grape sauce is to retain the flavour of the grapes. Use only red grapes of the strongest flavour like shiraz and be sparing with the apples.

1.2 kg black grapes (mataro or shiraz) ∣ 220 g sugar ∣ 2 tsp cinnamon ∣ ½ tsp cloves ∣ 2 tsp cayenne pepper ∣ 2 tsp salt ∣ 3 cloves garlic, finely chopped ∣ 550 ml vinegar ∣ 500 g mashed cooked apples

Boil all ingredients, except apples, for an hour in a stainless-steel pan. Add apples. Boil another 10 minutes, push through a sieve then bottle.

Apart from a grape-juice drink, that's about the sum of traditional grape recipes in the *Barossa Cookery Book*. People must have preferred to eat grapes fresh or drink the wine.

Many families did, however, make a hot grape tart. They simply filled an unbaked sweet pastry crust with grapes, probably with the big blue variety called grand turk, poured in a syrup made from a cup of water and half a cup of sugar, covered the top with pastry and baked until brown.

When it comes to counting up the recipes in the *Barossa Cookery Book* that use wine, the results are less disappointing. The English Christmas cakes and plum puddings contain small amounts, although you would really have to use your imagination to taste wine in the finished dish. The giblet soup recipe is thickened with a paste of flour and a dash of sherry. The jellied trifle contains a quarter of a cup of sherry, hock or brandy. And one recipe is a delicious filling of dried figs and sherry: not a traditional recipe, perhaps, but worth recording.

Fig Filling
Try this as a filling for *Berliner Pfannkuchen*.
6 dried figs | 1 wineglass water | 3 tbsp medium dry sherry | 1 tsp grated lemon rind

Chop figs finely. Stew in water until almost dry. Add sherry and lemon rind. Use to fill tarts, combined with other fruits like stewed quinces, or serve in a pot on the cheese board with matured cheese and water biscuits.

For one dish, however, red wine was essential and that was jugged hare. Like rabbits, hares had been introduced into Australia by Europeans, nostalgic for the hunt and for familiar game foods. Hares were more highly prized in the Barossa than rabbits, no doubt because they were much less common and possibly also because jugged hare was a dish of noble tradition back in Prussia, where it was called *Hasenpfeffer*.

At one stage men even formed a hunt club at Stockwell, in the northern part of the Barossa Valley. Members would go out on foot, accompanied by their hounds, to catch hares until the numbers of these dropped and so the club ceased to exist. Now, the population of hares is growing again.

People tried many different methods of preparing the hare for cooking. Some hung it until it was green, at least a week, and then soaked it in brine. Others preferred milk to brine for taking out the aggressive, gamey flavour. They often pot-roasted the hare then, wrapped in bacon with sage-and-onion stuffing, and cream in the gravy. When I had several hares given to me I was able to experiment with all the soaking methods. Some I cooked unhung, others hung and soaked, and yet others hung then cooked with no soaking. The last method produced the most tender, succulent meat.

Grant Schuyler and a couple of hares

Hasenpfeffer – Jugged Hare

A noble dish in a delicious sauce. There is a version in the *Barossa Cookery Book*. You need strong snips and a hacksaw for cutting the meat.

1 hare, gutted but with fur on | 250 g best bacon rashers, without rinds, cut in pieces | $3/4$ cup flour seasoned with 2 tsp salt and 1 tsp pepper | 500 ml red wine | 500 ml chicken stock | muslin bag containing 1 tsp peppercorns, 6 whole allspice and 4 bay leaves | 1 clove garlic, finely chopped | 1 onion stuck with 4 cloves | sprig rosemary | $1/4$ cup chutney, shiraz sauce or currant jelly

Hang the hare, wrapped in calico, in a cold place for at least a week.

Skin the hare and cut into pieces: the legs, the inner fillets attached to the backbone, and the back meat attached to part of the ribs. Remove the flaps, the main part of the ribs (both of which can be used for hare stock) and layers of sinews. Toss the pieces of hare in seasoned flour. In a heavy-based casserole, fry bacon pieces until just cooked. Remove pieces with a slotted spoon and set aside. Add more lard to the pan if necessary. Brown the pieces of hare a few at a time in the pan. Remove. Add wine and stock to the pan and scrape the brownings off the bottom of the pan. Add garlic, onion, rosemary and the bag of spices to the liquid and simmer for a few minutes. Add hare legs and bacon. Cover and simmer very gently $1 1/2$ hours. For the last half hour of cooking, add the fillets and back meat. The hare should be cooked but not falling off the bone and the fillets still a little pink. Remove meat from the casserole.

Strain the gravy and bring it to a rapid boil for about 2 minutes. Add any drained hare blood at this point. Check the seasoning. Add chutney, shiraz sauce or currant jelly to taste. Remove from heat and return the meat pieces to warm in the sauce. Serve with browned-butter noodles, green beans and a glass of Rockford Basket Press Shiraz.

If jugged hare or *Hasenpfeffer* was a dish to evoke memories of Europe, so were some of the hot wine drinks that are also given in the *Barossa Cookery Book*. As autumn approaches and the night air starts to feel chilly, it might be time to think about brewing some again. Members of the Tanunda Liedertafel certainly do. It's a welcome night of the year when they start making their *Glühwein* at their weekly meetings. The combination of singing, friendship and wine has kept this men's choir going since 1861.

Glühwein
The Liedertafel recipe (not this one) doesn't bother with diluting good red wine with water. Quite the contrary, it calls for an extra glass of brandy to be added at the end. This recipe makes enough for four tumblers.

500 ml water ∣ 2 cloves ∣ $1/2$ stick cinnamon ∣ $1/2$ cup sugar ∣
1 sliced lemon, skin still on ∣ 500 ml red wine

In a stainless-steel or enamel cooking-pot bring the water to boil with spices and sugar. Stir until sugar is dissolved. Add slices of lemon. Remove from the heat and add wine. Serve in tumblers or thick glasses. Put a spoon in each glass to prevent cracking.

In the *Barossa Cookery Book*, two recipes using wine were supplied by Miss Selma Seppelt of Seppeltsfield. One was for braised ox tongue. The other was for a light and elegant dessert that she called Hock Pudding.

Hock Pudding is actually a traditional German dish called *Welfenspeise*, from an area that did not supply many immigrants to South Australia. Not everyone in the Barossa Valley knew Hock Pudding but, interestingly, other local people who served it were, like the Seppelts, from wine-making families. They were putting a plentiful resource to use.

Welfenspeise – Hock Pudding
Wonderful dessert! The recipe fills 10 individual glass dishes.

3 cups milk ∣ $1/2$ cup sugar ∣ vanilla pod or 1 tsp vanilla essence ∣
$1/2$ cup cornflour ∣ $1/2$ cup cold water ∣ 6 eggs, separated ∣
1 scant cup extra sugar ∣ rind $1/2$ lemon ∣ juice 1 lemon ∣
2 cups white wine – nobody speaks of 'hock' any more!

In a saucepan heat milk, 1/2 cup sugar and vanilla. Meanwhile, put cornflour in a bowl and gradually add cold water to make a thin cream. When the milk is just boiling and the sugar is dissolved, strain the milk/sugar mixture into the bowl with the cornflour and stir rapidly with a wooden spoon. In another bowl whip the egg whites until peaks form.

Return the milk mixture to a gentle heat and stir constantly, allowing the mixture to thicken. Do not let the bottom burn! Remove from the heat. Let it stand for a minute. Stir in 1 tbsp of the whipped egg white. Fold in the rest of the egg whites while the mixture is hot. Place this bottom layer of the pudding into a glass dish or into individual dishes. Refrigerate.

In the top of a double boiler beat egg yolks and scant cup of sugar until thick and creamy. Add the finely grated lemon rind and the juice of the whole lemon. Whisk in the wine. Place the pan over a saucepan of simmering water, beating with a spoon until mixture foams and thickens. Remove the pan from the heat and continue beating with a wooden spoon until the mixture cools slightly. Let it stand and cool completely. Whisk it again. Carefully spoon this yellow layer over the white one, which must be firmly set at this point. Chill. Serve with cream. Maggie Beer loves hock pudding.

So many people have been involved in some aspect of wine-making from the early years of European settlement in the Barossa. Why didn't they use wine more in their cooking?

Someone has said unkindly that the wine they made in the nineteenth century was often made badly and rapidly turned to vinegar. Many, many local summer dishes contained vinegar!

Probably also a vast 'silent majority' of cooks did use wine frequently, without its ever being mentioned in a recipe, or without even using a written recipe at all, for that matter. At the moment of tasting the sauce or the gravy, their hand might reach along the kitchen shelf for the bottle to add a little wine where judgement called for some. They might slosh some red wine into the apple slices they were baking with brown sugar and discover that they had created nectar of the gods! This was all part of the secret of being a good cook – and you

Grapes and Wine

don't write down your secrets. You mysteriously achieve that appetising flavour that some people call a '*gut Geschmack*'.

Certainly, in many kitchens wine sat comfortably on the bench next to the stove, and on the dining-table as well. One wine-making family used to have a family joke that repeated what a winery worker sitting at the family dinner table had said when he tasted the soup: '*Mutter, reich mir die* bottle; *die Suppe ist zu heiß.*' (Mother, pass the bottle; the soup is too hot.)

The family thought it was a joke because of the mixture of English and German in the same sentence. But what the person said is interesting, too, because it shows that people were in the habit of adding wine to their food from the bottle that was on the dinner table.

This anecdote also leads to other questions. How much wine did local families actually drink themselves before the Second World War? Was it like the farm butter, too highly valued as a source of income to be consumed at home? Was it commonly seen as part of daily living or did people only drink it on special occasions? Did men and women consume wine equally? And was drinking wine acceptable in a community that held strong religious views about virtuous living?

All families are different and there are as many different answers to these questions as there are family anecdotes. It does seem that families surrounded by vines and wine-making were accustomed to drinking wine on ordinary days, not just on special occasions. This was at a time when families in most parts of Australia seldom drank wine with their meals.

Even children, coming home from school on a very cold day, might be offered *Glühwein* by their father to warm themselves after an icy walk along muddy country roads. On such a day, too, the midday meal might start with *Weinsuppe*: claret, spices and dried currants heated together and thickened with sago or cornflour. The remains of alcohol in the warm wines kept people going in bitter weather.

For many of the early grape-pickers, lunch was a piece of watermelon, accompanied by wine from a wicker-covered earthenware jar.

Any picnics out in the open air were times that called for beer or wine. In the old photograph of the Schlunke family picnic near Tanunda, about half the picnickers are serving themselves cups of coffee and half are pouring wine or beer from bottles.

It was naturally hospitable to share wine with companions. Visitors to outlying farms could expect to be offered a glass of claret. This could be dangerous for the baker doing the rounds from farm to farm with his delivery van. He sometimes had to rely on a well-trained horse to get him home again.

So wine really was a familiar part of life for many people. And for some, drunkenness was, as well. Many people who were children in the 1940s can remember walking past men staggering along the street. 'He's *schickert*!' they would say, in a matter-of-fact way as though this was something common. Which it was, for a few people, at that time (the word was known well by everyone then, as a slang word for 'drunk', and is really a Yiddish word). Some people drank so heavily that it altered their mental state and they spent part of each year in a city rehabilitation centre. People would nod wisely and say, 'Oh, he's gone for his annual holiday.'

People back then thought that drunkenness was amusing and told many stories about the town drunks and where they hid the brandy. A group of men were controlling the burning of wheat stubble. One seemed particularly reluctant to use his knapsack spray and when he was urged to douse the approaching fire, the others watched the flames spring up rather than die down. They drew their own conclusions. Another man hid his flagons in the garden incinerator, with spectacular results when his wife burnt the garden cuttings. For hardened drinkers like these, the ultimate job was to work in a winery – but watch out any of them who were discovered using a yo-yo, or piece of rubber pipe, to suck wine from the barrels! They were sacked immediately.

In all these stories, the drinkers seem to be men. Does that mean that wine was not touched by women, or that women did not approve of it? Not necessarily. In many families, men and women alike enjoyed wine socially with food. Women in some families had decided preferences for certain types of wine and bought their own stocks. Judging from the number of recipes they copied into their books, many women also experimented with making hop beer, which they presumably helped to drink.

Yet, another story is common, too. When visitors arrived, the men would go off to the shed for a good yarn over several glasses of port. (The practice that people are now calling 'shed culture', where the menfolk congregate out in the shed and the women dominate the house, has been a custom in the Barossa for generations.) When they were called for dinner, the men would come in with pink cheeks, grinning sheepishly and slurring their words. The women, busy dishing up in the kitchen, could scarcely conceal their anger. The scene was not one of domestic harmony and it was clear that the women did not approve of the men's custom of drinking heavily.

What did the clergy think about all the wine people drank? Early in the century, it depended of course on their religious denomination and once again the range of attitudes was huge. At one end of the scale were the Temperance groups associated with the Congregational Church in some small communities, while at the other were members of the clergy who enjoyed a glass of wine with their parishioners. One pastor, presiding over the funeral of the town drunk, pronounced in German, 'I now commit you to Satan,' and then went on to have a convivial drink with the mourners after the funeral was over.

Drinking customs have changed among Barossa people since the 1950s. Perhaps the biggest change is that wine is seen more and more as an accompaniment to food. Drinking beautiful wine and eating beautiful food are part of the same experience. People learned this when good restaurants began to make their mark. But the understanding of the partnership of wine and food was also influenced by certain individuals. Mostly they were people associated with the larger family wineries and one of them was Alf Wark, company secretary to Yalumba Wines from 1945 to 1971.

Through groups like the Bacchus Club, which he with friends from the other family wineries helped to set up in the Barossa, Alf conveyed his passions for food and wine to many people in the area. Alf became a legend when other Bacchus Club members took home stories about the pains he took to create special food for Club functions.

They said that Alf would go way up into the hills gathering wild asparagus and watercress along the creeks (the actual whereabouts of these delicacies he kept a closely guarded secret). They learned from him the correct serving of food and wine in post-war days when this knowledge was scarce. They saw that for him food could be relaxation, or an exacting project – as it was on the eve of the renowned Bacchus Club annual picnic when a team of female volunteers sprang into action making delicate hors d'oeuvres under his critical eye.

In 1969 Alf wrote a book called *Wine Cookery*, which celebrated 'harmony between the cellar and the kitchen'. It included recipes containing wine and advice about which wines to serve with different food. And since this is autumn and mushrooms are popping up in the early rains, let's end this chapter with one of Alf's mushroom hors d'oeuvre recipes:

Mushroom Caps and Chicken Livers
A good oloroso sherry is just the thing to serve with this nibble.
Sauté evenly sized small mushrooms until soft and fill the caps with chopped chicken liver pieces cooked in sherry. Serve on rounds of hot buttered toast.

Chapter 18

Mushrooms, Quinces, Nuts, Figs, Olives

Around Easter, when the leaves start to turn, the road takes you between long golden chains of vines. Out on the way to Seppeltsfield, the dates are bright yellow on the rows of palm trees and the stooks of hay are yellow in the paddocks. Then it may rain a little. The hills start to turn green and it is time to go walking.

Mushrooms appear after the early rains. 'Keep your eyes peeled,' my father used to say before we scattered over the paddocks, no sounds accompanying us except the birds, whiffling wind and the basket creaking as we stooped to gather a mushroom nudging through dewy grass. Then another. And another.

Back in the kitchen, cooking the mushrooms was simple: take off the brown, satiny skins, cut out the mites and fry the mushrooms in butter, stirring in a little flour, adding milk, pepper and salt before dishing them up on toast. The velvety flavour of dark, brown mushrooms is an unforgettable childhood taste. The white, button mushrooms produced commercially will never come near it.

Autumn is a time when many foods are ripe for picking, often in the wild along roadsides. As you drive over bridges or look down into creeks you see the sudden gold of quinces ripening on rogue trees that must have been seeded from gardens of earlier settlers. They rub shoulders with old fig trees and late plums, with almonds and walnuts. But none of them can keep pace with the olive trees, which race along fence lines and multiply every year in a frenzy for survival.

Early catalogues of garden plants in South Australia show that all these trees were grown almost as soon as settlers had arrived after 1836 and were able to get the ground ready. A catalogue of fruits and vegetables grown in the Province of South Australia published in the *South Australian Newspaper* of 7 December 1847 described each of these tree varieties as having grown well for several years. Only the walnut had not yet produced a crop – but then walnuts make a slow start, anyway.

The writers of the catalogue obviously had little time for quinces and it does not seem as though they were popular with other people in the city, either. The catalogue says, 'In a few gardens [the quince] is to be found growing under the burden of its fine-looking, but not very valuable fruit.'

If the writers had known how the Prussian settlers in the Barossa cooked quinces, they might have changed their minds. Quinces have always been popular in the Barossa, as they were back in Europe, and people still use them in many different ways.

For a start, a dish of them will give the house a fresh, tart perfume. In the 1980s when Margaret Zweck set up displays about pioneering women for the Vintage Festival, she always put a dish of quinces in the display because they were such a common sight in local houses years ago.

Quinces were often cooked as a vegetable to accompany pot-roasted meats. A spoonful of pink stewed quince, slightly sweetened, sat by the lamb or pork, an alternative to apple sauce, its tart flavour a good balance to the fatty, caramelised brown meat.

For many people quinces will always bring memories of Easter, especially for people who lived in the 1920s and earlier in the village of Bethany. On the Saturday before Easter people in the community would build a bonfire, burning off the summer weeds, the vine cuttings and heaps of pine needles. It was a cleansing ritual, to get rid of the old dross, to clean out the old life ready for the new. It was also time for a communal feast. In the hot ashes the people would bury pears, potatoes, onions and quinces and bring them out when they were soft and roasted right through, to eat with butter, pepper and salt, or, for the quinces and pears, a little sugar and cinnamon.

Other people remember the quinces being baked in the coals at times when there was a batch of bread at home in the bake-oven. The local bake-ovens had a unique design, with the oven opening placed at the back of the fireplace. When the firewood had burned to coals and heated the oven, the cook raked the ash and coals from the oven down into the fireplace before placing the trays of bread and cake in the oven. While the bread was cooking, quinces would be put in the ashes to roast, and the quinces and the bread would be ready to eat at the same time.

Children had their own ways with quinces. On the way to school you would pick quinces hanging over someone's fence, then bash them on the fence-post until they were bruised and soft. Then you left them lying there until you walked back home the same way that afternoon. In the meantime, the juices had started to run and the hard quince flesh had turned into an afternoon snack.

When sugar was plentiful, the most popular way with quinces was to turn them into jams and jellies. If people made quince jelly, they had the bonus of a dessert of ruby-coloured simmered quinces to serve with cream once the jelly had been strained into jars.

The following recipe for quince jelly came from Vera Bockmann, at the time of the interview a remarkable woman of ninety, who wrote about her varied experiences in her autobiography, *Full Circle*. Nearly everybody in the Barossa had a quince tree, according to Vera, and they all made quince jelly. Vera did not give exact measurements for this recipe. 'Just use your judgement,' she said. Some people cooked the quinces this way as a dessert using about two-thirds the amount of sugar, or less, without bothering to make jelly.

Quince Jelly
Some recipes specify that the quinces should still be slightly green.
Enough Smyrna quinces to cover the bottom of a large, heavy-bottomed stew-pan ⁞ for every quince allow 1 cup sugar and 1 cup water ⁞ juice of ½ lemon

Wipe the quinces but do not peel. Place them in the pan, cover with water and add sugar. Place on the stove, over the lowest heat possible. Simmer uncovered for 4 hours. The water should hardly be trembling. Do not stir them. In that time, the quinces will turn dark red and the juice will turn to syrup. Just before the end of cooking, stir in the lemon juice. Take pan off the stove. Allow to cool overnight. Remove the quinces, which can be eaten as a dessert (they freeze well: serve with cream). Boil the quince syrup rapidly for another 10 minutes, stirring constantly. Cool until set. Spoon the jelly into clean, dry jars and seal.

Quinces also make delicious jam:

Quince Jam
Easy to make!
Clean and wash 3 to 6 Smyrna quinces and put them in a large, greased pan. Cover with water and boil gently until soft. Take quinces out, reserving the water. Peel the quinces while they are still fairly hot (try not to burn your fingers). Halve the quinces and scoop out the centres. Dice the flesh and put back in the water. For every cup of the quince/water mixture, add 1 cup of sugar. Simmer gently until the mixture goes a deep pink. Be careful not to burn it. Watch it carefully all the time. When the jam is cool, put it in jars. This quince jam retains a strong flavour of fresh fruit.

Quince trees must have borne much fruit – recipe-books from the early twentieth century all have good crops of quince recipes. Of the recipes given next, the older is the one for pickled quinces. It is typical of recipes already known to the settlers when they first arrived before 1850. The recipe for quince chutney is more likely to have been an English recipe, introduced to German-speaking families by young English wives or English-language newspapers toward the end of the nineteenth century.

Pickled Quinces

Mild in flavour, these pickled quinces taste best within a year of being made. Excellent! Makes two or three jars

1 kg Smyrna quinces | 1 L water | 2 cups sugar | 2½ cups vinegar | ½ stick cinnamon bark | 6 cloves

Wash and slice the quinces. Put the cores and seeds in a muslin cloth. Simmer quince slices in water 10 minutes or until not quite tender. Drain and dry on a plate. Dissolve sugar in warmed vinegar, add ½ cup of the quince water, spices, muslin bag and drained quinces and simmer extremely slowly 20 minutes until the syrup thickens a little. Let stand until cold. Put quinces in sterilised jars, cover with juice and seal tightly.

Quince Chutney

This chutney has a good fresh flavour of quinces. Makes two jars.

455 g quinces | 150 g apples | 300 g onions | 230 g sugar | 2 tsp salt | 3 cloves garlic | ½ tsp ground ginger | ½ tsp cayenne | ½ tsp allspice | ½ tsp mace | red-wine vinegar to cover

Peel and mince the quinces and apples, add the other ingredients, cover with vinegar and boil gently in a stainless steel or enamel pan 1½ hours or until the desired consistency. Put in sterilised jars and seal tightly.

Quittensahne – Quince Soufflé

This was in the pioneers' 1834 *Bremisches Kochbuch*. I don't know if anyone made it in South Australia but they had the recipe, which is delicious and easy. The original made one large dish, but it's much easier with individual soufflé dishes.

2 or 3 quinces | water | 1 cup sweet white or red wine (for a milder flavour, use half wine and half quince juice) | 1 cup sugar | 1 tsp cinnamon | grated rind and juice ½ lemon | 4 or 6 egg whites (see below)

Wipe quinces and boil in water until just soft. Allow to cool, then peel and cut off the soft flesh. Chop it up to make 2 cups of quince flesh. Put flesh in a stainless steel saucepan with wine, sugar, cinnamon and lemon rind and juice. Simmer gently until tender, stirring at intervals. Taste and check the flavour. Purée in the blender. Pass the purée through a sieve. The purée can be kept in the refrigerator or freezer then softened with a little hot water and used as needed. Its flavour improves with keeping.

To make individual soufflés, set the oven at 180°C. For every cup of puree take two egg whites. Beat them until stiff and fold in the quince mixture. Spoon into greased individual moulds. Place on a tea-towel in a shallow pan and pour boiling water gently into the pan, to reach halfway up the sides of the dishes (the original recipe said to put the dishes in a bed of salt). Bake 20 minutes. Serve with runny cream.

A word about another quince dish before moving on. You can make quince paste. The sweetened puree of quinces is boiled until it thickens and turns red. You spread it onto trays and allow it to dry out, then cut it into blocks and eat it with cheese or as a sweet. This dish was a traditional recipe in Silesia, where it was called *Quittenbrot* or quince bread. People do not seem to remember it being made in the Barossa, however. Its enjoyment nearly a hundred years later is in part due to Maggie Beer's quince paste on sale in the local shops and to her recipe in *Maggie's Farm*. It is interesting, though, that Silesians and Mecklenburgers in Germany regard *Quittenbrot* as one of their traditional Christmas foods.

Quinces they may have had back home in Prussia, but figs had been an exotic fruit in Europe. Yet in South Australia by 1847 fig trees were described as 'most abundant and luxuriant everywhere' and figs were regarded as a possible food for export.

Many German farms in the Barossa had a fig tree, mostly of the variety that local people called *Zuckerfeigen* or sugar figs, although there were black figs as well. Sugar figs are the large green figs that turn brown underneath when they are ripe. Local people consider them to be very good for the digestion. People eat them raw, but more often crystallise them, pickle them or make them into jam.

Crystallised Figs

These are very good. Try adding even more vinegar. Try using a dehydrator to speed up the drying.

500 g figs | 1 cup of sugar | ½ cup water | 2 tbsp vinegar | caster sugar

Cut the ends off the figs and prick all around with a fork. Bring sugar, water and vinegar to the boil. Place figs in boiling syrup and boil gently for 2½ to 3 hours. Take figs out of syrup, place on a wire tray and allow to stand for at least 2 days in an airy place. Turn figs once every 24 hours. Keep outside, but not in the sun, till quite dry (3 to 4 days). Roll in caster sugar, then pack and press in boxes lined with grease-proof paper.

Preserved Figs

This preserve is a five-year wonder! Very similar to the previous recipe, it requires the figs to be stored in their syrup in jars. The lids should *not* be airtight. Old recipe books said that the jars should be covered with parchment paper dipped in vinegar or rum. Each year in storage makes the syrup thicker and the figs more succulent. Eat them before they start to dry out, however. Use them to stud a baked ham. Serve the ham on vine leaves surrounded by more figs.

6 dozen figs (preferably blue figs) with the skins left on | 3 cups water | 60 g whole ginger bruised and chopped | 2.75 kg sugar | 1 cup vinegar | zest of 2 lemons

Boil figs in water for 30 minutes. Add ginger and sugar and simmer very slowly 2½ hours. Add vinegar and lemon zest and cook a further 10 minutes. Adjust flavours. Place figs in heated jars. Cover well with syrup from cooking. Seal with cellophane paper dipped in vinegar, secured with a rubber band.

Pickled quinces and figs

Pickled Figs

The syrup should be sticky. Use the syrup in gravy to go with hare and veal.

25 figs | 550 ml vinegar | 170 g sugar | ½ tsp pepper | 1 tbsp salt | 3 cloves | 12 allspice | 2 tsp ground ginger

Soak figs in vinegar for one day. Remove figs and place in jars. Pour vinegar into enamel or stainless steel pan and add rest of ingredients. Boil a few minutes to thicken the liquor. Pour hot mixture into jars and cover while hot. The figs need to be left a couple of weeks, the same as pickled onions.

A tip from the Seppelts vinegar book: to your usual recipe for fig jam add ½ cup of white or brown vinegar to 1.5 kg figs. Do not use over-ripe figs. This will prevent the jam from fermenting and greatly improve the flavour.

Fig Jam

If you add the vinegar as suggested above, this is a very good jam. Be sparing with the ginger.

1.7 kg figs | 1.5 kg sugar | 125 g preserved ginger (optional) | 550 ml water | juice and rind 1 lemon, and grated rind of ½ lemon

Wipe the figs and cut off the ends. Cut figs into pieces, cover with half the sugar and allow to stand overnight. Next morning, peel the lemons as you do an apple and cut up rind into small strips. Squeeze the lemon. Chop the ginger finely. Add the rest of the sugar, the water, ginger, lemon juice, and zest to figs and boil 2 hours or until thick enough. Add grated lemon rind at the end. Adding vinegar really transforms this jam.

Dried Figs

This came from a newsclipping in an old recipe notebook.

A week or so before preserving the figs prepare a strong lye from ashes of fig wood; all cuttings from the fig tree should be kept for this purpose. Half a bucketful of ashes to 10 gallons of water will make a good lye. Stir well occasionally. When required, pour off the clear water into an open vessel such as a copper. Set to boil and keep at simmering point.

Gather the figs when they are fully ripe but not over-ripe or withered. Place them in a sieve or bucket with holes in it, one layer at a time, and lower them into the boiling lye for a minute. Remove the figs, drain, lay them in the sun and turn twice a day for three days. Place a calico awning over them if the sun is too hot, so that they will dry evenly. Cover up or take under shelter at night. Pack the figs evenly into boxes until you have one row above the top of the box. Place on the lid, press down and nail or place a heavy weight on it. Set the boxes in a dry place. In a few days a treacly substance will exude from the figs, which, when dry, produces the sugary appearance peculiar to dried figs.

The almond was another tree that the first settlers in the Barossa did not know well. They would have had almonds in England and Europe only if they had been able to buy them imported from Spain or the south of France. Here in the new colony the tree grew with ease. The *South Australian Newspaper* of 1847 sang the praises of almond trees that someone had planted in 1837 simply by sowing a few almonds they had bought in a shop. The trees were now 18 feet high, producing abundant crops.

It was not long before almond trees were growing in the first Barossa settlements. They made a pretty view for people in Bethany looking up the track towards the hills, especially in spring when both the almonds and wattles were in flower. Settlers across the Barossa planted almonds at the edges of their vineyards; shelling the harvested almonds was time for a party, with young people sitting round the kitchen table cracking jokes along with the shells. They were ordered to whistle so that they could not eat too many of the nuts, but most of the time they sat collapsed in laughter (which still prevented them from eating the almonds).

Yet for some reason almonds, especially the bitter almonds, remained a delicacy in Barossa cooking. (People knew exactly which trees in the orchard grew the bitter almonds. They looked out for the trees with the pink blossom.) A load of almonds was too precious as a cash crop to use often as food. People remember 1930s afternoon teas where a recipe containing bitter almonds was regarded as

Mandeltorte

exclusive. On one occasion the guests bit into the cake and nodded appreciatively, saying, '*Ah! Mit Mandeln!*' (With almonds!) The recipe was auctioned at a community card-party as a fundraiser for a local charity. Here it is:

Mandeltorte
This is a prince among cakes. Maggie Beer suggests that you serve it with plums or apricots poached in St Hallet Pedro Ximenez.

225 g ground almonds ❙ 7 or 8 ground bitter almonds or a few drops of almond essence ❙ 1 tsp baking powder ❙ 225 g caster sugar ❙ 7 eggs, separated

Grease a round cake tin 20 cm in diameter and 6 cm high. Line with baking paper. Beat yolks of eggs with sugar until thick and pale. Beat egg whites until stiff, add almonds and baking powder. Fold into egg-yolk mixture. Bake in slow oven (150–160°C) for about 40 minutes.

Other rich cakes made with almonds appeared in private recipe-books. Many people made the following recipe for *Blitzkuchen*, sometimes as a birthday cake. (Recipes for *Blitzkuchen* and *Mandeltorte* were both printed in the 1834 *Bremisches Kochbuch*.)

Blitzkuchen
Make it in March when the almonds are fresh. Instead of the jam, it would be fantastic with plums and slightly soured cream. You could even try cooking the plums underneath the meringue.

KUCHEN BASE
85 g butter ❙ 85 g sugar ❙ 2 egg yolks ❙ 85 g self-raising flour

Cream butter and sugar. Add egg yolks and beat until soft and fluffy. Add sifted flour. Flatten out in a greased, lined 22 cm springform pan and spoon over the topping.

TOPPING
2 egg whites ❙ 225 g sugar ❙ 1 cup minced almonds

Beat egg whites until stiff. Slowly add sugar and nuts until all mixed together. Spread on top of cake mixture. Sprinkle with more almonds. Bake ¾ hour in a slow oven (150–160°C).

Sandwich two of these together with fresh raspberry jam and cream as a birthday treat.

You would not often have found farm-people making recipes like the ones for these cakes in the nineteenth century, except for grand occasions. This was town cooking, fancy cooking for 'at homes' and afternoon teas, when people left their calling card and spent time playing croquet or painting pictures and worrying about where they fitted on the social scale. Farm-people shelled the almonds on their land and sold them as a cash crop, as they sold the butter. When it came to making cake, they kept to the one they had known all along, the traditional yeast cake of their ancestors, *Streuselkuchen*. Some people did, in fact, sprinkle chopped almonds on the *Streusel* before baking, a practice that had been carried out back in Silesia as well. But the majority of cooks made *Streusel* without almonds.

Discussion about almonds brings us to the subject of *Bienenstich*. Slabs of this tempting cake sit on the counter of every Barossa bakery, next to the pieces of *Streuselkuchen*. It has the same yeast base as the *Streuselkuchen* but its topping is a crust of caramel and almonds and it has a custard cream filling. People understandably think that it is a genuine part of the early Barossa Valley food history, especially if they have heard that this cake originated in Silesia and is something like *Streuselkuchen*.

Bienenstich, however, is quite a newcomer to the Barossa. The fact is, according to the most respected food historian in Germany, that *Bienenstich* only became known as a cake in Germany around the end of the nineteenth century. That means it could not possibly have been brought to Australia by Prussian pioneers. It scored no mention when the *Barossa Cookery Book* was first published in 1917 and although the third edition gave a recipe for honeycomb cake, subtitled

'Bienenstick', that cake bore no close resemblance to the Silesian yeast recipe in German cookery books. (Incidentally, the word *Bienenstich* means 'bee-sting' and *Bienenstich* sometimes has honey as well as almond slivers – meant to represent sharp bee-stings – on top.)

People who came from Germany or visited there from the 1890s onwards perhaps knew of *Bienenstich* but anyone who lived in Tanunda in the 1960s can tell you how the cake really came to be known there. It was because of a baker called Martin Meinel, who worked in various bakeries in Tanunda. A recent immigrant from Germany, in 1964 Mr Meinel introduced to his customers some of the recipes he knew from living in Europe but the one that immediately became popular was *Bienenstich*. Members of the Liedertafel choir remember especially the slabs of cake that he took along to choir practice. The few bitter almonds included in his recipe made it different from any other version that has been made since.

How could anyone forget Mr Meinel? He and his wife were very much a part of the town community and the children all knew him because he loved swimming. On lazy hot afternoons down at the pool, he swam with the youngsters out from school. He could use his hands like a syphon and squirt water metres into the air from his clenched fist. He was also impressive when he projected his large, doughy form off the diving board and did 'honey pots', spraying the pool with a shower of water droplets. Honeypots in the pool and bee-sting topping on the yeast cake: those were the achievements that made Mr Meinel famous in the town.

Bienenstich

This homemade version is excellent. To prevent the custard-filling from curdling, place the bowl immediately on a bed of ice to whip it. (A tip from Maggie Beer.) Make the filling first.

FILLING

4 egg yolks | $2/3$ cup sugar | 1 tsp vanilla essence | $1^{1}/2$ tbsp cornflour | $1^{1}/2$ cups milk | 8 tbsp butter

Beat yolks, sugar and vanilla in a heavy saucepan until the yolks are pale-lemon-coloured and sugar is entirely dissolved. Add cornflour and milk, then heat, stirring constantly, until the mixture is nearly boiling. Do not cook too long. Remove from heat and allow to cool, stirring vigorously at intervals over ice. Cool to room temperature but do not chill.

In a separate bowl, whip butter until it is light and fluffy. Beat the whipped butter into the cool custard mixture. It should be smooth and hold its shape. Chill it to make it firm while you make the cake (some locally adapted recipes use a mixture of copha and butter to make the filling thicker). Heat oven to 170°C.

DOUGH

In a warm saucepan mix together $1/4$ cup warmed milk, a scant dessertspoon of sugar and 15 g compressed yeast. Put the lid on the saucepan and put it in a warm place for 5 to 10 minutes. In a bigger saucepan, mix $1/3$ cup milk, $1/3$ cup plain flour, 1 tablespoon sugar and the contents of the other saucepan. Again, put the lid on the saucepan and keep it in a warm place for another 10 to 15 minutes.

Meanwhile melt 55 g butter.

Into a large warm dish sift $2^1/2$ cups plain bread flour, a scant $1/2$ cup sugar, $1/4$ teaspoon salt, $1/4$ teaspoon cinnamon and a pinch of nutmeg. Stir in the grated rind of 1 lemon.

In a smaller dish beat together 2 eggs, $1/2$ cup milk and a teaspoon of vanilla or almond essence.

Now combine the yeast mixture, the melted butter, the flour mixture and the egg mixture in a big bowl and knead it for 10 minutes, pulling the dough from the back and pushing it back down into the dish as you turn it. Put the mixture into a greased plastic container with a lid and put it in a warm place to rise for an hour.

Prepare a baking tray by lining it with greased baking paper. Pat the dough onto the tray, gently using a warmish rolling pin to make the dough level. Cover with large plastic bags and stand it in a warm place for another half an hour.

ALMOND TOPPING

7 tbsp butter | scant ½ cup sugar | 1 cup slivered blanched almonds | 2 or 3 slivered bitter almonds | 2 or 3 tbsp milk | few drops almond essence | 1 tbsp honey (optional)

Melt butter. Add other ingredients to saucepan, and stir constantly over low heat until the mixture thickens. Spread mixture on risen dough. Bake at approx 170°C for about 30 minutes.

When the cake has cooled completely, cut it in half horizontally and spread the custard filling over the bottom layer. Cover with the top layer.

Growing almonds may have been a new experience for the early European settlers, but some of the very old walnut trees we have in the Barossa no doubt began life as a few handfuls of walnuts from the old country tucked into someone's luggage. Walnut trees grew in Silesia, in Brandenburg and in England, especially in the south.

When Easter arrived, the walnuts on the Australian trees were ready for picking, which was best done by spreading hessian sacking under the tree and knocking the branches with long sticks to make the walnuts fall. If the dark outer skin on the walnut shells was still damp and sticky, the family would spread the nuts on an old woven wire bed frame to dry before packing them into sealed bins and storing them where rats and mice could not get to them.

Cooks put walnuts to good use in cakes and buns and biscuits. This recipe for date-and-walnut cake is typical of the way walnuts were used in the 1930s and 1940s on afternoon-tea tables.

Date-and-walnut Loaf
The cake has a good flavour. Do not over-cook.

1 cup chopped dates | 1 cup boiling water | ½ tsp bicarbonate of soda | ½ tsp vanilla essence | ½ tbsp butter, melted | ¾ cup sugar | 1 egg | ¾ cup chopped walnuts | ½ cup plain flour | 1 cup self-raising flour

Preheat oven to 180°C. Put dates, boiling water and soda in a basin. Cool the mixture, then add vanilla. Beat together melted butter, sugar and egg. Add date mixture and nuts then sifted flours. Bake about 45 minutes in a rectangular tin lined with baking paper. Test with a skewer. When the skewer comes out clean the cake is done. Butter the slices.

No one can talk about walnuts from Barossa Valley trees without mentioning the walnut liqueur made by Joe Pelligrini, a much-loved Italian man who lived in the district from 1928 until 1970. Generations later, people still speak glowingly of Joe and his liqueur. Joe made it to a traditional Italian recipe from green walnuts and his family have just a small amount left, which they bring out on special occasions.

Walnut Liqueur for Joe Pelligrini
The version made with gin is really good.
Wash 6 fresh green walnuts and dry them thoroughly. Put them in a jar, cover them with spirit (gin is an option, as I discovered when I ran out of spirit!) and add two cloves and a small piece of cinnamon bark. Seal the jar to make it airtight and store in a dark place with a mild temperature for 7 or 8 weeks. At the end of this time, heat half a litre of red wine and 1 cup of sugar over a medium heat, stirring until it reduces to a light syrup of half its original volume (about 40 minutes). Allow to cool. Strain walnuts, add wine to the liquor, and bottle. Wait a fortnight before using.

It was not just for his walnut liqueur that Joe was known to the local people. He loved company and his hospitality was legendary. Whoever you were, he always called you Charlie. 'G'day, Charlie,' he'd say. 'How about a drink?' Out would come the glasses and the claret – he was very good at making claret – and you would spend the next hour or so on his verandah or in his kitchen, sharing jokes and stories and planning the next fishing-trip or fund-raiser. Afterwards people would say, 'Where did you drink with Joe?' If you had been invited into the kitchen, you knew that you were favoured. That was how it was with Joe.

He was also a good cook, and was constantly being invited by his drinking friends to share their fishing-trips to the River Murray or the coast. The flavour of the olive oil that he used when making dishes of fish, chicken, duck or rabbit was new to local men, who learned to eat food of a different culture from their own.

His fishing companions still remember how Joe taught them to smoke fish on the beach in a little smoke-box. He hung the fish from hooks attached to the ceiling of the box and smoke came from smouldering sawdust and green leaves. The dishes he prepared were enhanced by the quality and freshness of the vegetables that he had grown himself.

I suggested to his son that Joe had influence over the people with whom he shared his love of food. Alf Pelligrini immediately said, 'Well, if he didn't influence them, he would certainly con them!' And he told me a story to show what he meant.

Once, a few days before Easter, a woman came to see Joe to buy a duck from his freezer. She was, incidentally, a person well-known in the Barossa community for her own hospitality and service to local charities. On this occasion she was wanting one of Joe's famous ducks to cook for her family for Easter dinner.

Joe reached down into his freezer and lifted out the last duck he had left. 'How about this one?' he asked.

'It's not quite big enough,' said the woman. 'Show me a bigger one.'

Joe put the duck back into the freezer, pushed it along a bit and pulled it out again. 'How about this one?' he asked.

The woman looked at it and considered. 'Yes,' she said, 'but it's still a bit small. I'll tell you what: I'll take them both.'

Joe thought for a second and then he said, 'No, you can't have the two because I've already sold one of them. I don't care which one you have, either this one or the other one.'

'Well,' she said, 'I'll have that one.' And she took the duck away, never realising that she had had no choice in the matter.

Many other stories could be told about this stocky man with a big heart whose enthusiasm for life helped him to raise wads of money for the local hospital. But since this book deals mainly with stories about food, we should spend some time talking about Joe and the local olive trees.

Even though olives did not feature in the food culture of the early settlers to the Barossa district, olive trees became part of the landscape quite soon after the Europeans' arrival. It is said that naughty children used to throw olives onto the Bethany schoolroom stove and cause a stink with the teacher in more ways than one. An old woman who could remember back to the 1880s recalled this story in 1968 and the chances are that olive trees had seeded themselves even earlier than 1880.

Olive tree seedlings spread rapidly in Southern Australia and olives were established in Adelaide plantations in 1839. In the 1850s Sir Samuel Davenport put in cuttings at Beaumont in the Adelaide foothills. They became the basis of the olive oil industry carried out by G.F. Cleland & Sons Ltd. This was the company that established Chateau Tanunda in 1890 and later planted olive groves at Gomersal in the Barossa, which were in production by 1919. But since someone's childhood reminiscences about olives hark back to an earlier time, we can only say that travelling birds or experimental gardeners must have been responsible for introducing olives to the Barossa area before then.

By the time Joe Pelligrini was looking around for a source of olive oil in the 1940s, there were olives along the roadsides all over the Barossa Valley. Some of them were large, old trees by then and Joe and his family set up a small business picking and processing. He let it be known that he would buy olives from other pickers and he went out and picked them from the side of the road himself. Most people said, 'Oh well, we don't want them. You might as well take them,' and so he did.

Every night after Joe had come home from work at Chateau Tanunda, his wife, Teresa, would have the copper boiling and they would do another can of olives. The olives were crushed in sewn bags under a press to obtain the first lot of pure oil. Then boiling water was poured on them for the next pressing. The vat into which the oil drained had a tap at the bottom from which the water drained off, leaving the oil to be strained and filtered before bottling.

The olive oil did not sell for an exorbitant price but Joe had a regular market for it in the city and it made enough money to build three houses: one for himself and Teresa, and one for each of his two sons. His clientele was fairly small in the Barossa, where olive oil was regarded as a medicine. When someone claimed that Joe's olive oil had helped him to pass a kidney stone without having an operation, Joe won customers intent on restoring their health.

Many people have harvested the wild olives in the Barossa since Joe died in 1970 and some have built up small businesses. It caused dismay when, early in 1996, a long row of olives, which had been a landmark in the settlement of Vine Vale, was suddenly grubbed out. Olives grow slowly and these were trees producing substantial crops. I went out sadly and counted the rings on the stumps before they were burnt. It is not easy to count exactly, because the rings through the trunk of an olive are fine, scribbly lines that often flow together. But it seems that those trees had been perhaps 80 years old. Other old olives in the district have had time to grow right around the pioneer post and rail fences passing through them so that the whole mass is fused into a tortuous bit of sculpture. I hope those trees never go.

In fairness, some people in the Barossa were from early on interested in pickling the local olives. Several people can remember their grandparents making jars of pickled olives, either to sell to companies like Cromptons or for their own table. This next recipe comes from the 1920s, from the notebook of Wanda Grosser.

Shirley Lindner makes pickled aubergines

Pickled Olives

Put green olives in solution of 3 oz caustic potash to 1 gallon of water. Try in 48 hours to see if bitterness is gone. Wash in clean water for 3 days. Then put olives in a brine, ¾ lb salt to 1 gallon of water.

For ripe olives, follow the same procedure but use less caustic, say, 2 oz to a gallon.

At the end of the twentieth century we have learned in the Barossa that olive oil makes food grown in our Mediterranean climate taste wonderful. Maggie Beer, who has been promoting olive oil for years, must feel pleased that the Barossa district, with a food culture originally favouring fats from the cow and the pig, is enjoying a change that represents a shift of cultural emphasis.

As a symbolic gesture I'll end this chapter with a delicious recipe for aubergine pickled in olive oil, on sale at Langmeil Wines in Tanunda and made by Shirley Lindner who, with her husband, Richard, and their partners, helped to establish this interesting winery.

Shirley Lindner's Pickled Aubergines
Try the ones with cumin and coriander, also sold at the Langmeil winery.

2 large aubergines | 2 tbsp salt | 1 cup virgin olive oil | 1 tsp turmeric | 3 cloves garlic, thinly sliced | 3 whole red chillies | 1 cup malt vinegar | 1 tsp fresh or dried oregano | 6 leaves basil | 1 or 2 tbsp brown sugar (or less, to taste)

Cube or slice aubergines and sprinkle with salt. Leave for approximately 30 minutes. Discard juices and pat dry. Heat oil in a large pan. When hot add turmeric and fry gently for 5 minutes. Add garlic, chillies and vinegar. Reduce heat and simmer for 10 minutes. Add aubergines, herbs and sugar and cook further 10 minutes. Remove from heat and allow to cool. Place in sterilised jars. Best after 3 weeks. Toss a few pieces through a green salad or serve with other salad vegetables and fresh bread.

Chapter 19

Autumn Reflections

We are approaching Easter with the speed of a popping cork, and afterwards this year comes the biennial Vintage Festival. Over the next few weeks, wine will flow and food will be dished up on many occasions: family meals, food in the street, sumptuous banquets to complement rare wines, lavish picnics recalling food of earlier times. The churches, too, will be decorated with food for Harvest Thanksgiving services. They will smell heavenly, decked with apples, quinces and pomegranates, sheaves of wheat and bread shaped like plaited anchors.

The dishes for each of these events will have some links with the traditional food prepared by the early European settlers in the Barossa. Remember Fiedler, who entertained Old Colonist with food and wine on his front verandah? If he were to come drifting back now he would still see the kinds of fruit, bread, meats and *Kuchen* that must have been on his own table 150 years ago.

But there are differences, of course; and noting some of the major changes has been one reason for this book.

Now, watering the garden, with the autumn sun on my back, I think about what gives Barossa food a special character.

Right from earliest white settlement, people followed the complete process of preparing food, from the ground up. Most of their ingredients were sitting all around them on their mixed farms. The people knew what was in their food because they themselves had produced it. In fact, they made almost everything they needed, even the yeast cultures they used in brewing and baking.

Their love of gardening translated well to a new land and a new climate. It did not take them long to start growing apricots and peaches, for example. And strangely, crops like grapes that they had grown only with difficulty back in the old country grew more easily in the new. The fermentation processes used for so many of their foods and for making wine were effective in this warmer climate.

They could continue the time-honoured peasant practice of gathering wild foods, too – before these grew scarce under the advance of farming land. Wild foods, at first kangaroo, native currants and yabbies in the creek, eventually came to include feral foods: hares and rabbits, quinces and almonds from the side of the road.

Along the way the Barossa people shed some of the rich food they had traditionally eaten in Europe, but kept many dishes that continued to serve them well, including ways of preparing salads and vegetables, eminently suited to warmer weather. Often they included a dash of vinegar and a pinch of sugar in savoury dishes, or combined tart fruits with smoked meats, making use of the faintly sweet-sour flavour dear to their palate.

Finally, Barossa food customs have always been very much connected with patterns of time: like the days of the week and the annual punctuation of festivals, all set to the rhythms of the climate. Every year, the pattern begins again. It makes people into philosophers who mark the turn of the wheel, who maintain a sense of timelessness as they go through activities again and again connected to the earth and the seasons.

In many ways, the peasant traditions of Barossa food have for generations followed similar principles to those that people are now praising in Mediterranean cuisines, although I do see a few fundamental differences in approach. One is a difference in the choice of some of their flavourings. Another difference is the kind of fat used as the lubricant to their cooking. Makers of traditional Mediterranean food use olive oil where Barossa people would turn to butter, cream and lard. In both cultures, though, the importance of the land and the seasons is the same.

That was how the situation remained until about the 1970s. Although by then most people in the Barossa were no longer practising the unrefined peasant food culture of the first generation of European settlers, elements of it did remain, especially in their attitude towards food. The quality had to be good, even though nothing was wasted. Seek out the best apricot tree! Find the best way to pickle cucumbers! The way people made and ate their food was important. And food was produced mainly at home.

Several critical changes have taken place since the 1970s that have put the identity of Barossa food under threat. (The same changes have affected food prepared in country areas throughout the western world.) It is hard to list them all or to put them in order. Many seemed to happen at once. But here are some of them.

Like the rest of the western world, the Barossa stopped looking inwards and through various media, came into contact with the foods of other cultures. Freezers came onto the market just at the time when many women were thinking of taking up more paid work outside the home. Fruit orchards diminished as the wine industry expanded. Foods from all over the world, both fresh and prepared, appeared in supermarkets, making culinary seasons and exclusive regional cuisines notions of the past.

It was no longer possible, necessary or even desirable to spend so much time preparing or preserving food. Convenience foods jumped in to fill a need. And other cultures beckoned – tastes and flavours and methods altogether different. You could try them out in all the new restaurants and in your own kitchen. You could mix them, too, as chefs in the restaurants were doing. Just as people were trying 'world music', combining instruments and patterns from different cultures, they could experiment with world food.

So what did that do to the food culture of the people in the Barossa, whose traditions from a certain part of Europe had made them intriguingly different from other parts of Australia for so long? Not a great deal to help it survive. Which is a pity because among foods prepared in the Barossa years ago were some gems of recipes that should not be forgotten.

But there are still ways to keep Barossa food traditions alive and flourishing.

First of all, I hope that this book will remind people about some lovely recipes that we seem to have forgotten in our eagerness to try foods that are new and different. I realise that I won't have gathered every single dish. Only yesterday my brother mentioned some that he particularly loved. 'What about Mum's liver and bacon?' he said. 'Or her stewed cabbage rolls?' Other people will no doubt say the same thing about recipes from their own families. Nevertheless this book may help to save some excellent dishes that would otherwise have disappeared.

Our restaurants in the Barossa may well help. Many Barossa chefs are keen to promote Barossa foods and make good use of the excellent local butchers and bakers. Perhaps some of the family dishes that see the light of day in this book will appear on the menus of Barossa restaurants and be saved from extinction. Perhaps they will even be served in restaurants across Australia, or even in other countries, as examples of Barossa regional cuisine.

Old cooking often meant long, slow preparation, to produce wonderful flavours. Now, who has the time to devote a whole day to preserves or to baking? Yet, what is the alternative, apart from to going out and buying impersonal products churned out in a distant factory? As Margaret Lehmann says, 'I still want to know who had their hands in my food!'

Her own answer is to supplement what is made at home with food produced on a smaller scale by local people who are known for their expertise. She will make sure that she has supplies of local breads, meats and smallgoods, Zimmy's horseradish, Wiech's noodles, Maggie Beer's quince paste, Rosenzweig's honey, Marjorie Coates' preserves, Farm Follies pickles so that she can rustle up a splendid meal in seconds flat.

Autumn Reflections

To survive without becoming impersonal and to protect the use of the word 'Barossa', many small-scale producers have formed Australia's first regional food brand called *Food Barossa*. As Mark McNamara, a spokesperson of the members, says, 'We are a distinct food region in our own right.' The members themselves have identified criteria relating to the geography, quality, food safety standards and history for each group of products, and signed a licence to use the distinctive cork-and-fork logo. Food Barossa aims to bring authentic local products to a wider market. The website, www.foodbarossa.com, is worth visiting.

The point Maggie Beer makes about food and wine in her foreword is an important one, too. Local people have become increasingly aware of the way food and wine work together. From the first wine and food appreciation groups, through all the national and international wine and culinary awards that have come our way, the marriage between wine and food has become more solid. Each has come to depend more and more on the other. The success of each encourages the success of the other.

Finally, the annual Shows in the local towns have their competitions for traditional Barossa foods. On the March Sunday morning of the Tanunda Show (and, around the same time, at the Angaston Show) the judges are helping to bring these to people's attention. The championships could be expanded to include a whole range of other traditional foods. And just so that people from older generations do not carry off all the prizes, the local schools could teach and encourage students to enter. It could make young people aware of the potential of our regional cuisine; it would be a new start.

So the pattern begins again: the wheel turns ...

Tanunda Show, 1999

Author's Note

A book about an entire community naturally owes much to many people. I wish to thank everybody who has helped in any way and hope that I have not overlooked anybody in the following lists.

Proof-readers and patient listeners

My own family, especially my husband, Peter, my sons, Henry and Tom, my sister, Frances Wells, my brother, Mark Eckermann, and my aunt, Winifred Schulz.

Maggie and Colin Beer and Margaret and Peter Lehmann, who read the manuscript at various stages and who as friends were guinea pigs tasting various dishes.

Lynn Martin and Robert Dare from the History Department at the University of Adelaide and food writer and scholar Barbara Santich, who read my manuscript and challenged me in useful ways.

Margaret and Pastor Cedric Zweck, Pastor Henry Proeve and Luke Rothe, who read sections and checked their accuracy.

Gerlinde Trappe, friend and travel companion, who helped with translations, provided material and checked the accuracy of the German words.

Michael Bollen and Gina Inverarity of Wakefield Press.

People who kindly agreed to be visited and interviewed

(Many of these also read sections, provided recipes and documents and made suggestions)

Rita Bartsch, Vera Bockmann, Mona Doering, Brian Fechner, Keith Fechner, Chris Flamank, Frank Garrett, Anna Geier, Gwenda Geier, Colin Gramp, Otto Grocke, Bertha Hahn, Helen Hill-Smith, Eileen Hoffmann, Vreni Kummerow,

Wally and Hilda Lange, Peter Lehmann, Gloria Leno, Ivy Miller, Muriel Nelson, Janet Nitschke, Rhoda Noack, Stella Page, Alf Pelligrini, Mark and Gloria Rosenzweig, Frank and Melva Rothe, Harry and Melva Schmidt, Winifred Schulz, Rhonda Steinberner, Wally Stiller, Nita and Frank Stiller, Maria Stiller, Linda Wood, Alma Zwar, Margaret Zweck (Other people gave me interviews over the telephone. They have been acknowledged in the notes on each chapter.)

People who gave me access to documents from their own collections or contacted me with information about sources

Yvonne Angove, Barry Backman, Bill Bampton, Barossa Valley Archives and Historical Trust, Reg Butler, Sue Comelli, Joy Dittrich, Alison Dolling, Bill Evans, Shylie Evans, Alan Gallagher, Ian Harmstorf, Harry Hennig, Prue Henschke, David Herbig, Merle Hoffmann, Audrey Kernich, Lee Kersten, Jan Kohlhagen, Nathalie Leader, Rae Lehmann, Lutheran Archives (Adelaide), Mark McNamara, Olga Nitschke, Agatha Pietsch, Evelyn Rothe, Pastor Clem Schmidt, David Schubert, Joan Schultz, David Smith, Raymond Specht, Joyce Steinle, Roger and Myrene Teusner, Colin Thiele

People in Germany who provided documents or checked information for me

Ulrich and Ute Brunnert, Inge and Günter Hunecke, Ulla Lynen, Marianne Macke, Philipp May, Renate Schach von Wittenau

People who assisted with the photographs

Yvonne and Les Burgemeister, Aaron Penley and Graham Butler, Edna del Fabbro, Mona, Tim and Michael Doering, Bill Evans, Brian Fechner, Colin Gramp, Bertha Hahn, Fay and Ron Herrmann, Penny Holmes, Kingsley Ireland, Margaret and Peter Lehmann, Doug and Ingrid Lehmann, Michael and Annie Lehmann, Shirley Lindner, Graham Linke, Rhoda Noack, Mark and Gloria Rosenzweig, Harry and Melva Schmidt, Vern Munchenberg and Steve Speaight, Grant Schuyler, Ian and Pauline Schwarz, Joylene Seppelt, Peter Wells

Design and Production

Eric Algra, photographer, Liz Nicholson of design Bite, Clinton Ellicott of MoBros, and the team at Wakefield Press, all of whose creative skills are evident in this book.

Sources

PREFACE AND CHAPTER 1

Bernhard, M. *Gnadenbringende Weihnachtszeit*, Süd-West Verlag, München, 1966

Doeger, G. *The Emigrant to South Australia*, Tangermünde, 1849. Also G. Hunckel *Berichte Deutscher Ansiedler in Süd-Australien,* Bremen, 1845

Gramp, C. Taped interview, Tanunda, July 1993

Grandel, H *Hannah Grandel serviert Schlesische Spezialitäten*, Verlag Gerhard Rautenberg, Leer, 1994

Harmstorf, I.A. *History of S.A. Tourist Districts: The Barossa Valley*, Broadcast for Radio 5UV, Adelaide, October 1974

Harmstorf, I.A. *Guests or Fellow Countrymen* Thesis (Ph.D) Flinders University of South Australia, 1989

Harmstorf, I.A. 'South Australia's German Heritage', talk given at the German Teachers' Conference in Adelaide, June 1974

Harmstorf, I.A. 'True Germans are Patriotic South Australians' in booklet No. 2 for students of German in the Graduate Diploma in Education (Secondary) at the South Australian College of Advanced Education, 1988

Krummenerl R. *Küchenrenner für Landschaftskenner*, Verlag für die Frau, Leipzig, 1986

Lutheran Rest Home For the Aged *Recipes*, Tanunda, 1977

Proeve, H.F.W. 'Like a Mighty Army: The First Two Columns of Settlers' in *The Barossa: A Vision Realised*, Barossa Valley Archives and Historical Trust, 1992

Proeve, H.F.W. *A Dwelling-Place at Bethany: the Story of a Village Church*, Lutheran Publishing House, Adelaide, 1983

Ross, D. 'Special Surveys in a Land of Hills and Valleys' in *The Barossa: A Vision Realised, op. cit.*

Santich, B. 'Regionalism in Australia' in *Looking for Flavour*, Wakefield Press, Adelaide, 1996

Schubert, D.A. (ed.) *Kavel's People*, Lutheran Publishing House, Adelaide, 1985, p. 161

Talbot, M. *A Chance to Read: A History of the Institutes Movement in South Australia*, Libraries Board of South Australia, Adelaide, 1992

Thèrmann, J.D. Reminiscences, unpublished, 1848, passage trans A. Heuzenroder

Wurst, E. Letters in *The Family Wurst 1860–1980*, Lutheran Publishing House, Adelaide, 1980

CHAPTER 2

The *Barossa Cookery Book*, 1st Edition, Tanunda Australia Day Committee, 1917

The *Barossa Cookery Book*, 2nd Edition, Tanunda Soldiers' Memorial Hall Committee, undated

The *Barossa Cookery Book*, 3rd Edition, Tanunda Soldiers' Memorial Hall Committee, undated

Falland, B. Telephone interview, Tanunda, December 1998

Lehmann, P. Taped interview, Tanunda, South Australia, 1993

Linn, R. *The Tanunda Club 1891–1991: a Centenary History*, Historical Consultants Pty Ltd, Blackwood, South Australia, 1991

Love, D. and Love, D. *The Linke Families in Australia 1838–1980*, Lutheran Publishing House, Adelaide, 1980

Scharfenberg, H. *The Cuisines of Germany*, Poseidon Press, New York, 1989

Schulz, W.E. Taped interview, Tanunda, South Australia 1989

Steinberner, R. Taped interview, Tanunda, September 1992

CHAPTER 3

Geier, A. Taped interview, Greenock, South Australia, June 1994

Hahn, B. Taped interview, Light Pass, South Australia, 1992

Harmstorf, I.A. *German Settlement in South Australia to 1914*, South Australian College of Advanced Education, 1988

Jaensch, J.C. Account in *Kavel's People*, D. Schubert (ed.), Lutheran Publishing House, Adelaide, 1985

Juers, G.R. 'The story of Old Hoffnungsthal' from a series of articles in *The Lutheran Herald*, Adelaide, 1939–9

Kavel, F. Letter to his brother in *Kavel's People*, D. Schubert (ed.), Lutheran Publishing House, Adelaide, 1985

Page, S. Interview, Greenock, South Australia, January 1995

Schubert, D. (ed.) *Kavel's People*, Lutheran Publishing House, Adelaide, 1985

South Australian Register, 6 July 1855

Steinberner, R. Taped interview, Tanunda, South Australia, September 1992

Teusner R.E. *Family History of Wilhelm Kleemann*, Lutheran Press, Adelaide, 1969

Teusner, M. 'Johann Menge, 1788–1852', *Barossa Historic Bulletin*, Vol. 1 No. 5, 1978

Yelland, E.M. (ed.) *Colonists, Copper and Corn in the Colony of South Australia 1850–1851* by 'Old Colonist', Published by the Editor, Adelaide, 1983

CHAPTER 4

Angas, G.F. 'Bethany Village', *South Australia Illustrated*, 1847 (South Australian Archives)

Gerstäcker, F. *Reisen*, Vol 3, 1854 English translation quoted from I.A. Harmstorf, 1989

Herbig, D. *The Family History of Friedrich Herbig, Frau Caroline and Their Sixteen Children*, Lutheran Press, Adelaide, 1968

Klein S. 'Our German Ancestors', *McGrath Family Reunion Book*, private publication, 1997

Leditschke, E.L.P. *A Short Autobiography*, unpublished

Lehmann, P. Taped interview, Tanunda, South Australia, 1993

Mackenzie, E.C.V. *Hoffnungsthal 1847–1972* unpublished booklet, Lyndoch, 1972

Schulz, W.E. Interview, Tanunda, South Australia, September 1995

Stiller, N. Taped interview, Bethany South Australia, September 1992

Tanunda Lutheran Rest Home For the Aged *Recipes*, 1977. The recipes come from elderly residents of the Home.

Teusner, M. *Daughter of the Valley*, Lutheran Publishing House, Adelaide, 1978

Teusner, R.E. *Family History of Friedrich Wilhelm Kleemann*, 1969

Traeger, R. (ed.) *The Family Wurst*, The Family Wurst Committee, Adelaide, 1980

Watts, J. 'Family Life in South Australia 1890' cited in *Kavel's People* by David Schubert, *op. cit.*

CHAPTER 5

Hahn, B. Interview, Light Pass, South Australia, January 1993
Hazelton, N.S. *The Cooking of Germany*, Time Inc., Netherland, 1971
Leditschke, E.L.P. *A Short Autobiography*, unpublished, *op. cit.*
Lehmann, M. Interview, Tanunda, South Australia, 1996
McKenzie, D. *Teutonic Myths and Legends*, Gresham Publishing, London, undated
Nelson, M. Interview, Nuriootpa, South Australia, May 1998
Schmidt, M. Taped interview, Light Pass, South Australia, September 1992
Schubert, D. *Kavel's People, op. cit.* The shipboard version of this was *Grütze* (grain) and prunes, mentioned, for example, in the shipping details of the *Prince George*, which brought the first group of Pastor Kavel's people from Hamburg to South Australia.
Thiermann, D. Unpublished diary, 1848
Zwar, L.A., Wood, E.L., Miller, B.I. Taped interview, Nuriootpa, South Australia, July 1993

CHAPTER 6

Bockmann, V. Interview, Glenelg, South Australia, January 1993. Prussians preferred coffee to tea. They roasted it in a cylindrical drum (often home-made) about 12 cm in diameter, which was perched on a stand over the hot coals, turning a handle with skill so that the coffee beans did not burn. An example is on display in the historical museum at Tanunda.
Fechner, B. and Fechner, K. Taped interview, Tanunda, December 1994
Graetz, C. *The White Wends of St Kitts,* private publication, Adelaide 1992
Gramp, C. Taped interview, Tanunda, South Australia, July 1993
Hahn, B. Taped interview, Light Pass, September 1992
Heinrich, R. *Kaesler Chronicles*, Kaesler Reunion Committee, Adelaide, 1988. Example of family trek to new settlements.
Jacob, A. Unpublished diary, Jacobs Creek, 1840
Klose, B. Telephone interview, Tanunda, 1995
Schmidt, H. and Schmidt, M. Taped interview, Light Pass, South Australia, September 1992
Stiller, M. Taped interview, Tanunda, South Australia, July 1982
Zwar, L.A., Wood, E.L., Miller, B.I. Taped interview, Nuriootpa, South Australia, July 1993

CHAPTER 7

Ey, A. *Early Lutheran Congregations in South Australia, 1904*, A.P.H. Freund, 1986 Describes Anna's own arrival at Port Adelaide with her mother in 1847.

Hahn, B. Interview and demonstration of making *Quarkkuchen*, January 1993

Nitschke, J. Taped interview, Greenock, November 1994. Since this time, Janet's busy life has meant that she no longer makes *Kuchen* for customers.

Noack, R. Taped interview, Dutton, South Australia, July 1995

Schach von Wittenau, R. Interview, Hannover, Germany, July 1996. Frau Schach von Wittenau is a food writer for German bagazines and author of books on German regional cuisine.

Schubert, D. *Kavel's People*, op. cit. The detail about yeast 'for baking cake' is given in a summary of a letter written by August Fiedler to relatives and friends in Prussia in 1839.

Stiller, N. Taped interview, Bethany, South Australia, October 1992

Vollmer, R. (ed.) *Universal-Lexikon der Kochkunst*, J.J. Weber, Leipzig, 1909 Describes two ways of making *Streuselkuchen* but makes no mention of a fruit layer. It makes a distinction between the *Streuselkuchen* of Saxony, with no spices, and that of Silesia.

CHAPTER 8

Jacob, I. Interview, Adelaide, South Australia, January 1999. At the first Immanuel College, founded in the 1890s at Point Pass in South Australia's mid-north, the recipe in *Davidis* cookery book was used to make *Lachsschinken* (*Mürberbraten*) (information supplied by Miss Jacob, whose mother helped Pastor Leidig's wife in the kitchen.)

Ross, P.G. Taped interview, Tanunda, South Australia, October 1992

Schmidt, H. Taped interview, Light Pass, South Australia, September 1992

Specht, R.L. Letter to A. Heuzenroeder, February 1998

Stiller, M. Taped interview, Tanunda, 1982

William, T.J. *The Australasian Butchers Manual*, Peacock Bros, Melbourne, 1912

Young, G. *Early Barossa Settlements* Vol. 1, Chap 3., Techsearch, Adelaide, 1978

Zweck, M. Taped interview, Light Pass, South Australia, June 1992

CHAPTER 9

Aeuckens, A. et al. *Vineyard of the Empire: Early Barossa Vignerons 1842–1939*, Australian Industrial Publishers, Adelaide, 1988

Anonymous *The House of Seppelt*, Adelaide, 1951.

Eckermann, W.P. *A Brief History of One Line of the Pioneer Eckermann Family*, unpublished, 1957

Geier, G. Taped interview, Greenock, South Australia, August 1994

Gramp, C. Taped interview, Tanunda, South Australia, July 1993

Hahn, B. Taped interview, Light Pass, South Australia, September 1992

Hale, M. Interview, Tanunda, South Australia, 1990

Ioannou, N. *Barossa Journeys*, Paringa Press, Adelaide, 1997. The book gives more information about how horehound arrived in the Cambrai district of South Australia, where two English veterinarians, Lambert and Harris, imported the plant to add to their garden of medicinal herbs. The book provides more details about the Wiech family business. It also describes hard balls of cheese being dried in the sun, mentioned by 'Itinerant', of 1849, who observed what he thought were goose eggs sitting on the roofs of some buildings. On inquiring, he learned that they were lumps of Quark being made into *Stinkerkäse*.

Ioannou, N. *The Barossa Folk*, Craftsman House, New South Wales, 1995. Describes the local makers and designs of butter churns. Chapters 9 and 10 also describe and give photographs of pottery bowls used to allow the cream to rise to the surface of the milk, and perforated pottery jars into which the curdled milk was poured to make *Quark*.

Jorgen, R. *The Flavour of the Hill Country, Texas-German recipes from the Sauer-Beckmann Living History Farm*, Stonewall, Texas, 1992

Kavel, A. and Fiedler, A. 'A Letter Home, 1839' in *Kavel's People, op. cit.*

Roennfeldt, M. Interviewed by R. and M. Teusner, Marananga, South Australia, 1974

Ross, D. 'A Land of Wheat and Vines', *The Barossa, A Vision Realised, op. cit.*

Rothe, F. and Rothe, M. Taped interview, Tanunda, South Australia, October 1992

Simpson, E.R. *The Hahndorf Walkers and The Beaumont Connection*, Beaumont Press, Adelaide, 1983

Thiele, C. Letter written to A. Heuzenroeder, September 1995

Women of St Michael's Lutheran Primary School Auxiliary, Hahndorf (comp.) *Recipes From My Grossmutter*, Hahndorf, 1975

Yelland, E.M. (ed.) *Colonists, Copper and Corn 1850–51, op. cit.*

CHAPTER 10

Barker, S. (ed.) *Explore the Barossa*, Royal Geographical Society of Australasia, (SA Branch) Inc., 1991

Carroll, A. and Tregenza, J. *Eugene von Guerard's South Australia*, The Art Gallery of South Australia, Adelaide, 1986

Chilman, J.K. *Barossa Aboriginal Heritage Survey*, South Australian Department of Environment and Planning, Adelaide,1990, p. 29ff

Grocke, O. Taped interview, Tanunda, South Australia, April 1994

Kraehenbuhl, D.N. Telephone interview, Adelaide, May 1994

Liebelt, J.C. Reminiscences in *Kavel's People*, op. cit.

Low, T. *Wild Plant Foods of Australia*, Angus and Robertson, Sydney, 1991

Proeve, H.F.W. *A Dwelling Place Called Bethany*, op. cit.

Ross, D. 'A Land of Wheat and Vines', in *The Barossa, A vision Realised*, op. cit.

Schramm, Alexander (1814–1864) 'A Scene in South Australia' c.1850, Adelaide, oil on canvas, 25.7 x 31.8 cm; South Australian Government Grant 1981, Art Gallery of South Australia

Seppelt, J. Interview, Marananga, South Australia, March 1998

Teusner, R. 'The First Inhabitants', *The Barossa, A Vision Realised*, op. cit.

Thiele, C. *The Picnic*, unpublished short story written c.1986 for the Lutheran schools in South Australia

Vivienne, M. *Sunny South Australia*, Hussey and Gillingham, Adelaide, 1908

Wendlandt, W. (Trans. P.A. Scherer) *Germans in a Strange Land: Tanunda in the 1880s*, Tanunda, private publication, 1986

Young, G. (ed.) *Early Barossa Settlements*, Vol. 3. op. cit.

CHAPTER 11

Anonymous *The House of Seppelt 185–1951*, op. cit.

Beer, M. *Maggie's Orchard*, Viking, Melbourne, 1997

Behn, V. *Reflections of Eckerville 1879–1979*, private publication, Waterloo, South Australia, c.1980

Bethany residents' taped reminiscences, Bethany, South Australia, 1992

Ey, A. *Early Lutheran Congregations in South Australia*, op. cit.

Gramp, C. Taped interview, Tanunda, South Australia, July 1993

Hill-Smith, H. Taped interview, Angaston, South Australia, October 1997

Jacob, A. unpublished diary, Jacob's Creek 1842

Lutheran Hymnal, Hymn No. 341

The *Barossa & Light Herald*, March 1949

Vivienne, M. *Sunny South Australia*, op.cit.

Zweck, M. Taped interview, Light Pass, South Australia, June 1992

CHAPTER 12

The *Barossa Cookery Book*, 3rd Edition, Tanunda Soldiers' Memorial Hall Committee, undated

Göock, R. *Deutsche Landschaftsküche*, Bertelsmann Ratgeberverlag, Gütersloh, Berlin, 1978

Hazelton, N.S. *The Cooking of Germany*, op. cit.

Rosenzweig, G. and Rosenzweig, M. Interview, Moculta, South Australia, November 1995

CHAPTER 13

The *Barossa Cookery Book*, 1st edition, Tanunda Australia Day Committee, 1917

Grandel, H. *Hannah Grandel serviert Schlesische Spezialitäten*, op. cit.

Lonie, J. *Keep Your Eye on Germany* play written by and performed by the Magpie Theatre at Yaldara Winery, April 1975

Morris, C.R. and McRitchie, G. (comp.) *Green and Gold Cookery Book*, Rigby, Adelaide, 1923

Rothe, F.O. Taped interview, Tanunda, October 1992

Vivienne, M. *Sunny South Australia*, op. cit.

Weber, J.J. (ed.) *Universal-Lexikon der Kochkunst*, Leipzig, 1909

CHAPTER 14

Cawthorne, W. *Menge the Mineralogist: a Sketch of the Late Johann Menge*, Shayer, Adelaide, 1859

Ellis, J. Telephone interview, Angaston, South Australia, June 1995

Grocke O. Taped interview, Tanunda, South Australia, April 1994

Kaiser, S. 'Zuckergeschichte in Schlesien' (The Story of Sugar in Silesia) in *Schlesischer Kulturspiegel*, Würzburg, April 1997

McGee, H. *On Food and Cooking: The Science and Lore of the Kitchen*, HarperCollins, London, 1991

Mintz, S.W. *Sweetness and Power*, Viking, New York, 1985

Schiller, B. Taped interview, Tanunda, South Australia, 1980

Schubert, D. (comp.) *Kavel's People*, op. cit.

Schulz, W.E. Interview, Tanunda, 1995

South Australian Newspaper 'Notice of Fruit and Vegetables Grown in South Australia', 7 December 1847

Stiller, W. Interview, Tanunda, May 1995

Symons, M. *One Continuous Picnic*, Duck Press, Adelaide, 1982

Tepper, O. Authentic Records and Autobiography, Mortlock Library, Adelaide, ref. PRG 313
Weber, J.J. *Universal-Lexikon der Kochkunst, Band II, op. cit.*

CHAPTER 15

Ahrens, M. Taped interview, Tanunda, South Australia, April 1986
Farm and Garden Newspaper, 21 February 1859 and 10 March 1859
Grocke, J.O. Taped interview, Tanunda, South Australia, April 1994
Lehmann, M. Interview, Tanunda, South Australia, September 1994
Tepper, O. Authentic Records and Autobiography, *op. cit.*
Thiele, C. *Heysen of Hahndorf*, Rigby, Adelaide, 1968
Weber, J.J. *Universal-Lexikon der Kochkunst, Band II, op. cit.*

CHAPTER 16

'Agricola' *Description of the Barossa Range and its Neighbourhood in South Australia*, Smith, Elder & Co., London, 1849, p6
Bremisches Kochbuch, Bremen, 1834, p502
Evans H. Letter to George Fife Angas, 1843
Evans, W. Interview, Keyneton, South Australia, January 1996
Gramp, C. Taped interview, Tanunda, South Australia, July 1993
Heuzenroeder, P. Interview, Tanunda, South Australia, 1994
Munchenberg, A. Telephone interview, Tanunda, South Australia, 19 May 1996. Mr Munchenberg recalled going as a child to wonderful Christmas parties put on for the Evandale workers, one of whom was his father. They had games and treats and presents for all the children. The parties were held in the hall of the Congregational Church in Keyneton, which Sarah Evans had built specifically for such functions.
Ross, D. and Munchenberg, R. 'The Everyday Way of Life', *The Barossa, A Vision Realised, op. cit.*

CHAPTER 17

Aeuckens, A. et al. *Vineyards of the Empire: Early Barossa Vignerons 1842–1939, op. cit.*
The *Barossa Cookery Book* 3rd Edition, *op. cit.* p126, 134
Bethany residents' taped reminiscences, Bethany, South Australia, 1992
Bockmann,V. Interview, Glenelg, South Australia, March 1993
Fechner, K. Interview, Tanunda, South Australia, December 1994
Lehmann, P. Taped interview, Tanunda, South Australia, 1993

Payne, P. *Dr Richard Schomburgk and the Adelaide Botanic Gardens 1865–1891*, Ph.D Thesis for Adelaide University, 1992, p473
Scharfenberg, H. *op. cit.* p402
Scherer, P.A. *Bethany Profiles*, private publication, Tanunda, 1993
Schmidt, H. Taped interview, Light Pass, South Australia, September 1992
Schulz, W.E. Interview, Tanunda, South Australia, 1997
Trojan, J. 'The Wines of '88', *Kreis Züllichau-Schwiebus*, (comp.) Curt Schelenz, Im Verlag das Viergespann, Frankfurt am Main, 1970, p137. Translated by D. Schubert
Wark, V. and Wark, J. Telephone interviews, Angaston and Tanunda, South Australia, April 1997. Recipe reproduced with the family's permission from Alf Wark's book *Wine Cookery*, Rigby, 1969

CHAPTER 18

Ahrens, M. Taped interview, Tanunda, South Australia, April 1986
Bampton, W. Address to the Burnside Historical Society, 15 June 1987
Beer, M. *Maggie's Farm*, Allen and Unwin, Sydney, 1993
Bethany residents' taped reminiscences, Bethany, South Australia, 1992
Bockmann, V. *Full Circle: an Australian in Berlin, 1930–1946*, *op. cit.*
Bockmann, V. Interview, Glenelg, South Australia, 1993
Falland, B. Telephone interview, Tanunda, December 1998
Hancock, R. Telephone interview, Adelaide, September 1995
Hentschke, W. 'Historical Notes on Bethany', *Barossa Historic Bulletin* Vol. 1 no. 1, 1969
Pelligrini, A. Taped interview, Tanunda, South Australia, June 1996
Scharfenberg, H. *op. cit.*, p432
Schulz, W.E. Interview, Tanunda, South Australia, 1985
South Australian Newspaper, 7 December 1847

General Index

A

Aboriginal people 30, 148, 151–2, 232
Adelaide 5, 24, 32, 42, 165, 197, 227
Almonds 26, 215, 275ff
Angas Park Fruit 216
Angas, George Fife 23, 232
Angas, George French 36, 133
Angaston 32, 151, 170, 216, 232
Angaston Cottage Industries 170
Angaston Hospital Auxiliary 168
Angaston Show 292
Apex Bakery 79ff
Apples 26, 93, 233ff, 239, 240, 240
Apricots 24, 26, 93, 206
Aubergines 287

B

Bacchus Club 168, 170, 265
Backobst 12, 45, 212
Bake-ovens 41, 74, 81, 215, 268
Bakers 3, 20, 79ff
Barley 73, 174
Barons of the Barossa 169
Barossa Cookery Book xi, xiii, 17, 18, 64, 69, 197, 198, 227, 256, 259, 260, 278
Barossa Journeys 126

Barossa Music Festival 145, 156–7
Barossa Picnic Baskets 146
Barossa Ranges 5, 35, 142
Barossa Valley accent and language 3, 27, 65, 66, 131, 230, 246, 262, passim
Barossa Valley Pheasant Farm pâté 21
Beans 7, 26, 28, 62, 63, 196, 223
Beaumont 284
Beer 144, 161, 222, 263
Beer, Maggie xii, xvi, 95, 156–7, 174, 232, 241, 255, 261, 271, 277, 279, 287, 291–2
Bees 174ff
Beetroot 26
Berlin buns 10, 159–161
Berlin 6, 9, 10, 11, 12
Berliner Pfannkuchen 10, 16, 159–161 (recipe), 210
Bethany 2 5, 24, 36, 142, 143, 212, 267, 284
Biele 97
Bienenstich 20, 278ff, 279–80 (recipe)
Billygoat Square 133
Birdwood 7, 8
Birthdays 159, 277

Black Forest cake xii
Black kitchens 41, 120
Black Pudding x, 113, 116 (recipe)
Blumberg 7, 8
Blutwurst x, xi, 10, 50, 113, 116 (recipe)
Bockmann, Vera 16, 45, 268
Bomst 251
Brandenburg 3, 4, 6, 9, 10, 11, 64, 281
Branson family 13
Breakfast 50
Bremerhaven 6
Bremisches Kochbuch xiii, 66, 70, 200, 206, 227, 243, 270, 277
Breslau 6
Burge, Grant and Helen 168
Butchers 3, 20, 100ff, 117, 196
Butter 7, 102, 134

C

Cabbage 7, 10, 57
Cake 19, 162
Calf 161
Camp oven 51, 52
Card games 73, 222
Celery 150
Cellars 41, 137
Chateau Tanunda 284, 285
Cheer-up Society 18
Cheese 7, 11, 14, 132ff
Children 35, 39, 42, 53, 73, 84, 86, 101, 106, 112, 114, 124, 127, 151, 163, 170, 188, 191ff, 202, 217, 263, 268
Chop picnics 144, 221
Christmas 14, 73, 179ff, 191ff
Chronicle, The 13, 31, 66
Citrus 68

Cleland, G. F. and Sons 284
Climate 56
Coates, Marjorie 291
Coffee 7, 73, 161
Company Store (South Australian) 216
Conrad butchers 124
Corella pears 206
Cottbus 6
Cows 26, 27, 28, 33, 134
Crawford, Miss 18
Cream separators 137
Cucumber salad 10, 197
Cucumbers 14, 16, 17, 26, 241, 242, 245, 246
Cuxhaven 4, 6

D

Daily meals 48ff
Dairies 27, 28, 137
Davenport, Sir Samuel 284
Devon sausage 124
Die Gallerie 170
Doecke 97
Doering, Mona 111ff
Dost, Ben 153ff
Dresden 6, 190
Drinks 70, 236
Drunkenness 263ff
Ducks 7, 24, 44, 161

E

Easter 133, 266, 267, 281, 288
Ebenezer 97
Eckermann, Jean 72
Egg industry 129, 130
Eichsfeld 124
Ellis, Roy 202ff
England 281

English 13, 14, 66, 69, 86, 140, 143, 230
Eudunda 86
Evandale 233, 239
Evans, Bill 232ff
Evans, Henry 232, 239
Evans, Sarah 233, 239ff
Ey, Anna 159

F

Falkenberg's winery 154
Farm Follies 170, 291
Fechner family 79
Federschleissen
Fennel 126
Fermentation 14, 58, 134, 242, 289
Fiedler, August 2, 24, 26, 203, 288
Figs 271ff
Fishing 222ff 283
Flamank, Chris 117
Flour mills 142
Folklore 29, 56, 126
Food Barossa 291
Fowl and noodle soup xii, 47, 48, 163
Fowls 7, 24, 36, 161
Fowler's Vacola 244
Frau und Mann fern 113
Friedrich Wilhelm III 4
Fritz sausage 124
Fritzsche, Johann Daniel 4, 42
Fruit 24, 26, 202ff
Full Circle 16, 268

G

Game 44
Gazpacho 171
Geier, Anna 27, 42, 237
German cake x, xi, xii, 3, 9, 161, see also *Streuselkuchen*

German influence 2ff
Gerstäcker, Friedrich 35
Gladstone 16
Glühwein 73, 260 (recipe), 262
Goat Square 133
Goats 36, 51, 132
Gomersal 284
Goose 161, 193, 194 (recipe)
Gourmet Weekend 156
Gramp family 21, 167, 170
Gramp, Colin 168, 169ff, 242
Grant Burge Winery 170
Grapes 9, 11, 32, 93, 215, 248ff
Greaves 107
Green and Gold Cookery Book 240
Greenock 42, 89, 150, 203
Grieben 107
Grosser, Wanda 285
Grünberg 6, 121, 251, 252
Gurkensalat 10, 197

H

Hackett, Max 168
Hage 2
Hahn, Bertha 95, 140
Hahn, Captain 6
Hahndorf 7, 8, 24, 140, 148
Hale, Margaret 129
Hamburg 4, 6, 58
Hannover 6
Hare 257–9
Harvest Thanksgiving 288
Harz mountains 6, 124
Heinrich, Annie 31, 159, 245
Henschke family 137
Henschke, Prue 199
Herbig Family Tree 42
Herbig, Caroline 42
Herring salad 168, 187

Herrings 7
Hessen 22
Heysen, Sir Hans 221
High tea 72ff
Hill-Smith, Helen 168ff
Hirschhornsalz
Historical Museum, Tanunda
   58, 144, 159
Hoffmann, Baker 79
Hoffmann, Erwin and Laurel
   157, 167
Hoffnungsthal 44
Honey 174ff
Honey biscuits xii, 10, 179, 180
   (recipe), 193
Honigkuchen xii, 10, 179, 180 (recipe)
Hore-hound 126, 237
Horseradish sauce 12, 63, 64

I

Institute Library 8, 9
Interdenominational marriages 8, 13,
   86, 87, 231
Ioannou, Noris 126

J

Jack family 13
Jacob, Ann 23, 140, 164, 197
Jacob, William and Jacob, John
   23, 171
Jacob's Creek 21, 22, 23, 140, 145,
   164, 170
Jam-making 32, 207, 220
Jones, Henry, Esq. 24
Juers, G. R. 44

K

Kangaroo Island 23, 234
Kangaroos xiii, 44

Kartoffelsalat 11, 199
Kavel, Pastor August Ludwig
   Christian 7, 57
Keil 2
Keyneton 137, 199, 232, 239
King's College, Adelaide 240
Kitchens 36, 39
Kitchener buns 10, 16, 159–161
Kleemann family 23, 30, 51
Kleemann, Mrs Edwin 66
Klemzig 6, 24, 42
Knackwurst 10, 50, 113, 121 (recipe)
Koch family 14
Kochkäse xii, 11, 138
Kohlhagen, Jan 236
Kronberger, Rudi 168

L

Lachsschinken 10, 132
Lange, Wally and Hilda 100ff
Langmeil Wines
Lard 27, 47, 102, 107, 134, 290
Leberwurst x, 10, 113, 114, 115
   (recipe)
Lebkuchen 180
Ledtischke, Emilie 36
Legnica 6, 11
Lehmann, Frau Pastor 19
Lehmann, Margaret 50, 167, 291
Lehmann, Olga 150
Lehmann, Pastor Franz 19, 54
Lehmann, Peter 19, 49, 50, 167, 194,
   198, 250, 255
Liegnitz 6, 11, 189
Liegnitze Bombe 189
Light Pass xiii, 3, 31, 34, 36
Limburger cheese 143
Lindner, Shirley and Richard 287
Lindsay Park homestead 232

Linke family 13
Linke's Bakery 182
Little Para River 22
Lobethal 7, 8
Luhrs family 36ff
Luhrs, Anna Rosina 39ff, 51
Lutheran 2, 4, 8, 73, 97, 144, 179, 190, 210, 226, 231
Lyndoch 35, 140

M
Machine biscuits xii, 10, 185
Maggie's Farm 271
Maggie's Orchard 157
Mandelbrot xi
Matthews family 151
McNamara, Mark 292
Mecklenburg-Schwerin 6, 9, 11
Meerrettichsoße 12, 64
Meinel, Martin 279
Melons 22ff
Men 131, 198, 218, 248
Menge, Johann 22ff, 164, 208
Mengler Hill 2
Meringues 10, 186
Mettwurst x, 10, 14, 50, 113, 121 (recipe)
Mickan 97
Milk products 132ff
Minge family 102, 103
Mixed farms 19, 26, 112, 288
Moculta 13, 174
Mohnklöße 14, 189
Mongols 57
Mrs Beeton xiii, 63, 66, 200, 227
Mulberries 26, 233ff
Muntries 150
Murnong 148
Mushrooms 265, 266

N
Name changes 16
Napoleon cake 19
Native cherry 151
Native cranberries 150
Native currants 148, 208
Nectarines 24, 226
Nehrlich, Dorette (Dorchen) 42
Nekla 6
Neu Mecklenburg 6
Neu Schlesien 5
Ngadjuri 152
Nitschke, Janet 89ff
Noack 97
Noack, Rhoda 97, 111
Noodles xii, 11, 127
Nuriootpa 8, 151, 169, 182

O
Oats 174
Ochla 121
Oder River 6, 45
Offe, Private 18
'Old Colonist' 24, 26, 203, 288
Olives, olive oil 283ff, 289
Onions x, 223–4, 268
Opium poppies 72
Oxley Farm goat cheese 146, 291

P
Parrots 44
Peaches 24, 226
Pears 24, 26, 268
Peas 7, 12, 26, 196
Pech 97
Pelligrini, Alf 283
Pelligrini, Joe 282ff
Pelligrini, Teresa 285
Peramangk 142, 148

Peter's Hill 97
Peters family 13
Pfeffernüsse 20, 180
Picnics 143ff, 220, 265
Pie-melons 30, 31, 32
Pigs 26, 27, 28, 47, 100ff, 161
Plums 24, 26, 93, 225
Plush, Gladys 69
Point Pass 164
Poland xiv, 6, 11, 63, 121, 252
Polst family 31
Polterabende 159, 161ff
Pompenbrei 9, 47, 46
Poppyseed 14, 72
Port Broughton 236
Port Parham 218, 222
Posen 3, 4, 6, 11
Post-war immigrants xii, 20
Potato salad 11, 199
Poultry 26, 27, 47
Presswurst 50, 113, 116, 117 (recipe)
Prussians xv, 3, 4, 5, 14, 19, 63, 133, 149, passim
Puddings 7, 66ff
Pumpernickel 20, 143
Pumpkins 22ff, 33

Q
Quandongs 150
Quark 11, 132
Quarkkuchen 11, 95
Quinces 26, 267ff

R
Rabbits 44, 153ff
Radishes 26, 200
Ratios of German names on electoral rolls 8
Recipe notebook xiii, 13, 222

Regional cuisine xii
Reiswurst 113, 116 (recipe)
Restaurants 21, 169ff, 264
Rice 7, 66, 114
Riches From the Vine 252
Rillons 107
River Murray 218, 283
Robins, Cecil 206
Rockford basket press shiraz 259
Roennfeldt family 33
Roll-mops 143
Rosenzweig, Mark and Gloria 174ff, 291
Rote Grütze x, 11, 145, 253, 255 (recipe)
Rothe 2
Rye 143

S
Saffron 94, 95
Salzgurken x, 11, 243
Sandy Creek 19, 151
Sauerbraten 20
Sauerkraut 7, 10, 14, 57, 58 (recipe), 60, 171, 230
Saure Gurken 11, 242
Saxony 6
Schlesisches Himmelreich 9, 45
Schmidt, Harry 74ff
Scholz family 65
Schramm, Alexander 152
Schrapel family 2, 212
Schubert, David 250
Schulz's butchers 117
Schwartenwurst 113, 121 (recipe)
Schwarze Küche 120
Schwarzkopf, Elsie 87–9
Schweineschlachten 100ff
Second World War 19, 28, 252

Seeds 27
Semler family 234
Seppelt family 137, 165
Seppelt, Benno 165
Seppelt, Joylene 146
Seppelt, Selma 260
Seppelt, Sophie 167
Seppelt's Raspberry 236
Seppelts Wine Vinegar Recipe Book 245, 274
Seppeltsfield 167, 266
Seven Sleepers 56
Ship-board provisions 6, 7, 57, 66, 94, 212
Shows x, xi
Siebenschläfer 56
Siegersdorf 134
Silesia xiii, 3, 4, 6, 9, 10, 11, 14, 44, 57, 64, 187, 208, 252, 271, 278, 281
Silk 234
Skjold 4ff, 36
Smokehouses 41, 120, 123
Soldiers 19, 86
Soroptimist International of the Barossa Valley 252
Sourbush 150
South Australian Newspaper 267, 275
South Australian Register 30, 207
South Australian Soldiers' Fund 16
Spreewald 6, 11
Springton 42
Spritzgebäck 10, 185
St Hallett 277
St John's wort 126
St Kitts 97
Stelzer, Harry 82

Stiller, Nita 96
Stinkerkäse 11, 138, 139
Stockwell xiii, 8, 257
Stollen 20, 189–190
Stolz, Frau Pastor 31, 34, 211, 227
Stoves 52, 54
Streuselkuchen x, xi, xii, 9, 20, 72, 86ff, 91 recipe, 159, 163, 193, 278
Sugar 7, 14, 208
Sugar buns 10, 159–161
Sulechów 6
Sundays 53ff, 71ff 102
Sunny South Australia 143

T

Tanunda 2, 8, 21, 42, 129, 150, 157, 158, 170
Tanunda Club 17
Tanunda Institute Committee 18
Tanunda Liedertafel 260, 279
Tanunda Lutheran Rest Home 96
Tanunda Show x, 224, 242, 292
Tanunda Soldiers' Memorial Hall 17
Tea 7
Temperance Movement 239, 264
Tepper, Otto 151, 208, 230
Thiele, Colin 133, 134, 144
Thiermann, Johann Daniel 7
Tin-kettling 159, 161
Tomatoes 197, 223, 227
Traeger family 207
Trojan Johannes 250
Turkey Flat Winery 26
Turnips 26, 49, 62

U

Universal-Lexikon der Kochkunst xiii, 197, 209

V

Van Dieman's Land 24
Veal 47
Vegetables 7, 22, 24, 26 27, 28
Vine Vale 254, 285
Vinegar 7, 27, 261
Vintage 248ff
Vintage Dinners 157
Vintage Festivals 133, 145, 146, 158, 255, 267
Visiting 71ff
Vivienne, May 143
Von Bertouch family 14
Von Mueller, Baron 148

W

Wallaby 44, 51
Walnuts 26, 281ff
Wark, Alf 168, 264
Water melons, *Wassermelone* 23, 28, 262
Waterways 232
Wattle bark 153ff
Weddings 161ff
Weekly routines 51, 74
Weinkeller Restaurant 21, 170
Weinstube Restaurant 21, 170
Wends 6, 11, 96
Wheat 24, 26, 73, 143, 174
White pudding x, 113, 115 (recipe)
Wiech, Marie 129
Wiech's noodles 129, 291

Wine 12, 14, 21, 24, 27, 41, 106, 130, 137, 144, 161, 162, 163, 170, 202, 239, 250ff
Wine consumption 262ff
Wine Cookery 265
Women 35ff, 100ff, 130ff, 168, 248, 263ff, 267
World War 1914–1918, 14–17 , 86–7, 187, 193–4
Wurst machine biscuits 10, 185
Wurst-making 111ff

X

Xeres 171

Y

Yabbies 171, 217, 218
Yalumba Winery 157, 168, 264
Yalumba Harvest Market 146, 170
Yam daisy 148
Yeast 14, 90
Yeast for baking 75, 76, 90, 94

Z

Zebra 13, 208
Ziegenmarkt 255
Zielona Góra 6, 121, 252
Zimmy's dill cucumbers 291
Züllichau 6, 251
Zwar 97
Zweck, Margaret 267

Index of Recipes and Described Dishes

SOUPS
Beetroot soup, *Rote Rüben Suppe* 49
Fowl and noodle soup 48
Sour cabbage soup, *Sauerkohlsuppe* 50
Turnip soup with dumplings 49
Wine and sago soup, *Weinsuppe* 262
Wurstsuppe 50

CHEESE AND CHEESE DISHES
Boiled cheese, *Kochkäse* 138
Cheesecake, *Käsekuchen, Quarkkuchen* 95
Hard cheese 140
Quark 132
Stinkerkäse 138–9

EGG DISHES
Arme Ritter 50
Buttered noodles 129
Noodles, *Nudeln* 127
Pickled hard-boiled eggs 130

SALADS AND LIGHT MEALS
Bean salad 198
Beetroot salad, *Rote Rüben* 199
Cucumber salad, *Gurkensalat* 197
Herring salad, *Heringssalat* 187
Joylene Seppelt's Barossa picnic loaf 146
Lettuce salad 198
Mushroom caps and chicken livers 265
Tomato and cucumber salad 198
Warm potato salad, *Kartoffelsalat* 199

VEGETABLES	Broad beans 63
	Glazed beans and carrots 196
	Layered pumpkin bake 33
	Mushrooms 266
	Onions and potatoes baked in the fire 268
	Potato pancakes, mock fish 66
	Sauerkraut 58
	Sweet-sour cabbage, *Dämpfkraut* 62
	Tomato pie, scalloped tomatoes 197
FISH AND SHELLFISH	Colin Gramp's garlic yabbies 171
	Herring salad, *Heringssalat* 187
	Yabbies 218
MEAT DISHES	Brawn 200
	Brine for pickling meat 111
	Jugged hare, *Hasenpfeffer* 259
	Peter Lehmann's roast goose 194
	Pie-melon stew, *Pompenbrei mit Klöße* 46
	Pigeons with brandied cherries 169
	Pot-roasted meat 51
	Rabbit pies 154
	Roast kangaroo with bacon and garlic 44
	Silesian Heaven, *Schlesisches Himmelreich* 44–5
	Sour offal, *Sauer G'schlinge* 47
	William Jacob's steak-and-kidney pie 172
SMALLGOODS	Bacon 111
	Black pudding, *Blutwurst, Reiswurst* 116
	Ham 111
	Kehlebraten 119
	Knackwurst, Schwartenwurst 121
	Mettwurst 121
	Presswurst, Zungenwurst 117
	White pudding, *Leberwurst* 115
BREAD AND DUMPLINGS	Bottled hop-yeast starter 75
	Bread sponge and dough 78
	Dumplings 45, 46, 64
	Horseshoe pretzels 84

Index of Recipes and Described Dishes

Lemon yeast 77

Potato dumplings, *Kartoffelklöße* 65

SAUCES, CONDIMENTS AND RELISHES

Anna Geier's tomato sauce 228

Apple cucumber chutney 245

Apricot chutney 226

Bean chutney 226

Evandale apple chutney 240

Grape sauce 256

Horseradish sauce, *Meerrettichsoße* 64

Mulberry vinegar 234

Nectarine chutney 226

Pie-melon chutney 32

Plum sauce 225

Quince chutney 270

Tomato relish 229

PICKLES AND PRESERVES

Barossa pickled onions 224

Bread and butter cucumbers 245

Candied orange peel 70

Colin Gramp's *Saure Gurken*,
	dill cucumbers 242

Crystallised figs 272

Green tomato pickle 229

Mrs Jansen's onion pickles 223

Pickled aubergines 287

Pickled cucumbers 242ff

Pickled figs 274

Pickled grapes 256

Pickled nasturtium buds 227

Pickled olives 287

Pickled plums 225

Pickled quinces 270

Preserved figs 272

Salzgurken from 1834 243

Shirley Lindner's pickled aubergines 287

Sweet-and-sour cucumbers, *Zuckergurken* 246

Sweet-and-sour pumpkin pickle 34

DRYING FRUIT

Dried figs 274
Fruit-dipping solution 212
Raisins 215

JAMS AND SPREADS

Apricot jam 209
Apricot butter 214
Fig filling 257
Fig jam 274
Gooseberry jam 211
Marmalade 69
Native-currant jam 150
Pie-melon jam 30, 31, 32
Plum conserve, *Pflaumenmus* 210
Quince jam 269
Quince jelly, *Quittengelee*, 269

DESSERTS AND CAKES

Apricot afternoon tea cake 214
Apricot or pear tart 207
Backobst with a champagne crust 213
Beer cake *Bierkuchen* 98 98
Berlin buns, sugar buns,
    Berliner Pfannkuchen 159–161
Bienenstich 279–80
Blitzkuchen 277
Bread and butter pudding 66
Bread pudding 66
Cream puffs, *Windbeutel* 166
Date-and-walnut loaf 281
Evandale apple pie 239
Evandale mince pie meat 240
German cake, *Streuselkuchen* 91
Grape pie 256
Griefen tarts 109
Hock pudding, *Welfenspeise* 260
Kitchener buns 159–161
Mandeltorte 277
Pear cake 207
Pie-melon roly poly 68
Poppy-seed pudding, *Mohnklöße* 189

Potato cake 98
Pot-roasted quinces 9
Quince soufflé, *Quittensahne* 270
Rote Grütze 255
Sugar cake, *Zuckerkuchen* 94
Waffles 159

BISCUITS

Almond fingers 186
Ammonia biscuits, *Weihnachtskuchen* 184
Griven biscuits 110
Honey biscuits, *Honigkuchen* 180
Machine biscuits, *Spritzgebäck* 185
Meringues, *Schaumkuchen* 186

DRINKS

Beer 237
Ginger beer plant 237
Glühwein 260
Lemon syrup 70
Mulberry syrup 236
Vinegar water, *Essigwasser* 236
Walnut liqueur for Joe Pelligrini 282

Wakefield Press is an independent publishing and
distribution company based in Adelaide, South Australia.
We love good stories and publish beautiful books.
To see our full range of books, please visit our website at
www.wakefieldpress.com.au
where all titles are available for purchase.
To keep up with our latest releases, news and events,
subscribe to our monthly newsletter.

Find us!

Facebook: www.facebook.com/wakefield.press
Twitter: www.twitter.com/wakefieldpress
Instagram: www.instagram.com/wakefieldpress

www.ingramcontent.com/pod-product-compliance
Lightning Source LLC
Chambersburg PA
CBHW060303010526
44108CB00042B/2624